A Magic Carpet Ride

*To Elisa
Enjoy!
Dina Michalopulos Kingsley*

A Magic Carpet Ride

༄

Gina Michalopulos Kingsley

Gina Michalopulos Kingsley

Copyright © 2016 Gina Michalopulos Kingsley
All rights reserved.

ISBN: 069271393X
ISBN 13: 9780692713938

Table of Contents

A Magic Carpet Ride · 1
Childhood Summers in Greece · 9
Teenage Trips in Greece · 13
Honeymoon in Greece · 20
The First Family Trip to Greece · 22
Exploring Athens · 25
Rhodes—Island of Sun · 27
The Tapestry of Turkey · 32
Seeing Queen Elizabeth and Jolly Old England · · · · · · · · · · · · · · 36
My Father's Village in Greece · 38
Ancestors and Cemetery Rituals in Our Village · · · · · · · · · · · · · 41
The Monasteries of Meteora · 43
Santorini Sunsets and Scuba Diving Calamities · · · · · · · · · · · · · 46
Mountain Towns in Greece · 51
Star Gazing Cruise in Lefkada · 53
The "Onassis" Cruise in Lefkada · 55
The Corfu Vibe · 57
The Tranquility of Greek Gardens · 61
A Farm Villa in Crete · 67
A Mountain View in Crete · 70
Greek Mythology on our Greece Trip · 72
My Son's Journals · 74
Greek Island Musings · 78
Midnight in a bar in Brussels, Belgium ....and the most medieval square in all of Europe · 80

Gypsy Family Travel Evolves ·83
Using Bloom's Taxonomy in Travel Planning · · · · · · · · · · · · · · · ·88
Castles and Cathedrals ·90
Cardio Chaos in Canada- Ziplining and Whale Watching · · · · · · · · · · ·92
Creating Gypsy Family Travel ·95
Irresistible Ireland ·98
Dazzling Dingle Peninsula in Ireland · 101
Majestic Muckross House in Killarney—A Victorian Mansion · · · · · · · · 103
Tantalizing Torc Waterfall · 105
Mohammed, Muslims and Mystical Morocco · · · · · · · · · · · · · · · · · 107
The Rock of Gibraltar · 116
The Alhambra in Granada, Spain · 118
Legendary Loch Ness in Scotland · 120
Saturated by Scotland · 123
The Highlands of Scotland · 126
Rambling Las Ramblas · 128
The Splendor of Seville · 132
Planning the next Odyssey · 136
The Alps, Alpine Slide and the "Willy Wonka"
wonder of Switzerland · 142
A Trance in France · 145
A Vineyard in Germany · 147
"Al-lo in Austria and Lichtenstein · 149
Magnificent Milano · 151
Mambo Italiano · 154
The Vatican · 156
Vividly Venice · 158
Organic Farm in Orvieto · 160
Hawaii Hedonism · 162
The Menagerie of Mexico · 166
A Sunset Cruise Gone Awry · 169
"Mother and Son Reunions...are only a ticket away"
Dominican Republic · 172

"Yes, I know how to operate a catamaran" Aruba, Bahamas, Curacao, Puerto Rico · 175
The First Baby Chick Leaves the Nest · 178
A Journey Within · 182
Intensely India · 185
An Indian Wedding Extravaganza · 188
The Pulse of India · 195
The Spectacular Taj Mahal · 198
A moment of Namaste in India: Udaipur · · · · · · · · · · · · · · · · · · · 200
Elephant Rides and Snake Charmers · 202
Blogs, Guest Blogging and Magazine Travel Writing · · · · · · · · · · · · 205
My Sons' Global Awareness · 211
My son's visit to Mount Athos, Greece · 214
Our Youngest Son's Interview on Travel · 224
The DNA of Wanderlust · 226
My Mother's Fabulous First Journey · 232
My Step-mother's Story: Surviving the Armenian Genocide · · · · · · · 236
A Peruvian Quinceanera in Tulsa · 240
"What's Down in the Basement?" · 243
Be Happy for This Moment · 249
The Greek Muses · 251
Philanthropic Connections and Opportunities · · · · · · · · · · · · · · · 256
Expanding my Gypsy Family · 259
Chicken Cacciatore ala Orvieto · 269
Greek Lamb Chops · 270
Dakos Salad in Crete · 271
Parsnip Soup of Ireland · 273
Tagines of Morocco · 274
Rabo de Toro recipe ingredients (Gibraltar) · · · · · · · · · · · · · · · · 276
Neeps and Tatties in Scotland · 277
Paella in Marbella....Sangria and Tapas · 279

A Magic Carpet Ride

I'M ON A sail boat in the Ionian Sea, somewhere between the islands of Skorpios and Lefkada in Greece, kissed by perfect zephyr breezes and the sun's rays. I'm sitting in a bathing suit and white tee shirt with my arm around my husband, watching my oldest son Greek dance with passengers, my youngest son pulling the masts up and "steering" the boat and my middle son enjoying ice cold watermelon slices being served to all the passengers. I've just had a shot glass of Ouzo and Greek olives. The sea is shockingly turquoise blue and I've just been to a bucket-list islet called Skorpios which had been Onassis's private island. I'm thinking out loud, "This is a perfect moment in life."

I think of the eloquent and famous quote by Omar Khayya'm, "Be happy for this moment. This moment is your life."

Choosing to go to the island of Lefkada came about after reading about the Epirus area of Greece's mainland. Lefkada is close to Epirus and peaked my curiosity. We had vacationed on the Aegean Sea side of Greece frequently and had not been to the Ionian side for decades. Furthermore, we had Greek-American friends who vacation on Lefkada every summer and there was an opportunity to meet up with them which we knew would be fun for our sons.

The verdant, rolling hills of Lefkada eased and reposed us into the landscape after being on a twelve hour overnight ferry boat ride from Bari, Italy. This lush, forested island was very redolent of the Ionian beauty we experienced on Corfu two years before. The Ionian Side has a unique beauty in the manner that the islands are not as barren and rocky as many other island clusters of Greece.

Our mountain villa, ensconced high up into the mountain village of Vafkeri was a luxurious weeklong retreat for us. The staggering views from our pool patio made us facetiously imagine how the gods felt on Mount Olympus. Everywhere you looked, there were trees, rolling hills and islets in the sea. Knowing we'd be going to Skorpios on this trip and being able to see the nearby islets was an exalted feeling for me as the trip planner. Connecting all the dots to achieve the perfect vacation is a challenge that I gladly accept. Seeing my husband relax on a chaise lounge after he drank in the views was my ultimate reward. Later, he'd lean over the railing of the villa property to enjoy the vistas. It is unusual to ever see him totally relax as he loves to go, go, go. Only in Greece does Patrick relax fully.

After settling in, one of the first activities we did was meeting up with our Greek-American friends who were vacationing there. The meeting point was brilliant on my friend's part. She suggested we meet at Porto Katsiki beach. We were not expecting to find what we did there. The sparkling and gleaming water on this sun saturated beach blew us away. Porto Katsiki (Port of the Goat) beach was so blue it looked like a blue paint can had fallen over into the sea. We had to reach the beach by staircases of a hundred steps or more.

The reunion with our friends was filled with nonstop photos as they were proud and excited to show us such a beautiful place. In this atmospheric and convivial moment, I was reminded of how my mother made these remote connections happen for us when we visited Greece in childhood summer trips. She was the master of social networking and charmingly bold and friendly. Is this what was happening to me? Was I now the Greek mother networking with fellow Greeks and showing my children a more "native" side of Greece and Hellenism? The irony of my sons greeting their Greek-American camp friends on another continent in their ancestral homeland made them laugh as they greeted and hugged each other. The day was dazzling and the moment was brimming with excitement. No matter how many times both of our families had been to Greece, we just kept staring at the view of the ocean. It kind of knocks the wind out of you, visually---but also, emotionally. There is no denying it---we are just so overwhelmingly proud of our magnificent ancestral homeland.

Our villa was near Karia, a village which is nicknamed the "embroidery capital of Greece." Nydri is the larger town nearby. It was a good twenty minute drive down the mountain to get to the port town of Nydri. Excursions on Lefkada were totally different from any of the other Greek islands we've toured. Lefkada is old-fashioned in the way that it's not touristy and it has an authenticity to it. When you look onto the port from the mountainside, it looks like a 1950's postcard. A full week there was perfect. You can walk right up to any boat on the port and ask for the two cruises I recommend. *Captain Gerasimos's boat with the huge eye on the mast is the one I recommend.*

Our villa was a paradise to come home to everyday. The boys plunged into the big pool in the Ionian heat of the sun and we lounged in our chaises sunbathing and taking photos of the florals. We'd lean over our fence and stare at the mountains surrounding us as we identified the island of Skorpios in the distance. This was a thrill for me as I am fascinated with the history of Ari Onassis who owned the private island of Skorpios.

Every morning when Patrick and I had our coffee and tea on the patio, Yianni would feed and play with three tiny kittens who would find us and the bowl of milk we'd put out for them. Stray cats are everywhere in Greece and they are part of the restaurant scene, too. This was a perfect way to start the day for our youngest son because it gave him some continuity to a feeling of recreation back home with his own pets that he was surely missing. Animals at your own private villa sure beats being at a hotel in this regard. With there being five of us in our family, the villa and rental car combination was the way to go since most European countries don't permit more than four people to a hotel room or to a taxi. Because of this fact, we enjoyed bigger residences and roomier cars and vans during our trips and this worked out fine for a family of five with three sons!

The trip memories of our time on Lefkada may be the centerpiece of our family travels; our magic carpet ride. The trips before and after this one are significant, too, and have influenced my passion for travel writing and my desire to create educational travel planning lessons for families.

Sorting through the memories of the trips and organizing the information peeled back layers of a story. Our story has felt like a magic carpet ride through so many glorious countries. We've been transported physically, emotionally and mentally through the journey of global awareness. Each destination is its own story threaded within a bigger tapestry of the story of our family spirit....our gypsy family's travels. While writing this book, I was playing background music and the lyrics jumped out at me.

> *"No one else can feel it for you; only you can let it in.*
> *No one else can speak the words on your lips. Drench yourself in words unspoken; live your life with arms wide open. Today is where your book begins. The rest is still unwritten."*
>
> (Natasha Bedingfield)

Today IS where my book begins. I have always adored those lyrics from the song "Unwritten" because it is so apparent how illuminated the singer is and how much she celebrates expression and evolution. The song breaks open with an ethnic melody which makes it universal and instantly, I'm riveted. It is said she wrote it for her teenage brother who was on the brink of his life and self-discovery. She is full of hope and soul stretching. It if full of sisterly love and, in my interpretation, an appreciation for ethnic musical beats and vibes...a perfect background melody for me as I wrote this book. I interpret is as the singer being filled with curious hope for her brother, a young man, to feel his spirt, take risks and fly off into the world. I relate to that since I'm raising three young men with my husband. Parents give their children "roots and wings" and ironically, I feel that my sons helped me find my wings.

When I put together the photo albums after the family trips or took excerpts from my travel journals to insert into my travel blog or magazine writing, I realized that the photojournalism of those trips was my open love letter to my sons and my husband. This project wasn't a song like what the aforementioned singer accomplished for her brother---but an artistic expression, nevertheless, hoping to paint with my words and edit our photos into a storybook for them. *The progression of voices in the book reflects the progression of voices within my journals, depending on my age at the time.*

The fictional Aladdin took Jasmine on a flying magic carpet to sights unseen. Their relationship embodied discovery, freedom and wanderlust. Patrick and I had already traveled extensively before we became a couple and we had even met up with each other briefly in Greece when we were teens. But now, as a family, we started new travels together with our sons. Because of Patrick's nomadic flair to sometimes traverse several countries in a day by rental car or my desire to ferry to a new continent on a day trip from Europe to Asia or Europe to Africa, I facetiously started to compare our family to a band of gypsies.

The gypsy spirit is found in the vagabonds who roll up their tents and move camp. Like the nomads who used Persian carpets as their flooring to ground their tents, we had the spirit of a magic carpet. We took our curiosity on a magic carpet ride in the form of planes, trains, rental cars and ferry boats.

Traversing four continents with our sons was never ending information, knowledge and adventure and some locations were more exotic than others. This season in our family life is what might have defined our spirit. It was that pivotal time as a family when your personalities collaborate and the synergy pushes you to reach goals. This particular season was when the children were out of infancy and not yet into the young adult stage. Touring so many countries together left us mentally and physically breathless, in a good way. When we'd return back home from our trips, we tried to copy recipes from many countries and even hold dinner parties with friends showcasing these recipes. I'd set out tablecloths or tea towels from those countries, play the regional music and run the slideshow of that trip on my computer. I've included some of the recipes in the book.

Writing this book developed because of many revelations that convinced me it was time to organize my travel journals and records into a story and travel guide. I struggled a little with how the intention would be perceived. I asked myself, "will people find it useful?", "Will it encourage traveling?" "Will it spread a positive global message?" I wanted my experiences to become useful knowledge to others considering travel---not to come across as pretentious. I still struggle with that possible perception. I know how fortunate my family of origin was to see so many places because of my father's flying privileges as an airlines employee. I never take that for granted. Later, in my own family with my husband and sons, we prioritized traveling by making financial sacrifices in other areas. I am grateful for that spirit of adventure.

In a season of purging and editing my home to prepare for an impending empty nest, items began to reappear in my life that seemed to point to an opportunity to delve into travel writing. Those will be revealed in later chapters. My life was also experiencing changes and transitions in my roles and my psyche seemed to be redirecting to new purposes. A journey to India motivated a makeover in my goals and a transformation in my attitude in taking new risks. I wanted to write and edit all of our photos from all of the countries we traveled to together as a family and some that we traveled to independently. I would call the blog Gypsy Family Travel and it would contain travel tips, itineraries and lesson plans on how to research trips with your children. Those explanations will be explained throughout the book as well as descriptions of the origin of our wanderlust and global awareness.

You may have read a travel book about the divorcee starting a new chapter in her life or a travel writer from a prestigious magazine being sent on assignment with only twenty four hours notice. You may have read travel books or articles about the young millennials backpacking around the world. I am none of those people and all of those people. I have *some* qualities of those aforementioned people, for example, I am starting a new chapter in my life; but I'm not divorced. I am a travel writer for a magazine. I am backpacking sometimes to exotic places with my sons and husband, but I'm not a millennial and I don't stay in youth hostels. My story of wanderlust is different. I am a mom in a happy marriage and partnership, raising a family and having adventures with my husband and three sons. SHOCKER! It can be expensive, logistically challenging, full of random complications but it's also priceless, adventurous, thrilling, risky, transformative and magical.

Every country held special meaning and memories but the country that remains deep in our hearts is our ancestral homeland of Greece. Another quote I read once that was powerful for me was *"Greece is God's love affair with the planet Earth."* I don't know who said it and I know the combination of words is odd but I understand how someone could compare the creation of Greece to a love affair. Greece has everything a country should have: islands, mountains, villages, metropolitan cities, delectable cuisine, glamorous shopping, impressive history and leisure at its art form. The colorful personality of the country and the vibe of the culture makes Greece approachable and addictive.

Greece is the destination retreat for much of Europe because of its southern location and its thousands of islands. Frolicking in Greece and reveling in the sensuous sunshine is therapeutic and intoxicating. It *never* changes—whether you are a child basking in it, a honeymooner playing cards and splashing in the waves with your soulmate or enjoying it with your children---the Greek beach is something to behold and worship. It's hard to believe that water can be that blue or the temperature can be that perfect. Just when you think you're ready for a break from sun and sand, you stroll over to a beachfront cafe where the smells of delicious Greek food awaits you. Your body and mind are in complete relaxation mode and you kind of lament the day that you have to return home to reality.

That's how I felt about drinking the quintessential Cafe Frappe in a tavern on the island of Rhodes. I remember tasting that sweet concoction, staring at its swirls and thinking, no matter how much I try to duplicate this drink back home, (I asked the waiters for the recipe) I just know it's not going to taste the same without a Greek beach in front of me or a white-bloused Greek waiter to serve it to me. These coffee moments in complete relaxation mode are like a meditation. Everything in Greece is like a meditation. I'll use that word often throughout this book. After all, what is a meditation for?... it's for bringing one to a level of intention and peace. *It's a reverie.*

I wasn't born in Greece; I was born in Oklahoma. I'm first generation from my father's side and second generation from my mother's side. So to say, my "returns" to Greece should not imply that it is my birthplace. It is my country of origin; my ancestral homeland and the heritage that defines so much of how I live today. I've heard Phil-Hellenes describe Greece the same way for them and they are not even of Greek descent. Greece is just somewhere that people find their essence, somehow. It's a way of life ; you don't have to have a drop of Greek blood to embrace this country and culture. I can list many a friend who would attest to this. There were times in my life that my non-Greek friends embraced my heritage and identity almost more than I did. They gravitated towards the affectionate ambience, the smells in the kitchen, the family bonding and lively rapport constantly going on in the home or community. They became attached to the elderly, gentle grandparents in the mix and the role they played in the family constellation. I tried to sneak by all of this commotion when I brought my friends home, as if to ignore it and it might go away but my friends were politely transfixed with the interactions of my family members and they carved out their own friendships with them.

Childhood Summers in Greece

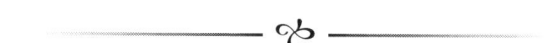

EXPERIENCING GREECE BEGAN for me in 1972. I was four years old and basically remember two things---the commotion of Athens and meeting my youthful new aunt who was joining our family by marrying my favorite uncle. She was the picture of the 1970's "that girl"--she had the hair flip, was skinny and she wore minidresses. I loved her youthful energy and I immediately clung to her —physically and emotionally. Other than that memory, I also remember asking everyone to carry me because I was not fond of all the walking in the heat. This habit continued on my next trip at seven years old.

On the trip in 1975, at seven years old, the memories were more vivid. On that trip, I discovered the sensuousness of the smells of Greece—the diesel in Athens from all of the mass transportation going on, the toasty goodness of the huge grilled pretzels on the street food stands and the village smells of the family farm. Other senses were engaged, too. The sounds of the traffic below us as we lounged on my grandmother and aunt's apartment balcony and the laughter of the school kids playing on the concrete playground of the neighborhood school became my auditory memories. So the memories of sights, sounds and smells increased with this second trip but a new sense that came about was the *feeling* I encountered in my father's village. At seven years old, I was old enough to engage in more activities on the trip. I could venture out a bit more crossing the gravel road of my relatives' house to the other side of the street to explore. Looking at the animals grazing behind the fence was better than any petting zoo I could imagine. These animals were part of my family---my father's childhood property now owned and run by caretakers who were part of his childhood. When you're seven years old, you don't necessarily interact and converse that fluently with everyone in a foreign country so interacting with the animals was perfect for me.

There's a level of confidence and success children feel with animals. My interaction with the animals turned into something adventurous and free spirited for me because rather than just peer at them through the fence or pet them, my brother and I decided to take a donkey out for a ride through the village. My brother was sixteen years old so naturally, I felt confident in his capabilities. Everything started out alright and the donkey took us on a leisurely ride through the village. This was on the morning of our departure to Athens which was three hours away from our village in the Peloponnesus. I don't recall if we asked for permission to do this but we were off on a last minute village adventure while our parents said their goodbyes and packed up. Still, to this day, that donkey ride with my beloved big brother remains one of my most thrilling childhood memories. Clomping along the gravel and dirt roads of this mountain village with the sun on our faces and the fresh mountain breeze not even really knowing where we were going was thrilling!

I trusted my big brother and he trusted that donkey. Donkeys are stubborn, however, and when Dori the donkey decided to halt, she was not going to be convinced otherwise. There we were in the middle of nowhere and we could not convince that donkey to move. We couldn't abandon her either, though. So, we didn't panic but we were worried.

One distinct memory I have about this tribulation is that my brother and I couldn't remember the correct commands that we were told to give Dori. We tried both terms for "go" and "stop" but nothing was working. Around this time, my mother was back in the neighborhood of the village, yelling out our names to find us because it was time to depart. "Gina Marie!!", she called out. "George?!" We couldn't hear her because we were quite a distance away but we heard all about it from our sister, dad and others. It was a legendary story for awhile. When my mother cried out "Gina Marie!", the villagers thought she was calling me "Gina Mori" and

"Mori" is a negative and insulting term. They thought, "this rude Greek-American woman is calling her seven year old an inappropriate term". Lost in translation! It's something we all laugh about now.

The other sense that was engaged on this trip was our sense of taste. Visiting so many relatives, one has to go through the customary rituals of sitting in someone's apartment and being served Greek delicacies. One sweet, in particular, that was served to us often was "vanilia" (va-nee-lee-a). I did not like it but you could not be rude and decline it so I learned to take tastes of it so as not to appear rude.

Vanilia and the milk in Greece were the only tastes I did not enjoy. The tastes that were other-worldly to me, however, were my yiayia's (grandmother) augolemano soupa (chicken soup) and Greek french fries cooked in olive oil. I could cry right now remembering the taste of them---and the smell of her Athenian apartment kitchen. The soup is chicken, rice and egg-lemon broth and it was so thick you could eat it with a fork. I thought of it as love in my stomach. That love was made more intense by the fact that I loved and adored HER. She was the grandmother I was named after—Yiayia Evyenia.

Evyenia is "Eugenia" in English. It means well born, queenly and courteous. To us, she *was* the Queen; queen of the kitchen and queen of our hearts. I only knew her for eleven years but to describe the loss I felt on the night we learned that she had died, would be impossible to put into words. She was more than a grandmother to me. She was a playmate when she lived in America with us for a few years.

According to my family, she really raised me in my infancy and stayed on in our hometown for three years. She was the first person to pick me up when I cried and she had the energy and adoration for me that grandmothers often do when mothers are so busy with older children and responsibilities. She and I went on walks to the convenient store and sat together while she knitted.

I first comprehended unconditional love when I noticed that she fed us watermelon but she herself could not eat it because of her diabetes. She chewed on the watermelon seeds only. I could not understand how she could feed me and my baby cousin the "nectar of the gods" when she could not eat it. How did she resist this temptation? I knew why....because she was the perfect and supernatural Yiayia who loved us unconditionally and wanted us to enjoy cold, sweet watermelon on a hot summer day.

So the 1972 and 1975 trips to Greece gave me memories of sight, sounds, taste, smell and feeling in all of those latter descriptions. It gave me the understanding and experience of another country and started to build my appreciation for global awareness. Not everybody drinks cold soft drinks. Not everybody has big backyards and houses. Some people eat vanilia rather than popsicles for snacks. I learned this and I survived! While the 1970's trips shed some light on me as a child, the 1980's trips were my teen years and brought about a level of understanding that only a teen can comprehend.

Teenage Trips in Greece

GOING TO GREECE as a fourteen, seventeen and eighteen year old made me look forward to the activities that teens look forward to---beaches and shopping. Most teenage girls jump at the chance to worship the sun and shop. Many teens, however, cannot be pulled away from their social lives and familiar routines to go somewhere foreign. This choice was made for me during my 1982 trip. I was going to Greece with my family for a month-long trip and that meant I would have to miss a week of summer camp in Wyoming with my youth group friends. I wasn't thrilled about it at the time and my mother took us on what felt like a pilgrimage to go visit everyone's relatives in some remote towns and villages of Greece. My sister and I joke about it now. We weren't even that acquainted with some of the hometown friends whose relatives we were going to see!

Yet, it was important to our mom and thank goodness we took that family trip together because three years later, she died. She felt a sense of purpose on that trip; networking and connecting people to each other. We learned from the master. Sometimes, when we drove to these remote neighborhoods, we had to ask for directions and this ended up becoming a comedy one day! Two Greek men argued with each other about who was giving the correct directions to us. We felt awkward about the ensuing fight and as we drove off, we looked behind us and saw the men still arguing and waving their hands at each other. Greeks are lively, passionate and dramatic so this goes with the territory! Observing these characteristics were part of the education of being among the Greek culture and vibe.

Another bonding event that happened for my twenty year old sister and I during this trip was that we were forced to become closer because we only had each other to converse with in English most of the time. Our big brother was working back home in Tulsa. This particular trip was the first time I went to Greece without him. We missed him—but we definitely had more room in the rental car. On those long drives between locations, my sister and I found Greek advertising vocabulary so charming and funny. We kept a journal of just these terms. Grilled cheese was called "toast" and a dance hall was called a "discoteria."

Some nights, when I stood out on my aunt's balcony in Athens, decompressing from all of the family togetherness, I would stare at the moon. I was always pretty poetic and I think I wrote several love poems on that trip, longing for my current crush. I never sent those poems, thank God, but it was cathartic to express myself. One particular night I stared at the moon and realized---that's the SAME moon that my loved ones back home in Tulsa see. I'm on the other side of the world; yet *we share the same moon.* It made me feel closer to everything. I realized how connected we all are on this Earth. No matter how different characteristics can be—like advertising vocabulary and how foods and drinks taste differently, we share the same moon. *It was cosmic. A cosmic revelation.*

This was also the first Greece trip that I first realized how much more fashionable Europe is than America---in terms of latest styles. Because the styles hit Milan, Paris, London, and Rome first ....Athens is on this route much faster than Oklahoma. Trust me. This was a huge bonus for me as a fourteen year old on the verge of creating my own style identity. For us, in America, we were on the cusp of the Madonna explosion years; a time when clothing and hair styles would reflect Madonna's eclectic style—big bows, bangle bracelets, neon midriff shirts and pumps. Self-expression was huge and emerging out of the recent preppie style years of Laura Ashley and Ralph Lauren conservative dress.

On one particular shopping day in Athens, I discovered a nuance about customer service that made me realize the differences in how countries handle this. My aunt took me to a popular sweater store that was all the rage in the mid-80's both in America and Europe. I looked through each shelf or display and proceeded to unfold sweater after sweater to examine them and decide if I was going to buy any. My aunt was treating me to an outfit that day. The saleslady came over to me and, in Greek, asked me rather confrontationally, "Miss, are you going to buy anything or are you just going to unfold every sweater??" I looked at her, puzzled by such a brash question and quickly answered, "I'm sorry."

My aunt, who does not have children but is attached to her nephews and nieces, took on a "mama bear" protective attitude and snapped back to the saleslady, "Miss! My niece is from AMERICA! And in America, the salespeople do not ever say anything like that to their customers. In fact, they tell them, "Thank you for shopping with us and have a good day!" The saleslady withdrew a bit and answered, sheepishly, "Well, this isn't America." In this awkwardness, I realized how much I should appreciate the American customer service work ethic. I admired how my aunt defended me and it was probably a little bit out of her pride of all her trips to America but also because she was trying to give me some affection and attention after my mother's death. This shopping trip was a gesture and a bonding activity for us and she felt it was spoiled by the saleslady's attitude. I found it kind of humorous but it also taught me so much that day about cultural differences but also about the side of my aunt which I had never seen before in terms of defending her niece.

I slowly accumulated some Euro-styles to my wardrobe but not much. It wasn't until the 1985 trip, at seventeen years old, when I really found my flair. I was on a mission to bring back cow hide leather purses, wool fisherman sweaters and knock off designer bags to my girlfriends and their curious mothers. Off I went to the market districts of Athens—a young amateur stylist/buyer/exporter--- prepared to please my hometown clients. While I bought them the traditional Greek items, I discovered unique "punk" accessories of safety pin bracelets, heavy hardware belts, sashes and baggy, crisp, white pants. These novelties were a hit back home. Of course, the best accessory was the deep, dark Aegean Sea suntan that is acquired while vacationing in Greece.

On this trip, it was just my father and I going for a couple of weeks to heal after my mother's death and her ten year battle with cancer. Daddy and I retreated to Greece into the loving arms of relatives and Mediterranean sun. God on Earth. I was numb from surviving what cancer's toll took on our family but I wasn't dead inside. I was seventeen and knew how to find my happy place and that was the beach and the markets. In the market places, all of the newspaper and magazines had headlines of the news of Rock Hudson having AIDS. Many acquaintances in Greece asked me if everyone in America was dying of AIDS. I had to reassure them that we were not all walking time bombs of HIV and AIDS. It became annoying to me but I found it funny, too...the hysteria of how things get exaggerated in the media. Daddy and I got our much-needed sun, squid and sulphuric hot springs of Santorini.

In 1986, we returned to Greece. It was summer again and I had just graduated from high school. I went to attend the wedding of my father to my new stepmother. I felt like someone needed to be there to support him in his big new step. I was somewhat taking the role of the parent, in a way. Maybe selfishly, it was my way of not letting go of Daddy, *physically*. I was going to be with him every step of the way.

He was surprised I wanted to go and he hadn't planned on it but being the eternally loving father that he is, he accommodated me. I was with him every day up until the wedding. At the wedding, I stood with my aunt from my mother's side of the family fighting back tears because it was the first time I realized what was really, actually happening. My father was getting married. I mean, physically, literally, in real time—my father was *getting* married---in a church---to another woman who wasn't my mother. My mother was gone. Seeing it in person was probably the best way to accept this. I was the only family member to witness this as my older, married siblings were back home with my grandfather (my mother's parent) just awaiting our new family member but not really ever seeing this marriage happen in person. I realize now how young my dad was –he was only fifty-two years old at the time. I am almost that age, now. I was glad to be there for him. My dad and my new stepmom had their backs to us, facing the priest and receiving their marriage sacrament. It was unusual for me to watch my father have his back to me. There is a statement regarding family dynamics, "sometimes you stand beside your child but sometimes you stand in front of them"--one connotes supporting your child; the other connotes protecting them. Defending them. In a way, with my father's back to me, and me standing in a pew behind him, I wasn't being left behind in his first steps to a new relationship and life.... but rather, I was protecting and defending his choice; his choice to heal, to move forward, to rebuild and to experience love again.

The tears I fought back were just as much about embracing that I was becoming more of an equal to my father; becoming an adult. I was a few weeks away from being eighteen; an adult old enough to vote and be independent. I would always be his youngest child, his baby; his "last frontier," he lovingly called me. But in this event, in this case, I was learning adult concepts, like maturing and understanding that change is inevitable. I was learning that you and your parents and siblings experience moments in life that are monumental. You survive them. You succeed or you fail. We deserved to succeed at surviving what cards we were dealt. We were a family that survived cancer even if our mother did not.

That night, my cousin and her husband, who live in Athens, took me out to keep me occupied. They kept me company as I stared in silence trying to process what just happened with this new marriage. We sat in a huge plaza with a crowd of people, tables, waiters, plates of food, maybe music and yet, I felt like I was in a vacuum of silence. I wasn't lonely but I was alone; alone in my thoughts and experience in that day. I was singularly dealing with this huge and new change. My sweet cousin kept checking on me, emotionally. I didn't have much to say which is always unusual for me. I am a loquacious person and I know it. At nearly eighteen, I was boisterous, enthusiastic for life and talkative.

This may have been one of the first times when I was solemn and speechless. I wasn't deflated though. Nothing much deflates me, at least, not for very long.

That night, I spent the night at my aunt and uncle's apartment. This aunt was my dad's sister and it was one of the ways his family rallied around us in the aftermath of our tragic loss of mom.

Before I went to bed that night, my cousin told me words of support and acknowledged that she knew I was going through something difficult on this day. Although I couldn't emote and preferred to stay numb and tough, she will never know what her support and love meant to me that night. I have always tried to pay that kindness forward to others in the same shoes.

The rest of Daddy's honeymoon week, I spent with my other aunt on a short trip to a nearby coastal town for her business trip. While she and her colleague went to a business conference, his teenage son and I walked around the coastal town and beach, bonding over American bands and trivia. It was nice to have another teen to converse with amidst all the loving relatives. On this walk through the coastal town, I could forget everything and just focus on the fact this new acquaintance, a virtual stranger, and I both liked the the band The Violet Femmes. Although this boy and I came from different parts of the world, a love for music is universal. Teens can be so different and yet so alike. After small talk and courteousness, we sat in the rental car just to enjoy The Violet Femmes in mostly silence with a few critiques here and there about this popular new album. The week was soon over and there were some difficult good byes with relatives as it was an emotional time.

So the 1986 trip was definitely an eye opening and intense week. It brought about some maturity or "pre-maturity" as I like to refer to it. My term for when someone has to grow up fast and before their time in some ways. I witnessed intense emotions and other dynamics that often happen in a big family. My father's family is big, loving, beautiful and intense. With my father being one of five children, his is the family that gave me my treasured aunts, a loving and influential Godmother and my uncle who has always been an important presence in my life. My mother's family is also loving, influential, driven and religious. She was an only child but her cousins are my treasured aunts as well and so very influential in my life. It is said, "It takes a village to raise a child"--and how grateful I am to have this village. I got to see relatives from both sides of the family that week and I was ready to come home to my hometown friends and relatives. I returned home with a wonderful new stepmother and some new funky merchandise that was a hit with my friends. I bonded right away with the step mom and we strolled through the streets of Munich on our layover to America. So far, so good. I found her pretty, shy and affectionate. It was all pretty amicable on this transition week. Once at home, there were adjustments of course. But overall, she was our angel and we still feel blessed to have her in our lives.

Honeymoon in Greece

THE NEXT FOUR years were about college, getting engaged and married. What a whirlwind college is for a female. You enter college as a teenage girl, usually and exit as a woman. In my case, I exited as an almost twenty-two year old woman, with a degree and a marriage! I married in May —at the end of my senior year with one more year to go in a double major. My husband, also a Greek-American, suggested we go to Greece for our honeymoon and not only was it an appropriate way to culminate our formal and festive Greek wedding but it was also romantic and elaborate. Two twenty-somethings going off to Europe with two big borrowed backpacks, winging it on ferry boat rides to whatever island we picked that day and staying in pensions and bed and breakfasts. A three week honeymoon in Greece with my perfect husband, mate and lover far exceeded my expectations. Patrick knew how to navigate all over Greece and he practically memorized the streets of Athens as this was his third trip there. He spoiled me rotten and indulged me in every possible way. Everywhere we went, the Phil Collins song rang out, *"It's just another day for you and me in paradise."* So appropriate. The song is about homeless people and how the rest of us should not take our lives for granted. Here we were, traipsing around the true paradise on Earth, island hopping and going home to a house full of unopened wedding gifts, getting ready to fluff our nest and start our life together.

This three week long trip in Greece exposed us to six islands, time with relatives and fun adventures as we immersed in the culture. We rode on our Athenian friend's death-defying motorcycle through the hectic streets of Athens clinging to each other for dear life. We revisited important sights, spent time with relatives and made new friends along the way.

We met an artist friend who taught us about the custom of "pikilia." He had one of the most posh apartments I had seen at the time---with a view of Lecavito on one side and the Acropolis on the other. This artist friend in his chic apartment was enjoying hosting us (the young, casual, Greek American newlyweds)---and in his hospitable way, he announced "Let's have some pikilia!" and dashed off to his kitchen.

My husband and I looked at each other puzzled. We had never heard this word before. Our friend came back to the table with a beautiful display of what we would call in America "charcuterie" or appetizers. *Doesn't it sound more charming, however, to say "PIKILIA"....it was like a little tune.* I say it all the time. Now, it's our custom to make a pikilia platter often....whether at home entertaining, or while traveling.

Later in the trip, we made friends with a shop owner on the cliff of Santorini and went out with him and his Canadian girlfriend to the discos and taverns. They introduced us to "Captain", their friend who took us out on a boat ride to the hot springs and fumaroles of the active volcano of Santorini and let us steer the boat. Greeks are so hospitable that way. You can meet a shop owner, make friends with him and next thing you know he is introducing you to his girlfriend, going out to the bars with you and giving you information to contact his friend who will give you a personal boat tour of Santorini!

There were so many other wonderful connections we made as well as the quiet moments together playing Gin Rummy on the topless and nude beaches. We drank in the sun and we drank in the fresh squeezed orange juice, beer and cocktails. No matter how much good food we ate daily, we still went home thinner from all of the walking and lack of snacking. Greece is so good to you in that way. You return home thinner, with a better haircut or style and with a deep tan. The relaxed look on your face makes you look like you've been to a spa and the chic new clothes you usually end up with make you look Euro-fabulous.

The First Family Trip to Greece

IN THE SEVENTEEN year gap until I returned to Greece, there was a flurry of marriage, career, new houses, three babies and trips. It was time to return to Greece. We always thought about it but we were waiting for the right time. Relatives came and went to Greece. Friends came and went to Greece. We knew when our youngest son turned a certain age, it would be the right time to go. He was going to be six soon and our other two sons were nine and eleven. I bit the bullet and told my husband I was buying the airline tickets with money I saved up from my part time psychometry job. I cut corners on household expenses and my husband's pride perked up when he purchased the remaining airline tickets and provided us with a glorious vacation in wonderful hotels, villas and excursions. I know if I hadn't pushed for this trip to happen, there might never have been the "right time" to go. But it was heavy on my mind for me to see the boys' faces when they saw Greece's soil for the first time. I had a vision in my mind of how I would feel, vicariously, when I observed them seeing the Acropolis for the first time and for them to understand their roots. I used to get teary about it all the time. They liked this emotion in me and they felt a connection to me in this moment. I was their "Greek School" teacher for several years and I tutored them at home in Greek language. They looked to me for those traditions and my husband supported this and contributed to it with his own Greek customs and traditions.

The preparation for this trip back to Greece was overwhelming. Logistics, itinerary, tools to make the flight easier and the host gifts you to take to the relatives are all part of the preparation and cargo to have a successful journey to Greece. It's a good thing I didn't think about all those logistics before I bought the airline tickets or it may have prevented me from going. Once these details were set in place, I was able to emotionally connect again to the motivation to go in the first place. This was going to be the full circle moment trip for me. A mother with her husband taking their sons to their ancestral homeland. I opened my heart and soul up for what this adventure would have in store for us.

We touched down in Greece at the Athens airport and my heart was racing. I knew my relatives were waiting for us at the gate. My dear aunt, her daughter, and her family awaited us. My sister and her friend were with them, too. After a long flight, it was a little overwhelming emotionally to comprehend this moment. As I hugged each person lovingly and introduced my sons to my aunt and their cousins for the first time, I was filled with the realization that our journey to Greece had officially begun! My sons had met my cousin three years prior in America to this but they had never met her husband or daughters. It was an emotional moment and I could feel the love my aunt was emanating.

After all, my sons were the grandsons of her brother. What a flood of memories she must've been thinking about regarding her childhood with her siblings, and my father, specifically. Now, the next generation was building memories together. My sister was anxiously awaiting her hugs, too, as she was excited to show her nephews "her Greece." We were going to be staying with my sister at her Athens apartment for the first time and she had been preparing it for our stay.

The next few weeks in Greece were balanced with meeting family and island hopping. Upon meeting each relative, the connections grew for our sons and they began to identify with who they were in the family tree. Even with the language barrier (because the boys read and write Greek but can't speak it fluently), it was impressive to watch how cousins interact with each other. Words don't seem necessary—there is just a bond through body language, smiles and togetherness. The trend that summer was a craft called "scoobidoo" that kids would weave together much like the friendship bracelets of the late 1980's. My sons and their girl cousins sat for long periods of time together in silence making these crafts and communicating through "Greenglish" and sign language. When children are left to their own devices, they keep each other entertained. They find their peers among the crowds of adults and the long car rides while sightseeing. I also observed that my sons just sensed that they were related to their cousins and that was good enough for them. There was an importance in that realization to them. There was a trust that they released themselves into which allowed them to accept and fully engage in this journey of family.

Exploring Athens

AMIDST ALL THE bonding with relatives and introducing the sons to family members, we also introduced them to Athens, the capital of Greece. Millions of people live there and it's everything you expect a capital city to be---populated, busy, exciting, full of monuments, shops, restaurants and traffic.

In the approximately eleven million people who live in Greece, approximately 3.75 million live in the metropolitan area of Athens. (665,00 in the city proper). Mass transportation and parking are stressful situations but the pulse of the city is exciting. We can't help but love our visits to Athens.

Taking my sons through Athens was daunting as we had to be careful with subways, crossing streets, etc. My husband and I had seen Athens many times before as individuals or as a couple but seeing it through my sons' eyes for the first time was precious to me because we had studied Athens for years and I was eager to show them our ancestral homeland.

The Parthenon can be best understood and appreciated when you watch the video about it in The Acropolis Museum. To know what the Parthenon actually looked like in its original design is important because the stone color of it now is from years of erosion and pollution. Observing the marbles and the sculptures within its top layer is something you can appreciate best in person. The architectural design of the styles of columns of various temples and buildings is explained so well at the Acropolis Museum exhibits and film presentations.

The Parthenon Marbles (referred to as the "Elgin" Marbles) are housed in the British Museum in England. The controversy of the "Elgin" Marbles is a heated subject as there are philosophical problems with these marbles not being in their original home of the Acropolis. The history behind Lord Elgin taking them to England to preserve them is an intense subject. <u>Stealing Athena</u> by Karen Essex is a good book for adults to read about this topic as it weaves back and forth between the stories of Pericles, the architect of the Parthenon and Lord Elgin and his explorations. This topic of the "Elgin Marbles" received international attention when a celebrity recently became an activist for this cause. As a Greek-American, I paid close attention to this information in the news and I admire the effort behind the activism.

On our first day in Athens in 2007, my sister encouraged my husband and I to go take a jog while she settled into her apartment with our sons. She looked forward to time with her nephews and she wanted us to stretch our legs after a long flight. We weren't far from the Olympic Stadium of the 1800's and we thought it would be very appropriate to jog there. Greece has Ancient Olympia, home of the first games ever, the Olympic stadium of the 1896 games and the modern Olympic Stadium of 2004. We saw them all and they are a source of great pride for me. Walking to the 1896 Olympic stadium from my sister's apartment was very special and memorable as I was so happy for her that she created this second home for herself in her beloved land of Greece. Jogging on this track with my handsome Greek-American husband was poignant for me because not only was Greece our ancestral homeland and honeymoon destination but now we were here with our three Greek-American sons for the first time to show them their roots. It's hard to be in Greece and not burst with pride at all of the legacies within us.

Rhodes—Island of Sun

After we did all there was to do in Athens, we flew to the island of Rhodes. I had always wanted to see Rhodes, or as the Greeks call it: Rodos. Flying into Rhodes (Rodos) from Athens was spectacular because you could see Turkey as well. Two continents in one glance --Europe and Asia.

We rented a car and drove to Pefkos which was forty five minutes away. We didn't mind being "lost" or unsure of directions because Rhodes is so mind-blowing beautiful. This gave us an opportunity to observe the terrain of Rhodes. We were so surprised at the greenery of this island! It resembled Colorado with its pine trees everywhere! I remember thinking I smelled eucalyptus trees, even.

I seem to remember reading somewhere about this "island of Helios (sun)" because it gets 300+ days of bright sunshine a year. Our rented villa's garden was full of fruit trees which excited our six year old so much. He checked to see if the figs were ready. (He's learned this skill from his Papou (grandpa). We relaxed on our villa balcony while the boys played ball in the garden. In perfect timing, a billy goat from the adjacent property came right up to our fence. How perfect!

We found a Panorama Cafe which remains one of the best views of Greece I've ever seen. The royal blue water turns purple out in the horizon. Rodos takes my breath away like so many places in Greece. I know it's the top three of islands for me. Our youngest son found lizards everywhere we went---this was his mission on the trip. While we absorbed other cultural highlights, our youngest remained focused on the flora and fauna of this geological wonder called Greece.

We bought local honey at a street side food stand--native Rodos honey--which is inexplicably delicious due to the unique cultivation of the area and the herbs from which the bees pollinate. A dollop of this clover honey became part of our breakfast ritual---in tea, on biscuits, etc. and of course, we brought some home as gifts. Rhodes has a uniqueness to it because of its Medieval influences. We walked through Medieval town's cobblestone paths, fortifications and we saw where the Colossus of Rhodes once stood in the harbor. Although it's not there anymore, to envision where this statue (one of the seven wonders of the world) stood, was a moment!

Our daily walks included a stroll to the zaharoplasteion (a bakery of artisan sweets), a purchase of tiropita (cheese pie) and spanakopita (spinach-cheese pie). One day, the boys all went to the beach in the late afternoon while I stayed at the villa in Pefkos, called Milos Villas. I wrote in my journal, tidied up the villa, walked through the garden and enjoyed the *sea breezes, ocean view, safety, tranquility, and privacy of this existence.* At night, I listened to the crickets and the late night parties in the distance as well as the occasional odd bird or animal sound.

Our favorite memory of Rhodes was riding the donkeys up through the village of Lindos. Looking into the shops and villas gave us an idea of the town combined with a recreational activity! I gasped as I peered into each shop or home. Rhodes was utterly beautiful and delightful. At night, we danced in Nikolas's Taverna in the city of Pefkos (not far from our villa). As we ate our dinner and heard the soulful Greek music beating out of the speakers, the feeling overcame us to just get up and dance. The waiter called out to the owner inside, in Greek, saying, "The Greek-American mama is dancing with her sons" as my husband took our video. He eventually joined in the dance line along with the waiter and owner, too. The other customers enjoyed this spectacle. It was a great impulse in the middle of my journal writing while the family ate dessert. I asked myself, "This was what it's all about, isn't it?" The Greek school lessons, the Greek dance lessons, ---they shouldn't just be *lessons*---they should be a lifestyle; moments in reality. I knew my sister, back home, would be thrilled beyond words because she is my sons' Greek dance instructor. This moment wasn't about costumed dancers on a stage at the Greek Festival back home in Tulsa, but about feeling the impulse to get up and dance, in casual clothes, out in the sea breezes in a taverna atop the sea.

It was hard to comprehend how blue the ocean was on these Rodos beaches. We parked our rental car on the side of a village road to take photos. Outside of a restaurant called Panorama Cafe, we stood there in disbelief to take in the panoramic view. It was at that moment that I first realized that the ocean water in Greece has layers to its hues. Closest to the shore, the water is clear, then green, then mediterranean blue, then navy blue and then, miraculously, purple. Together they make that Grecian blue but if you look closely, it's layers of blues, except on the island of Lefkada, where it is solidly the most turquoise blue the eye can ever absorb. It was opaque, thick, sensuous and shockingly turquoise blue. On the boat cruises through the Ionian islets off Lefkada, all I can remember feeling is the ecstasy of physical feelings of happiness. The body was totally consumed with the feeling of happiness; separate and together with the mind and soul. Every fiber of my being was out there in that sea of turquoise, lapping up every breeze, every wave crashing, every beam and ray of sun shining on us. But Lefkada is another chapter. I digress. Let's get back to Rhodes which was just as insanely magnificent.

On Rhodes, we discovered the lovely city of Lindos. The donkey rides up the winding roads through Lindos beckoned to us. We waited on the town square for this magical donkey ride but what happened during that wait was even more magical for me, as a mom. My oldest son, eleven years old at the time, was conversing in a slow and carefully thought out Greek speech with a nine year old native boy. I listened carefully and intently from a few feet away to hear them. Luke asked him, "Pos se lene?" (how are you called/what is your name?) and the boy answered, "Me lene Nikos." (I am called Nick) Success! Luke built up to "Poso hronon eisai?" and Niko answered, "Emai enaia hrono" (I am nine). Lastly, Luke asked him "Apo pou eisa?" (Where are you from?) and Niko answered, "Apo etho —Lindos" (from here, Lindos.) Three sentences! A conversation, nevertheless. My Greek-American son was *communicating* with a foreign child in Greece....a complete stranger; not a relative....and he was understanding him!

The boy, in turn, asked Luke some questions and I assisted Luke in his answers. This exchange could not have made me happier; not only as a mom but as a Greek School teacher, too. My sons were my Greek School students and this was the ultimate field trip we were on! We were immersing in a culture, *our* culture, our heritage and one of the most beautiful countries in the world which happens to be one of the most influential civilizations in the world.

The conversation that took place in the city center while we waited for our donkey ride was the first of several splendid moments in Lindos. No one could have prepared us for what was about to transpire next. The trail of donkeys lined up for us and others to join was so exhilarating for me vicariously with the boys. My husband trailed behind us on foot, as he preferred to run up the hill beside us. Each shop or pension we looked into on the right and left of us as we rode up the hill was a perfect lesson in Grecian architecture. The design of each alcove was a stunningly simple but breathtaking aesthetic of art and living. Everything about the shop or residence we peered into was designed to look out onto the view of the sea. Atop our donkeys, we looked through each shop, home or art gallery with a view that spilled out onto the open navy blue sea of Rhodes. I kept looking back at my husband, gasping at the beauty and asking him if he was catching all of this.

When we reached the top of the hill, we explored the Acropolis of Lindos -Temple of Athena which is a Doric structure and archeological site. We stretched our legs and caught our breath after that visually stunning donkey ride up the hill of this most posh town of Lindos. The donkey ride was a perfect excursion for the boys and a little archeology is always fascinating but ending the day at the beach in Lindos was perfectly appropriate. While the boys ran off ramps and jumped into the water, I caressed the sea shells and ran my toes back and forth in soft sand. I showed my husband each piece of what seemed like sea glass. The shells and glass were as clear and vibrant as the water. Lindos was a gorgeous surprise but it was time to return to our rented villa in Pefkos.

One of the things I always appreciate about Greece and other trips, is the fact that you can live simply in your villa, not dependent on each gadget or appliance you have at home. Our villa in Pefkos was three stories high with balconies, a full kitchen and a big yard full of fruit trees. Even though it had a washer and dryer, I was intrigued with the circular clothesline outside. It made sense to me to dry our clothes and bathing suits out there in the fresh Rodos air everyday rather than use the electricity of the washer and dryer. Something about being in such a natural beauty of a country like Greece, makes one more aware of environmental courtesies. Environmentalism is very big in Europe out of necessity for this small continent's resources and as part of their political beliefs. My cousins' school plays and musical programs are actually about protecting the environment. Their schools curriculum teaches this environmental awareness. In our poshest rented villas, I saw no problem with simply rinsing out our clothes in liquid soap in our sink and then hanging them to dry outside on our balcony or clothesline. Not that this is the method of the locals, but because as a vacationer, I simplified my own routine in order to feel the break from home chores...and finding a laundromat or paying the thirteen euros to have the pension owner do our laundry for us. After all, we were living in swimsuits and cover ups all day, anyway, it seems.

Our time in Rhodes ended with an enchanting day meandering through the streets of the Medieval town, sipping sweet and cold cafe frappe in a taverna and buying an ornate gold ring with a medieval cross on it for my birthday. The handmade ring was full of intricate details, Grecian royal blue lapis and enamel and even the band had details on it. The ring is always a symbol to me of our time in atmospheric Old Rodos Town in the middle of a majestic medieval fortress town draped under magnificent bougainvillea.

The Tapestry of Turkey

ONE DAY, ON a walk through Rhodes town, I saw a flyer on a travel agency window advertising excursions to Turkey. The Turkish port of Marmaris was a one-hour ferry boat ride from Rhodes. This strongly enticed me, for various reasons. My husband was hesitant but I pointed out to him the benefits of this idea. "Our kids and us can add another continent to our list---ASIA...and another country!" I also felt it was important to see and experience the exotic country that has so much historic connection to our ancestral homeland of Greece. Sure, the connection is mostly negative and tragic but as an educator and a humanist, I feel there is something important in *understanding* other cultures and experiencing it first hand—not just believing it from a book or lesson. My husband knew he wasn't going to be able to convince me otherwise, so, hesitantly, he agreed to this excursion. The expense was going to be worth it in my eyes. As strange as it sounds, I was fascinated to see the country of the people who inhabited my ancestors' village and island and drove them out as political refugees in the 1920's. Centuries before that, the Greeks endured oppression from the Turks for four hundred years, approximately.

Back then, hidden Greek schools, held in caves, had classes in the middle of the night to continue instructing their children to keep their Greek language, traditions and religion alive. This oppression made us who we are today. The poem is one of the first Greek poems we learn as children. It describes how the students walked in the moonlight to their hidden schools to learn their lessons.

The translation of it is:

> My little shining moon,
> Light my way so I can walk
> To go to school,
> To learn my lessons,
> Reading and writing,
> God's wishes.

Other tragic events in Greek-Turkish conflicts occurred all the way up to modern times but I was not deterred by this fact when it came to seeing another country or continent. I have lovely Turkish-American friends back home in Tulsa and we respect each other and find our own unity and bond.

The tour in Marmaris offered a variety of things to see and experience: a visit to the Gold Center, a Persian rug factory, a loukoum factory and a Turkish bazaar. I was told for years that the gold in Turkey is exquisite! We toured through the Gold Center and admired the unique design settings of the gold jewelry. The rug factory was a favorite for my youngest son. He sat and watched the ladies at their looms for an hour straight—just fascinated at their technique. I bought two kilims from the rug factory and was so ecstatic to take them home in their own little duffel! There are many styles of rugs, kilims, etc. The rug factory tour explains the differences in detail. They are all works of art! Delving into the subject of ethnic rug making, I learned so much about its history. Persian rugs, Indian rugs, Turkish rugs----they are all stunning! Upon entering most rug factories, you'll be treated to a coffee or beverage and a guide will explain all of the different styles of rugs. It's quite an experience!

A fascinating fact I learned while reading about the history of carpet weaving is that the carpets were invented to serve the purpose of practicality for the nomads. The thickness of the carpets was out of necessity to protect people from the cold conditions of the climate. By using carpets, they didn't need the hides for this purpose that would've come from their animals. They needed their animals for other things. These carpets served as their flooring rather than the ground. Carpets helped decorate and beautify their rustic tents. The carpets were easily transportable when their nomadic lifestyle needed them to move on. There are so many styles of rugs from so many origins. I felt like I could stay in one of those rug stores for hours and hours studying the different designs. *Just to name a few:* Turkish, Oriental, Persian, Indian, Kilim, Tabriz, Kazak, Heriz, Sarouk, etc.

 The loukoum factory was fulfilling for us because when we used to read <u>The Lion, the Witch and the Wardrobe</u>, I used to tell my sons that the Turkish Delight that the White Witch would feed Edmund was probably a loukum! Although we've had many loukoumia in Greece, going to our first loukum factory was unique! They make the loukoum in the traditional, eight hundred year old method like they did for the Sultans years ago. We learned that Turkish Delight used to only be for royals; not commoners. We watched them string the cubes and dip them which fascinated us. We tried a Turkish gyro which has cabbage in it unlike Greek gyros. Lastly, we heard a call to prayer for the Muslims who prostrated on their prayer mats at 3:00 pm. to pray together in the square. My oldest son ran over to watch it all take place. It was the first time he had observed people prostrating on prayer mats and this was in a mass group in a public place. He was fascinated and came up to us at the gyro shop table to express his newfound knowledge. Coming from a religious family like ours, he was comfortable with public and open prayer in the formats that he was familiar with---at our iconostasion at home, together in church, aloud or in the form of reciting long prayers and hymns in front of the congregation. Yet, he had never witnessed this exact type of public group prayer, especially in the middle of the afternoon in a town square. He shared his curiosity and interpretation with us, "Are they more religious than us?" My husband answered him in his own way. He had, after all, relented to all of us sailing over to Turkey for this excursion, much to his hesitation to do so. He was expanding his horizons, too, and his doubts were not unwarranted because when you're traveling, you do have to be aware of the risks and negative interactions that can take place. In the bazaar, if we didn't purchase something, we did experience a salesmen confront us with "You're hurting us….for one lire." That was his way to pressure us to buy something, as if guilting us to use our American money on his goods. As much as we enjoyed buying the authentic items---kilim rugs, loukoums, Turkish coffee, Turkish gyro, etc…we just simply did not want pirated items. So, that was not a positive experience but it was a lesson in travel.

When we boarded the ferry to sail back to Rhodes, it felt like a successful and informative day in a new land. Patrick read <u>The DaVinci Code</u> while the boys napped in the breeze. The boys bellies were full from loukoumies and Turkish gyro and their minds were full from new cultural lessons of the bazaar, rug factory, loukoums, gold center and the public call to prayer. I triumphantly held onto my duffel of kilim rugs from the Turkish rug factory and felt the sun's rays on my neck and shoulders taking in the view of the turquoise waters and unique mountain landscape of Turkey's border. On the ferry ride there, the view looked like what I had envisioned of China; pointier mountain peaks, unlike the rolling mountains and hillsides of Greece. It may have been my excitement upon entering a new continent and a way to distinguish the demarcation of two places. We set out to see a new country and absorb its culture and uniqueness and that was what we accomplished that day.

Seeing Queen Elizabeth and Jolly Old England

London, England has been the layover city for many of our trips to Europe and we enjoyed it so much, it started to become familiar to us....a familiar and bustling metropolis. As a married couple before children, it was a fantastic trip but taking the sons there was even better! Riding along the River Thames, doing the double decker bus tours, eating fish and chips near Buckingham Palace....it is a bright and boisterous city and our young sons gobbled up the pomp and circumstance!

The street artists and musicians made our sightseeing playful and entertaining for the boys but just riding on the double decker bus, absorbing the new environment, was good enough for us. Jokingly, my ten year old son asked, "Can we just keep riding the bus and not "hop off"?" Luckily, we did hop off and we timed it perfectly because what happened next was the surprise of all surprises! We got off the bus at Buckingham Palace and saw a huge crowd forming. We made our way into the crowd and asked people around us what was going on. Everyone was gathered in the square staring up at the balcony of the palace as antique war planes flew in formation over us. Someone told us it was the queen's anniversary of her "official birthday"---the day of her coronation. The entire royal family was about to come out on the balcony to wave to the crowd below. We were going to see the Queen!!!--and the Royal Family! Patrick put six year old Yianni on his shoulders and we huddled the boys close to us. The Royal Family appeared and the crowd started cheering. Queen Elizabeth was wearing the most vibrant chartreuse suit and hat I have ever seen. I could tell from even such a distance what high quality this suit must've been because the details stood out to me from high up there on the balcony. We took a photo of them and as far away as it was, we could identify the various royal family members. This was so exciting for us and poignant as it was ten years after Princess Diana's death so to see her sons, the princes, grown up like this, carrying out their formal royal duties, was touching for me. Patrick had Yianni on his shoulders to see above the crowd and it reminds me now of the time my brother held me on his shoulders (decades before) to peer above the crowd to see the Pope in the Vatican. I stood there telling Patrick and the boys, "We saw the Queen! We saw Queen Elizabeth and we weren't even planning to get off the double decker hop on/hop off bus!" I looked at Patrick and said, "I have seen the Pope at the Vatican in 1979 and I've now seen the Queen of England."

My Father's Village in Greece

AFTER TIME ON our own, we picked up my sister in Athens and headed for a three day trip to our father's village in the Peloponnesus, the peninsula of Greece. A village, called a "horio", is always the most powerful of memories for any child visiting Greece....especially when it's one's ancestral homeland like it is for us. Pyrgaki is the name of my father's village and it was beckoning as much to my husband to see it as it was to the rest of us. My husband has always felt a curious bond to Pyrgaki just from the special conversations he's had with my father. Now, he had a particular investment to transport my father's daughters and grandsons to Daddy's birthplace. My connection to Greece is so current and frequent as I converse on a frequent basis to my aunts in Greece and correspond with relatives (even one in the village) through birth announcements and Christmas cards over the years.

After many trips to Pyrgaki as a child and a teen, the most meaningful trip was when I returned there decades later to take my three sons for their first time. The family olive grove is the centerpiece of this village experience. The hundreds of olive trees with their wavering silver tipped leaves are a source of great pride for me as they yield the extra-virgin olive oil our family gets shipped to us back home, in America. When the olive oil arrives, it is so darkly hunter green before it is filtered into the olive colored oil. It's not the pale yellow oil you get in the grocery stores--it is *FIRST PRESS and peppery good!* The grapes must be harvested too every August I think. I was there in August of 1985 participating in this grape harvest (which migrant farmers do now, I believe) and it was hard work! I was bitten by so many mosquitoes and suffering quite a bit! But I knew then what a valuable experience this was. Not many American teenage girls can say that they have harvested grapes in Greece on their ancestors' property. (except, of course, Greek-American girls, maybe) In fact, as a young girl, my father and I made homemade wine by smashing grapes (with our feet) off of our own grapevine and fermenting it !

Birthday parties were held under the grapevine pergola and now I have my own homegrown grapevine pergola.

Our bee hives were another agricultural wonder in our backyard, growing up. When Daddy acted as beekeeper in his official beekeeper outfit with snuffer and mask, etc....it was excitement all over the house. Sucking the honey straight out of the beeswax was the most intensely sweet (again, peppery!) taste, that I felt like I was in a sugar coma. Nothing will ever taste like homegrown honey from our backyard.

When we visited my Father's village in Pyrgaki on childhood trips, we stayed at the home of a family friend who had been the caretaker of my grandparents' property. This family friend was more of an uncle to us than a former employee. We referred to this couple as Theo and Thea (uncle and aunt). His wife had been the nanny of my father and his siblings and their whole extended family had suffered through the war together when the village was under attack and my grandfather lost his fortune. The home we stayed in was very basic and simple in amenities and appliances but so larger than life because of the memories it held for us. The complex grapevine pergola out on the patio, the animals at the fence, the huge succulent fruits on the vines and the mountain pine smell in the air. My sister and I plopped down on the feather bed in the "guest room" we were given and it reminded me of passages I had read in the Little House on the Prairie books. This was a true country house. I could see our "aunt" in the kitchen boiling water in the vriki for coffee. A vriki is a small copper pot used to boil espresso. My brother, sister and I were both fascinated and a bit disturbed by the serious black and white portraits of ancestors on the walls. Such serious faces. All of these touches added to the character of the village home.

Now, my sons were getting to sit outside under the patio grapevine pergola and eating the juicy fruits but we stayed in a hotel this time. The boys had a well-rounded experience in the village on that trip, beginning with meeting family and friends and ending with an interesting visit to the family cemetery....

Ancestors and Cemetery Rituals in Our Village

PART OF THE "pilgrimage" of taking our children to Greece involved visiting the relatives and connecting with our ancestry. We visited my husband's relatives in a major city on the mainland and we visited my relatives in my dad's village on the peninsula of Peloponnesus. My maternal ancestors' island is not as accessible. Everything about the village experience was delightful....but there was one specific day and activity that connected my sons to their ancestry in a somber and powerful way. Just as I went to the cemetery when I was a child, we took our sons to the village cemetery where our ancestors are buried.

My husband, sister, and three sons went with a relative of ours to the cemetery on a perfect June day.

Our relative brought the necessary accessories for honoring and commemorating the deceased at their tombstones. My sons watched with curiosity at any differences in the way that it's done in the village. Back home in the states, I take my sons to the cemetery frequently where we visit the tombs of loved ones and light incense as we make the sign of the cross with our censer at each tombstone. The boys noticed that family members in the village keep oil in recycled soda bottles ---something they had never seen before as a use for a soda bottle. The purpose for that is to have oil ready to light the candles. According to my father, they may want to light the lanterns if they are there at nighttime.

There were many differences about the burial process, too. We learned that three years after the burial, there is an excavation and a service in which the bones are washed. This is done to make more burial space. The family places the exhumed bones in a box. The box is stored in special room room called "osteofylakeio". "Osteo" is a Greek word for "bones" and "fylakeio" is like a keepsake or storage; a place of safekeeping.

We walked through the cemetery and talked about various ancestors with my sister and relative. *It keeps the memory of that person alive.* It also adds more to your child's identity to find out how they are connected to someone's story or life. (This was the grave of my paternal grandmother who I was named for and who lived with us for the first three years of my life. She is the one I refer to in the first few chapters of the book.) My sons grew increasingly attached to the village cemetery and where they fit into the ancestry. They studied the iconography of the village chapel which my family members helped build. To see a tiny chapel like this was different and significant because we had been in so many massive cathedrals on our European trips. But this tiny chapel held so much meaning for our sons when they learned and understood its history and ancestral connection. *We saw a beautiful tree growing into the window of the chapel.* We spoke to a nun whom we've known for years.

At the end of the cemetery visit, my oldest son heard a bell ringing …steadily. This happened at the moment that we were incensing my grandparents' graves! He was perplexed by this because we observed the bell tower when we arrived to the cemetery. The rope was tethered to the fence, had not been loose at all and no one was ringing it. My son ran up to our relative and asked, *"How can the bell be ringing?"* Our relative whispered back, with no eye contact, "it's just the wind." We were not convinced by this because there was no wind! It never happened again while we were at the cemetery--only at that particular moment. My son still recalls this mysterious moment. I will always remember it as the moment I "introduced" my sons to their great-grandparents graves. This day was a good example of how Greece engages your senses like no other place, it seems. Your mind, heart and soul will never be the same.

The Monasteries of Meteora

Since we spent time on the Greek islands in 2007, our "magic carpet" took us to the mountains the next time we returned to Greece. In 2009 and 2011, among seeing other countries on our itinerary and my husband thought it was important to include Meteora on our touring. I had never been before, (that I can remember) so it was an opportunity for him to show us all the wonder of Meteora.

Meteora, on the mainland of Greece, is a destination that inspires for many reasons. The geological features are just some of the details to explore. The religious significance of it brings a whole new appreciation and awareness of monastic life. The word "Meteora" means "suspended in the air or heavens". The monasteries are built on sandstone rock pillars in an area of Central Greece. We stayed overnight in Kalambaka, the nearby town, and enjoyed a delicious meal. We reached Meteora by rental car from Athens but it would also be smart to hire a tour guide to take you there in an air-conditioned van or car.

Eastern Orthodoxy is a religion that dates back to Apostolic times. The sights, sounds, smells, feelings and tastes inside of an Orthodox church are powerful and engage all of the senses. Icons for visuals, hymns for sound, incense for scent, communion for taste and candlelight for feeling are all part of this process. Meteora is both a religious and geological experience. Because it is so rich in meaning and beauty, there are so many facets to its brilliance! I wonder what our sons were thinking when they experienced Meteora and its breathtaking views. When you first arrive, you take in the altitude and the geological impressiveness of Meteora. You take photos, you explore the hillside, and then you ascend to the monasteries. This can be challenging ---Greece has many steep roads and inclines. In the pictures, my son is just a speck in the stairway. The physical breathlessness doesn't even compare to the emotional breathlessness of the solemn and faith-filled ambience of what you find inside the monasteries.

The roads were very steep and the view is breathtaking and unlike any other. The icons, candles and monks graced the religious ambience of Meteora and filled us with prayer and a feeling of reverence for our Orthodox Christianity. Walking up to the monastery at Meteora makes you experience this view and be part of it. Walking through this most peaceful, holy monastery with no tour guide makes it a meditative process. Seeing our sons light candles in this dark chapel is a full circle experience for us as parents knowing this is why you bring your kids to Greece as Orthodox Christians and Greek children. Leaving the monastery, a guide gives you a loukoumi, probably symbolizing the sweetness of this experience. Outside, I was touched to see a Greek flag standing proudly in the rocky ground. Rooted.....like me.

Some women go to a yoga retreat in Costa Rica or learn transcendental meditation in India to find their mystical purpose and I applaud that quest. While I'm curious about those trips and delve a little into those concepts, I am not that woman. I am the Greek-American mother who, with my Greek-American husband, took our children back to our ancestral homeland as a pilgrimage and showed them firsthand where our rituals originated. Our mystical purposes come from a variety of traditions and practices. We learned about the osteophylakeio in cemetery rituals. We experienced lighting candles in monasteries. We broke out in spontaneous dance in Greek tavernas. We swam nude in secluded coves on a beach in Rhodes when they were little boys. The boys ran though olive groves in my father's village and picked lemons and figs from trees. We posed at the well where generations have posed before us. We felt and experienced the continuity of our heritage on these long trips in Greece. We did not just read about them in diaries or look at old photo albums of my childhood trips there. These experiences *were meditations*. They were epiphanies and they are now our reveries. Our gurus were not yogis; they were our family elders passing down traditions and stories of our origins. At Meteora, and other monasteries, it was the priests and monks who were our religious guides leading us through our spiritual path. It's not a blind quest of faith and curiosity of many different foreign and exotic lands and experiences--it's simply passing down to them what was meaningful for me and what I still know to be true.

Santorini Sunsets and Scuba Diving Calamities

It was so exciting for me to plan a side trip to Santorini for our sons. I had been there as a teen and my husband and I had been there on our honeymoon. I made sure that our trip to Greece would be a balance of visiting relatives, doing historic sightseeing but also relaxing and "lolligagging" on beaches. Santorini is a legendary Greek island that defines everything you think about an island in the Aegean Sea. It is the most photographed island of Greece (if not the most photographed island in the world). The historic volcanic eruption that occurred more than 3,500 years ago has created the breathtaking caldera views. We swam in the healing hot springs which reveal a tinge of yellow water containing the sulphur that is considered therapeutic for swimming. Having made homemade erupting volcano projects with my sons was a milestone for me as a boy mom but now, getting the opportunity to experience a volcano in person was going to be a unique and significant "field trip."

We explored the active volcano, rode donkeys, parasailed, swam in hot springs, explored wineries and museums and Patrick and two sons even went scuba diving one day. Akrotiri museum (a buried settlement) is a thrilling archeological site that I had enjoyed immensely as a teen with my father. I wanted my sons to see it but it had been closed for renovation for several years.

Santorini is considered "touristy," but locals still live there. Near our villa, we met a local man sitting outside of his villa. I was surprised to see a local man in this resort area. A magnetic force pulled me over to him and we started conversing in Greek. We visited with him while he cleaned green beans under his pergola. I conversed with him in Greek and translated it to my family. I was drawn to this elderly man because I fondly remembered cleaning green beans outside under our pergola with my grandfather when I was a young girl. My husband watched me entranced by this old man, riveted by his aura, as I sat myself down in the patio chair across from him as he cleaned green beans. Patrick asked me, "You miss your papou, don't you?" (Papou is the Greek word for grandfather.)

I didn't even realize until then that this man did remind me of the loving presence that is a Greek grandfather, for me, especially because my grandfather lived us when I was growing up. Looking back on this moment, I realize now that my husband was speaking from his own experience---he, too, missed his grandparents and the influence they were in his life.

Artemios, the Santorini villager, spoke to us on the importance of family and told us his philosophy: "A man without children is like a tree without branches."

Santorini at night is a whole other experience. We took siestas so we could conserve our energy for walking around the port town to shop and dine. We also spent the siesta times staring out onto the view of the caldera. The cruise ships, ferry boats, and the endless horizon was a fantasy. It was hard to comprehend such beauty....such calmness. We liked staying in Imeroviglio for our villa location. Its cliffside, breath-taking views made us realize how perfect it must have been for an historic pirate look-out point.

At night, we walked down to Fira (also called Thira), to get exercise and avoid parking hassles. The Imerovigli or Oia (pronounced "eeya" or "Ya") views are worth it and a nice break from the city center. Driving up to Oia took nearly twenty minutes, and we timed it perfectly so we could catch the world famous sunset. Our villa was called Irinis Villas, and we were so pleased with it, we stayed there on two trips.

We took sunset family pictures, ate dinner and strolled through the boutiques. I have been to Santorini four times, and I know I'll return.

People gathered around dusk to watch the sunset and capture it on film. There we were, tourists and locals gathered together, waiting pensively for that moment when something incomprehensible like the sun works its magic in the form of a sunset. It's a rhapsody and a kaleidoscope all in one. Like the starlight and moonlight of so many other nights I've enjoyed while traveling, it brings me back to the epiphany again, that we all share the same moon… the same stars. This cliffside view of the caldera has beauty that is ironic. The volcano that was so disastrous all those years ago, reached distances clear across the world. Yet, here in Santorini, all you see is beauty in the horizon. It's hard to equate that something so disastrous and naturally violent can originate from a place of such beauty and calm.

In the village of Oia, we went to a terrace cafe for dessert just to take in the caldera view. Our sons were asked by some local boys to form a team to play soccer in the plaza by the church. It was so charming to watch this interaction. The local boys took charge and yelled passionately as our Greek-American sons were passively engaged, polite but still into it and having fun.

Other tourists watched this game and took pictures of our boys playing with the dogs in the path. Our sons were lying on the ground playing with the stray dogs, oblivious to the world. Far out on a promontory, there was a couple getting dinner served to them. We saw a group of people assembling to watch the famous sunset. The sun was still shining on the side of a church so we posed for a family shot. We drove back to Fira and had dinner at Naoussa Restaurant, which was recommended to us.

One particular afternoon, my sons and I relaxed in our rooftop hot tub which looked out onto the ocean. Patrick had returned our two oldest sons to the villa after their scuba diving excursion that morning. As soon as he arrived to the villa, he realized that he accidentally left behind his backpack which contains several valuable items inside. He drove the rental car back to the port, hoping to find the scuba instructor. After he discovered the backpack was missing---which contained the passports, money and dive certification cards, he drove to the port and the boat was gone. The scuba instructor there told him to go up the road to the Old Port and he'd find the steps to go there. He drove the rental car there to the road at the end of the island. He stopped at a restaurant to get directions to the old port but there was no one there. He heard people in the back and walked into a back room and startled a lady. He asked her in broken greek, "Pou einai to limani? Paleo limani?" (where is the port, the old port?)

He asked, "Polles skales?" (Are there many steps?) and she motioned some directions which looked like "drive and take a left." He drove down the road which dead ended onto a cliff. He had taken the wrong road- a one lane road. He didn't want to drive backwards up this road that went the wrong way so he drove backwards to a turn off area. He backed into it but his car was lodged on a level that was leading up a little bit. The car got sideways with him on an angle and his door flew open next to a cliff. He put the car in reverse to go backwards to get off high center. He revved up the car and rocked it off of there. It came to a thud and didn't flip over.

He still hadn't retrieved the backpack yet because he wasn't on the right road. He drove up the road to another turn off but didn't want to get stuck again. Instead of driving the car down there, he decided to jog the two miles down to the port. There was an abandoned hotel where a chow dog started running towards him, biting at his heels. He saw all the steps to the cliff. ---to nothing…to his death, he thought. He climbed all the way down, found the Old Port and his backpack and everything inside. He drank the water bottle inside the backpack out of his extreme thirst. Next, he had to get past those dogs. He walked up the steps that he could've fallen off of, got on a road and thought, "Now I have to find something to fight the dogs off." He found a stick—the only wood in all of Santorini. He hit the ground with it when he saw the dog and the stick disintegrated. He started cursing at the dog and said, "Okay!....here I am!" and the dog started growling at him. The steps were behind him and the dog was in front of him. If he ran towards the dog, he thought he could get on the steps leading to the hotel. The dog was running towards him, barking, so he jumped on the stairs with the dog on his butt. Patrick jumped over the fence but the dog couldn't jump over it, so Patrick escaped fairly unscathed. When he made it back to the villa, he told us his harrowing tale and as much as we felt his fear, we nervously laughed at his descriptions.

    I wasn't with the guys when they went scuba diving and an aura came over them that seemed to let go of all precautions. One of the boys experienced a tough spot but managed through it. It's part of the process. But what happened later that night at the sunset viewing in Oia was not part of the process. The boys were playing around and we noticed that ten year old Mark had passed out and appeared to be shaking like a seizure. Jokingly, he had convinced his almost twelve year old brother to choke him. The nitrogen gases from the scuba adventure compromise divers anyway and the choking made the situation worse. It caused a scene during the peaceful and idyllic sunset and a crowd gathered. Needless to say, it was parental moment that unnerved us and embarrassed us. Oh, Santorini---so many memories!

Mountain Towns in Greece

In 2009, we showed the boys mainland Greece along with the islands of Corfu and Crete. The mountain towns in Greece have a beauty to them that highlights different details from the islands. The architecture varies and takes on influential styles from the settlers of various regions. We focused on chapels, monasteries and monuments while traveling through the mountains.

Our route was fantastic! My husband is wonderful when it comes to navigating these routes.

Delphi- to tour the Oracle of Delphi
Arahova- the quaint town of wools, embroidery, flokati rugs
Meteora--the monasteries atop rock pillars
Metsovo-stone paved streets in a ski village, a one-time Vlach settlement
Ioanina-capital city of Epirus
Igoumenitsa-coastal city

After some time at Meteora, we drove on to Metsovo with its high roads and hairpin turns. My husband asked me to read something from the Greece guidebook so would be distracted from the danger. We came upon some tunnels through the mountains that were three miles long! Metsovo was quaint and had a German and Austrian feeling to it. The village was full of specialty cheeses, costumes, wines, honey, wool and unique cuisine. The village architects have done an incredible job keeping the integrity here.

Men were making a cobblestone road there and we found a haunting, old, moss-covered church set back in a fenced park on a panoramic hilltop.

We ordered kokoretsi (a meal of lamb or goat intestines) from a restaurant where all the locals were--and that is always a good sign! On to Ioannina, we found a fortress (Aslan Pasha) with Arabic writing on the tombstone, cannonballs, dungeons, ruins, etc. It was an overcast day. We walked by the first lake we've seen on this trip and watched boats from a cliff by the fortress. My husband has fond memories of this city from his childhood trip to Greece so it was nice to see hear his memories.

Star Gazing Cruise in Lefkada

AFTER SEVERAL TRIPS to the Aegean Sea side and the Cyclades cluster of islands, we felt the urge to return to the Ionian Sea side of Greece on our 2011 trip. It had been decades since I vacationed on the Ionian side and various reasons influenced me to schedule some time on the Ionian side. It's true what people say, "every Greek island has something special" and you can't go wrong in selecting any of the islands to visit. Lefkada left its mark on us and I consider it among my top four favorite islands. One unique excursion we encountered (that I had never heard of before in any country) was a star gazing cruise.

Our Greek American friends told us about the cruise and we joined them for one of the most uniquely unforgettable nights we've experienced as a family. On the ferry boat ride to the remote, uninhabited island, we sat around a table with our friends and watched the dusk views over the sea.

The lull of the boat ride seemed to set the tone for this pending activity. While our other moments and activities with our friends were lively dinners at the port or beach time fun, this activity transported us physically and emotionally to a unique evening of bonding. Our conversation on the ferry ride became meaningful and intimate in its moments of reflection. I felt an instant bond to their youngest child due to similar family experiences we shared. Remembering how she laid on the lap on a family member during this slow and somber ferry ride (listening to our serious conversation) now reminds me that it was a metaphorical way to prepare for the atmosphere of the pending star gazing experience on the remote island. We'd be reclining, lounging, quiet, reflective and contemplative as we were about to listen to the astrological and astronomical lessons of star gazing.

We climbed off the boat, down a ladder and were handed a beach mat. We set up our mats, waited for the Greek food picnic buffet to be set out. We skipped rocks, ate our picnic food and waited for the sun to completely set.

Once it was pitch dark, our captain started his lecture about the skies….the astronomy and all its glory! He pointed out satellites, comets, constellations, space station, (with the naked eye) and Saturn through a telescope. *Again, the moon and the stars played a powerful role in my travels.* The captain told us stories of mythology and astrology to coincide with the lessons in astronomy. The passengers and spectators on the beach that night were from all over the world. The captain asked us to identify what countries we were from. We spanned Finland to Turkey to America and places in between. I thought, how symbolic we all were this way—-the *cosmos learning about the cosmos.* The Greek word for people is "cosmos" and yet it's also the word for the universe.

Many people fell asleep but I stayed up for the whole thing. To lie there with my ten year old son fast asleep in my arms was something I'll never forget. All of us alone at midnight on a beach of an uninhabited island; gazing at the stars and listening to stories and astronomical stories….in beautiful Greece?!--- nothing like it!

The "Onassis" Cruise in Lefkada

As if Lefkada wasn't already a perfect enough island visit with its breathtaking star gazing cruise, there was still one more excursion for us to encounter that I had planned out before the trip. The Onassis cruise was a "bucket list" event for me because I've always wanted to see Skorpios--which had been the private island of Onassis. Ari Onassis married Jaqueline Kennedy Onassis, "Jackie O", on the island of Skorpios. This cruise's captain had worked for Onassis as a youngster and was able to tell us anecdotal tales. He had photo albums onboard with newspaper clippings of the famous couple...and of Maria Callas, the opera singer, too. We learned details from our tour guide about Onassis's relationship with the island of Lefkada. Reportedly, when he was building up his private island of Skorpios with resources, he had to draw from Lefkada's resources to do so. In order to not have the situation be controversial in terms of taking advantage, it is said that he helped fund school programs and other generous resources back to the island of Lefkada and possibly the neighboring islets we saw on this tour.

Onassis married Jackie Kennedy on his private island of Skorpios so naturally, that interests me because I nostalgically and facetiously tie that event to Jackie somehow "becoming one of us Greeks". To think that in this idyllic setting, America's former First Lady was calling a part of Greece her home. Skorpios is where she retreated from the public world, swam in secluded coves and must have enjoyed the best of everything life has to offer. America could not give Jackie this privacy and protection—and she had been "America's Queen". As someone who has always admired Jackie Kennedy Onassis's iconic culture and style, I especially am influenced and beguiled by her because of our "dual heritages" as I like to think that she adopted the Greek heritage by marriage and residence. We visited four islets, swam in a cave which was rumored to have hidden a submarine (how??), went to an islet with an ancient olive press "factory", had a picnic on a beach and snorkeled and ended up on Skorpios --a public access beach on the private island. I looked at my husband when we descended the boat's ladder into the beach cove and said, "I did it. We are swimming at the beach Jackie Onassis did on her private island." I was connected to my idol and icon in this moment.

On the rest of our cruise, we drank espressos when we set sail, mojitos in the afternoon, and had Greek "caviar and champagne" as the captain called it, which is really olives and ouzo shots. The captain let our little son pull the masts up on the sails and pretend to drive the boat. In the afternoon, as everyone rested and basked in the sun, we all lounged in various corners of the boat while the staff passed out pieces of the juiciest watermelon wedges I've ever had in my life. Pure hedonism.

I looked out onto the turquoise blue Ionian sea with the wind in my beach-waved hair, the sun on my face, wearing a tee shirt and bathing suit, relaxed on beverages, with my arm around my husband. My gaze was on my sons dancing and steering the sailboat (which was a pirate ship replica) and I thought, "This is a perfect moment of life." People were Greek dancing in their bathing suits, everyone was relaxed and intrigued at the same time for what was around the corner as we toured the four islets.

Sailing, walking, hiking, drinking, eating, snorkeling.....reading scrapbooks, steering a boat, pulling masts, learning about an olive press and taking photos of native island women in their traditional dress....it was an assault of the senses in the best way. I accomplished my bucket list goal of visiting Skorpios.

The Corfu Vibe

Another Ionian Sea island gem is Corfu. Corfu is also referred to as "Kerkyra" which is a Greek word symbolic of the myth of Poseidon who fell in love with a nymph named Korkyra. Legend states that Poseidon kidnapped Korkyra and brought her to the bucolic island and named it after her.

Corfu is a resplendent Greek island in the Ionian Sea. It is diverse, picturesque and has beaches that you see in your dream! For years, I have heard recommendations to go there. An excerpt from my travel journal reminded me about our reaction to first arriving there: My husband was so excited about the Corfu coastline---not realizing what a huge island it is. We are so close to Italy and Albania. You can see Albania on a clear day.

We drove to Paleokastritsa which I had been reading about in my travel guide. It's an area with secluded coves and water sports and I knew the guys wanted to scuba dive since they were newly certified in it. My husband loved the countryside---rustic and mountainous and I found it unspoiled and full of flowers, blooms, and foliage.....very lush. When we found the Hotel Fiorita, I looked up the steep hill to find studio apartments/villas with white and blue lacquered shutters, doors and trim and the most fuchsia bougainvillea spilling all over the balconies. Tropical plants and bushes landscaped around a tree in a planter box and little purple martins flying under the ceiling of their taverna on the property. Heavenly!

Corfu is so lush because of the rainfall this island gets. Most Greek islands are rocky and barren but Corfu is green, lush and colorful with its florals. I found Corfu to be as lush as Hawaii. The flavor of the island was

Italianate and Venetian since it is so close to Italy. We loved Paleokastritsa area and its magnificent beach. The caves off Paleokastritsa beach were so breathtaking. Patrick decided we should rent a boat and sail through the caves. Seeing fish this way was fun for the boys and the colors on the rocks of the caves were stunning. We stopped at various caves and let the boys jump off to swim and explore through them. Although time on the beach was heavenly, exploring the villages was just as divine. The mountainside villages we drove through were darling! Patrick kept winding his way through each village road and corner in the effort to not miss one single detail. (especially near the village of Lakones) Our villa in Paleokastritsa was called Villa Fiorita and the bougainvillea was the focal point of this picturesque scene.

In Corfu, no matter where we sat to dine and take in the view, we were surrounded by beauty. The landscaping of any restaurant garden was artistic and aesthetic. One particular town we drove to, at the recommendation of the villa proprietor, was called Perouales. We drove up to Perouales to have lunch there and we were stunned by what we found when we arrived. Our restaurant was on the cliff's edge overlooking the sea. There was a ledge you could walk out onto, with a railing around it, to "become" a part of the view. I am not a fan of heights so I let my husband take our sons out onto the ledge. As many times as we've been to Greece, we had not observed a view of the sea quite at this angle. It felt like a 180 degree view. Every Greek island has a vibe to it of ultimate relaxation. Corfu had this vibe, of course. We dined for a long time, enjoying each other, laughing, savoring the meal and cherishing the vacation pace.

The truth is, however, that the locals appear to dine this way, too! They were not on vacation like we were, yet, they treat mealtime as if they are. That's one of the things people love about Greece---leisure is an art! Coffee breaks last for hours in the town squares. People converse, debate, and discuss politics passionately. Village people sit in silence peering out onto the mountain landscapes. This baffled my husband at first---how people could sit in silence but be together? I pointed out to him that with a view like that, how could someone NOT sit in silence, relishing the moment? What is there possibly more important to talk about that just observing the beauty of a Greek island? We, too, would be distracted by such beauty in our hustle-bustle pace of a life if we lived on a Greek island.

Lunchtime was a good time to test out Greek words and phrases on the boys to see if they were hearing, learning and applying the vocabulary. Although they hear Greek language spoken back home, the pace of the language is much quicker in Greece.

Another nice aspect about lunchtime was that it was the natural break in our day of sightseeing. We used the mornings to visit museums, churches, monuments, etc and we used the afternoons to hit the beach and do beach excursions. Lunch was time to recharge from all the walking and sightseeing. Kassiopi, a village up north in Corfu, had a colorful, scenic port and offered day trips to the neighboring country of Albania. You need to have your passports on you, though, and if you have them locked up in the hotel or villa safe, then it's not too convenient to go back and get them. We had driven all over Corfu in our rental car so this was the case for us that day. Corfu was a kaleidoscope of florals, vistas, textiles, marina boats and landscape.

In Corfu town, we went to the church of St.Spyridon which houses his relics. We happened to arrive right as a christening was happening. In the Greek Orthodox religion, we call it a baptism. What a beautiful church in which to have a baptism! How meaningful it will be for that infant to look back on his or her baptismal photos one day and know the significance of this church. The afternoons on the cove were perfect! There was light rainfall which upset me at first but it dried up quickly and the sunshine was a welcome sight. Of course, it's the rainfall that contributes to the lushness of Corfu!

Going into town for dinner was the end to a perfect day. The restaurant we went to, which makes my mouth water just thinking about it, was called Neraida. I believe that means "mermaid." Every restaurant on a Greek island serves delicious food. You can choose any one of them and you're going to be satisfied. Most menus serve the same variety of food perfection. When we walked into Neraida near Paleokastritsa Beach, we instantly felt like this night was going to be unique. It's not as important to judge a Greek restaurant by décor as it might be back in the states because the landscape is the décor. Neraida had a very special ambience, though. We walked down into a patio of tables with romantic lighting and a beautiful wine bottle display in the alcove of a wall. The menu was more developed than your typical tavern and we loved every bite, as usual. But it's what happened next with the entertainment that topped off the evening! Music started and two waiters dressed in crisp white button down shirts with black pants came out dancing around a table on the dance floor in the middle of our patio. We've seen these "wine tricks" as they are called back home at Greek Festivals in America. My husband and sons do these wine tricks, too. A "wine trick" is when one male dancer jumps onto the other male dancer and balances with his legs wrapped around the other dancer's waist.

 He dangles backward onto the floor and sets a glass of wine on his forehead. As he steadily lifts his torso up without losing the wineglass, the other male dancer, supporting him, takes the wine glass into his teeth and leans his head back to drink it. The other man jumps off the dancer and one of them smashes the wine glass with his shoe.

 These Corfu waiters did not do a typical wine trick; they danced on top of the table while plates were smashed around the dance floor. Then, a fire was set under the table and the waiters danced on top of the table and fire. It was a stunning scene. We alternated between taking photos of the fire table dancers and our sons' wide-eyed expressions staring in amazement at the dancers. The fire dancers of Corfu lit up the night! We haven't seen that fire dancing trick since Corfu. It definitely "raises the bar" for Greek dancers like us. We might do our wine tricks and we may even break some clay plates but I doubt we'll ever incorporate fire into our stage shows. We will leave that to the magic of Corfu and the legend of Poseidon and Korkyra's passionate union.

The Tranquility of Greek Gardens

AMONG THE GRANDEUR of Greek island and mainland visuals, the heart of Greece might be best expressed through the simplicity. One example of the latter is the simple beauty and tranquility of a Greek garden. Greece offers so much beauty in its views, landscapes, flora, beaches, mountains and picturesque villages. The most common images of Greece are probably the blue and white buildings of the islands.

However, there are other colors of Greece that are captivating. The terra cotta buildings and rooftop gardens are charming and bring so much tranquility to the village life. The potted geraniums in Greece must be the happiest flowers in the world! What more could a plant need to thrive than Greek sunshine and a loving Greek gardener to care for it? Sometimes, on our walks or drives, we saw villagers sitting on their balconies in pleasant company with their beautiful plants. We could *feel their tranquility,* vicariously.

It was apparent that they valued simplicity and truly applied the philosophy (that we all should) *"Happiness consists not in having what you want, but in wanting what you have."* Gardening to the Greeks is like breathing. They don't just want beautiful flowers around them, but also useful herbs to garnish their meals. Vegetable gardens for their homemade meals and fruit trees for their preserves and desserts are perfected skills of the Greeks. Even a grapevine serves a multi-purpose need. The leaves can be picked and brined for stuffed grape leaves (dolmathes) and the vine itself serves as a pergola for Greeks to sit under for shade. Grapevine pergolas are probably one of my favorite visions of Greece because for me, they symbolize a gathering place, togetherness and a way of making something natural into something architectural!

For me, it wasn't enough to just duplicate favorite recipes back in our hometown to remind us of our special times on vacations in Greece. I felt compelled to duplicate the grapevine pergola experience back home. I did it and it remains one of my favorite projects ever. I sit under the grapevine to receive its healing effects on my psyche. I cherish it for its nature and tranquility.

In my opinion, these tranquil Greek gardens lend themselves to the ambience of the Greek family homes and estates. I think back to my own Greek-American home garden that my father created. I used to follow my father around in his garden when I was a kid. I watched him turn manure into compost and seeds into plants, flowers, even trees. Trips back and forth to the nursery or the lumber store were highlights of my childhood; not because of the experience of the project itself but because of the one on one time I had with him in his pick up truck. We talked about all kinds of subjects in those conversations and one in particular that taught me something unique about Daddy. I asked him why he listened to country music on his truck radio. He was European, after all, so this perplexed me. He said, "country music songs tell a story." That was his simple way to tell me that he related to those stories. (Hardship, obstacles, etc. but expression and emotion, too).

Every spring, when I plant my vegetable garden, I wait for Daddy to plant with me. I know I can do it by myself or with my sons but I prefer to have Daddy there for his guidance but most of all so my sons can have this bonding activity with me and their papou. Three generations shoveling, scoping out the right spot and "home" for new growth, patting down fresh potting soil around a new plant and sitting back to admire our newly planted treasure. The best part of all is being with him and hearing his soothing Greek accent as we converse. His presence, his smile, his twinkly blue eyes and most of all his wisdom are the qualities we crave in Papou.

As a kid, I'd watch him take guests around his garden and point out his 6-foot tomato plants. People marveled at his garden. All kinds of vegetables, fruits, herbs, trees....and even a homemade greenhouse adorned our old backyard. Once, I told him I was interested in growing okra so we planted okra in little pots on our garage patio. It was satisfying to fry your own homegrown okra, especially when you're a kid. Ours was a garden to table experience in the summers as Mom would tell me to go pick some eggplants for her to fry for lunch. Our beehives made the most intoxicating honey each year and we briefly had chickens in the yard, too. One time, my dad and I even made homemade white wine by smashing green grapes with our feet and fermenting it for three weeks. We served it at a party and I still remember the look on one guest's face when we told him we smashed the grapes with our feet. He wasn't too thrilled!

A few years ago, Daddy happily told me that he bought us a pomegranate tree for our yard. He and yiayia love to clean pomegranates for my sons and put the seeds in little baggies for them. He thought a pomegranate tree would be a great addition to our yard. Whether it bore fruit or not, it grows beautiful flowers and would also be a great symbol of their traditions and memories of enjoying the fruit together.

He used to prune our rosebushes annually. Every February, he prepared the vines for the new growth and every May, the roses would bloom so brilliantly because he had carefully tended to them.

Rose growers know that you can't ignore this important step in having rosebushes, otherwise, the vines get clumsy and drape over with the weight of neglect. If you trim them up, they'll sprout better buds.

Another summer, he planted cherry tomatoes in his yard and told my cousin that he planted them "just for Gina because she loves cherry tomatoes." My cousin was so touched at this sweetness when she told me this story. Seeing it through her eyes, I realized how lucky I am that my dad thinks of me in those gestures. I should never take it for granted.

Recently, I desired to build a grapevine pergola in my own yard as an homage to the ones in Greece and also the one we had at my childhood home. So many birthday parties were held under that grapevine. My husband and I did this project by ourselves and it was successful. In two short years, the grapevine blossomed and thrived. My daddy came over one day when the grapes were in full bloom and he exclaimed, "I've never seen grapes like that! Not even in Napa Valley!" I bursted with pride and emotion. You would've thought that I won the Nobel Peace Prize. Something as simple as that comment made me prouder than major accomplishments in my life. I'm not sure why....maybe because gardening with Daddy has always been the zen thing in my life and I wanted to emulate it someday.

Daddy has been known to give container plants to people as gifts; basil, dill, rosemary....the gifts that keep on giving. People love to walk through his garden and have him identify the different herbs and figs. I found myself doing this with guests at my house, too. There's something so relaxing about rubbing mint together to release the oils and handing someone a bouquet of herbs to take home.

When I became a mom, I started to realize some parenting mantras when I was digging dirt on my hands and knees and preparing a flower bed. I realize these parenting lessons were never told to me by my father---but through his *example,* and him walking the walk....I think I analyzed and internalized them better.

"Bloom where you're planted." - (Wherever you go, there you are. Make the best out of your situation.)

"If something has good roots, it will thrive." (A good foundation will prevent you from being uprooted.)

"Keep the weeds away." (Weed consistently or a bad one will choke your growth. Watch the bad elements around your kids. Weeds creep up quickly.)

"Prune your trees and vines." (If you want something to keep growing healthy, you can't neglect it. You need to support it and pay attention to it.)

"Talk to your plants." (The vibrations are supposedly good for your plants. This statement reminds me of how important it is to talk to our kids....really talk. Don't expect them to read your mind and know life's lessons. Keep the good vibrations going.)

"You can take manure and turn it into compost." (A bad thing can be turned into something good; like mistakes into lessons, etc.)

"Wear sunscreen or a hat." (Just because your are having fun and being outside, you still have to proceed with caution. All things in moderation. The sun is great but the sun can be damaging, too.)

There are so many more lessons and comparisons I can think of that relate to gardening. But mostly, I think its best value comes from the act of being outside, soaking up the Vitamin D from the sun, making something beautiful and useful...nurturing a hobby.

Possibly, the best part of gardening is that it creates something that will keep growing, blooming and sustaining you. If you rely on only the sun and occasional rainfall, a garden might survive.....but vitamins, potting soil, regular watering, pruning, weeding, etc....will make gardens thrive. I've had several garden experiments: vegetables, rose bushes, hens to lay eggs, a grapevine pergola and hopefully, soon bee hives. I am constantly learning and reflecting back on the unspoken lessons I learned through gardening. …..*And I still love to follow my father around his garden.*

Gardening is one of the national pastimes of many Greek men, it seems. Back home in the states, in my community, it was the Greek immigrant men who tended to such amazing gardens. My best friend and I both had fathers who meticulously labored over their vegetable gardens in particular. My distant relative who lived down the street from us also had an impressive garden of vegetables, herbs and apricot trees. Our childhood years included growing up running around each other's backyards surrounded by potted plants, container gardens, vegetable beds, greenhouses and fruit trees. Fresh, crunchy cucumbers and tomatoes plucked from these gardens, cut up into Greek horiatiki (country) salads was a regular habit of our cuisine.

It was more than just gardening for our fathers, however. One afternoon, I walked down the street, back into my relatives' backyard garden looking for my playmate/distant cousin. I found something else instead. There, hanging from a tree, was a slaughtered lamb and my uncle, standing next to it with a butcher knife, draining its blood and skinning it. I screamed and took off running back home.

Another afternoon, my best friend and I were playing in the house and looked outside the window when we heard my dad's pick up truck pull up. Our dads were in the front of the truck and in the truck bed was a group of several live sheep. Our eyes were as big as saucers and it was difficult to see this dramatic scene out of context. We had driven many times with our dads in the truck out to various farms, acreages, even communal property we owned for their agricultural projects and quests but this time, it was strange---the farm animals were in my driveway! We jokingly laugh about this memory now and call this "Greek girl problems." It was a rich experience growing up this way.

A Farm Villa in Crete

CRETE IS GREECE'S largest island. In 2009, while looking on the internet, I found a villa on a working farm. There were actually two guest villas available to rent. The owners drove us around in a choo- choo train and they made us a meal delivered to our villa which was wild boar, squash courgettes and homemade ice cream made from their goats' milk. Fresh eggs and goat milk for our morning cereal were also delivered to our refrigerator in the mornings. The highlights of this villa stay were milking the goats, collecting eggs from the hens and discovering wild sage on our evening hikes.

Our first morning began with me waking up when the sunshine filled our bedroom through the shutters. I had the shutters opened slightly and loved watching the grapevine from the pergola waving at me in the breeze. Waking up with a grapevine outside of your sun-splashed bedroom window is intoxicating. The pastoral view from the mountaintop villa took my breath away each and every morning that I'd throw open the balcony doors to take my coffee and toast outside to breathe in the mountain air (and gasp!) Herds of sheep moving through geometrically landscaped roads awakens your soul in such a different way than a beach lapping up the surf and waves. The best part was knowing that in just a few hours, we would be at the beach, too! A perfect combination! Every night, back at the villa, we took walks at dusk up ascending roads surrounded by the fragrant breezes of wild sage growing on the hillside. I made the boys stop, sniff the herbs and try to identify the various ones---dill, oregano, sage, just as they do in Papou's garden but this time, in Greece, on Greek soil.

We interacted with the villa owners daily as they checked in on us. The young adult son mentioned that he would be milking the goats with an employee. I bursted with excitement and enthusiastically asked him if the boys could join him and learn how to milk the goats, too. He was happy to include them and I knew it was part of the perks of staying there when I read about the villa on their website.

Patrick and I tagged along, too, of course, to take photos but also because I was so eager to get back into the farm environment of Greece after decades of immersing into village life. As soon as we approached the sheep, goat and wild boar pens, I smelled the manure and hay. I had a visceral reaction immediately of being a kid again in my father's village in Pyrgaki. I didn't even make time to change my clothes. I ran out in my white sweatpants, hoodie, flip flops and grabbed my coffee mug to follow the boys. Patrick and the boys had a hard time deciphering which animals were goats and which were sheep! I had to point out the differences to my "city slickers." The goats were jumping high into the air and over each other! We were fascinated and curious. The proprietor and his employee showed our sons how they corral the goat up against the fence to milk it. Our sons each took turns crouching next to the goat to find the utters and squeeze the warm milk into the bucket. I was over the moon with elation. Although we live in the heartland of America with farms everywhere in our home state, we had to travel all the way to Greece to experience the simple act of milking a goat!

Next to the sheep and goat pens was a wild boar pen and shed. Those ominous creatures snorted and charged. I asked the proprietor if they have to shoot the boars in order to kill them as there's probably no time to try to capture and wrangle such a wild and forceful beast. He confirmed my suspicion and said yes, in fact, they shot the boar that they served us one night for dinner. It was quite paradoxical to think that while we were staying at such a luxurious mountain top villa, we were experiencing rustic details like having a dinner meat from an animal which had to be shot with a gun!

We had breakfast and snack foods delivered to us which were also farm fresh eggs, goat milk and unpasteurized ice cream.

Villa Creta gave us a parting gift which was a CD of Greek music with a picture of the villa pool on it and a bottle of Villa Creta wine. Such panache! I told the owner that I'd play the music while sipping Villa Creta wine when I was back home, remembering Crete.

Our youngest son was wistful as he waved goodbye, with a sad grin on his face, to the owner who dropped us off at the port. The owner looked nostalgic, too. *It was apparent these two bonded* over the magical goat milking lesson. Our boys are forever changed by this stay. Luxury + simplicity.

A Mountain View in Crete

I ALWAYS THOUGHT of myself as someone who loves islands but staying on a mountain top villa in Crete made me realize I might be addicted to both----islands AND mountains! I found this excerpt from my journal after staying on a farm villa in Crete.

> *"As much as I worship the scenery--white, blue, the Cyclades, cruise ships, windjammers, speedboats in the sea, exquisite shops, beautiful beaches, white marble floors and winding streets, chaise lounges, etc....I think I am realizing that I love the countryside too. The scented herbs of a hill meadow, the crow of a rooster, the maaaaa-ing of goats, the taste of goat milk, cheese, the swirl of wine you taste, grown from the vineyard you are staying on---all part of the country charm...We've heard birdsong and watched seagulls flying in groups off the cliffs. We've seen layers and layers of white umbrellas that look like statues on this cliff and huge pots of geraniums and other flowers on every balcony. It's a visual overload. It is worth all the sleeplessness, travel planning, costs and saving to get here. Exhaustion before relaxation...but utter relaxation once you get settled. No emails, no phone messages, no sorting of mail, no dishes or laundry, no feeding of pets....just meeting your basic needs and desires."*

My happy hour Pikilia recipe at our Cretan Villa consisted of the following: toast with herbs, feta cheese, drizzled olive oil, balsamic vinegar, Villa Creta wine and my husband's frosty mug of Mythos beer. I chopped up some sage, toasted the bread fried the Cretan cheese on butter. I squeezed lemon on it put salt, pepper, oregano, rosemary and wild sage….and olive oil!

Evenings were spent sitting in our villa gazebo, drinking Cretan wine and listening to Greek music while our boys swam in the pool or kicked around a soccer ball in the yard. We had complete and utter privacy in our walled villa property and grounds. When we wanted a view of the town, we sat on the balcony facing the pastures, streets and tractors. When we wanted a rugged view of pure nature and no urban signs in sight, we took off on hikes up the mountain behind us, only observing sagebrush and other herbs growing wildly along the trails. We were in such a steep and remote location that we noticed a jeep laying wrecked and abandoned in a valley below us. At this steep level, it must have careened down a road at an uncontrollable rate.

As with any mountain at this elevation, the air was so pure, I was so enriched to know that my sons could experience this quality of the outdoors that brings clarity, peace and simplicity to their souls and senses. They were "unplugged" from their hand held electronics or usual routines. Only the soil and the atmosphere were at their fingertips. I loved that. It brought me back to the summer moments I had as a child in Greece---on Dori the donkey, getting lost on a village road, smelling the village life, feeling the fresh air and internalizing the simplicity.

Now, my sons knew a part of me. They shared a part of my past; the innocent childhood wonder of a Greek summer.

Greek Mythology on our Greece Trip

A FOND MEMORY I have of a day in Crete is when my eight year old son and I discussed Greek mythology. I asked him if he knew that the father of all gods, Zeus, was from the island of Crete (according to mythology). My son then went into a long story about "Muthaw Ewth" (Mother Earth) and Kronos, etc. He told me about all of the murders of Zeus's siblings and the goat who suckled Zeus as a baby on Crete. We also talked about King Minos and the minotaur. We went to see the Palace of Knossos which is on Crete. I was impressed at his ability to recall long lessons of mythology. He thought he was teaching me and I let him think so. I used to teach Greek mythology to my third graders---but he doesn't know that. It must be very tangible for the boys to apply their knowledge of Greek mythology to the environment here.

When we visited Ancient Olympia on the peninsula of Peloponnesus, we saw the Temple of Zeus (one of the seven wonders of the Ancient World). That, too, must've been beyond impressive to the boys because Olympia was the site of the first Olympic games done in honor of Zeus. They had to decipher that the games were real; while Zeus was not. Yet, the ancient Greeks' mythology was their belief system for an era.

Seeing the Palace of Knossos in Crete connected us to the mythology of King Minos, the minotaur, Theseus, Ariadne, the ball of string, etc. They've read the story before but now, they were seeing where it "happened."

It helps to know historic facts ahead of time and/or have a tour guide while there because otherwise, it is possible you'll be walking through this site thinking "it's just a pile of rocks". The latter is true for many tourists. But when you realize the incredible history of Knossos and the advancement of this place for its ancient time, it is spectacular! Flushing toilets back then!? A sewer system? Minoan plumbing? hundreds of residents? Incredible!

My Son's Journals

It is never too early to model for your children how to keep a travel journal. This is something they will cherish years and decades later. At least, that's how my children reacted upon finding their journalizing from our travels. It's even possible to have the youngest of children start this journalizing habit. My youngest son had finished kindergarten when we took our first family trip to Europe.

Because he hadn't started first grade yet, all he knew how to do was "pre-writing". Pre-writing is a combination of phonetic writing and illustrations. I found his journal entries and they are precious to me now that he's in high school!

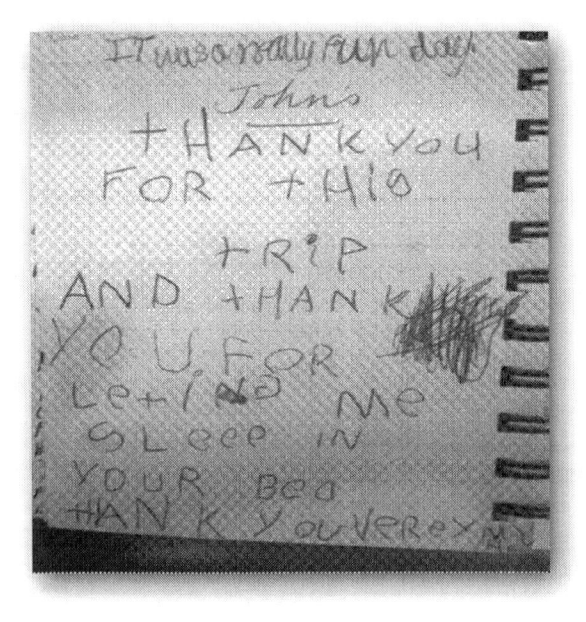

Translation: "Thank you for this trip and thank you for letting me sleep in your bed. Thank you very much." (This may have taken him a long time, too, now that I am remembering this trip. When our nights were winding down, I had the boys write some reflections in their journal. Another good time to do this is at restaurants waiting for your dinner.)

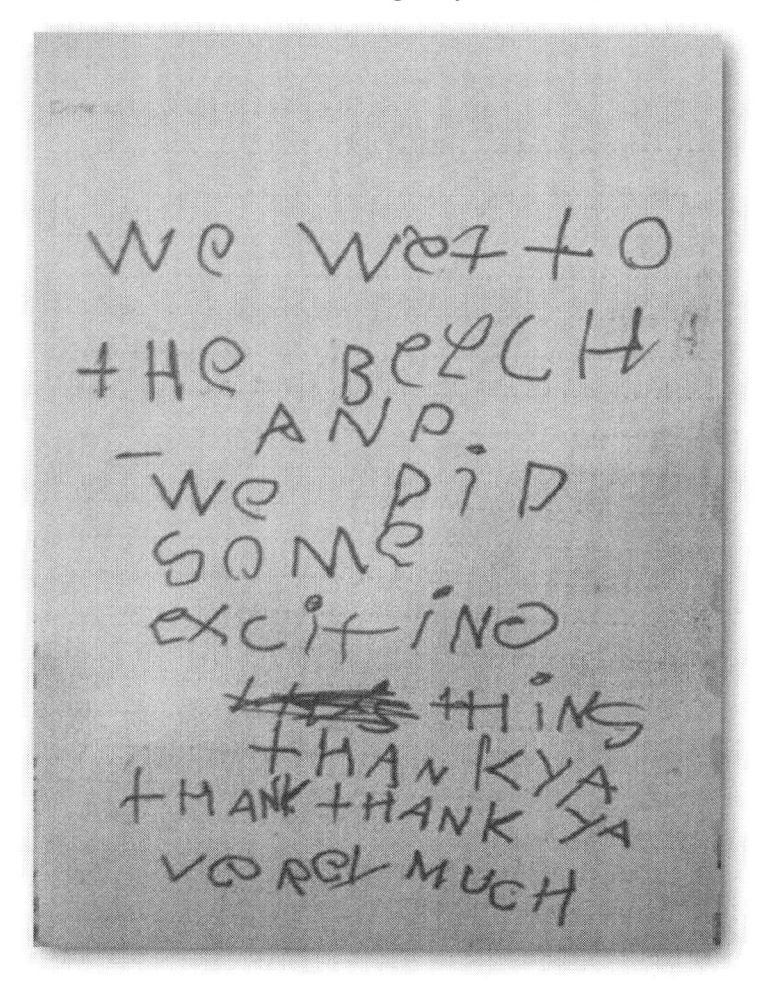

Translation: "We went to the beach and we did some exciting things. Thank ya, thank ya very much".
(Elvis impersonation...really.)

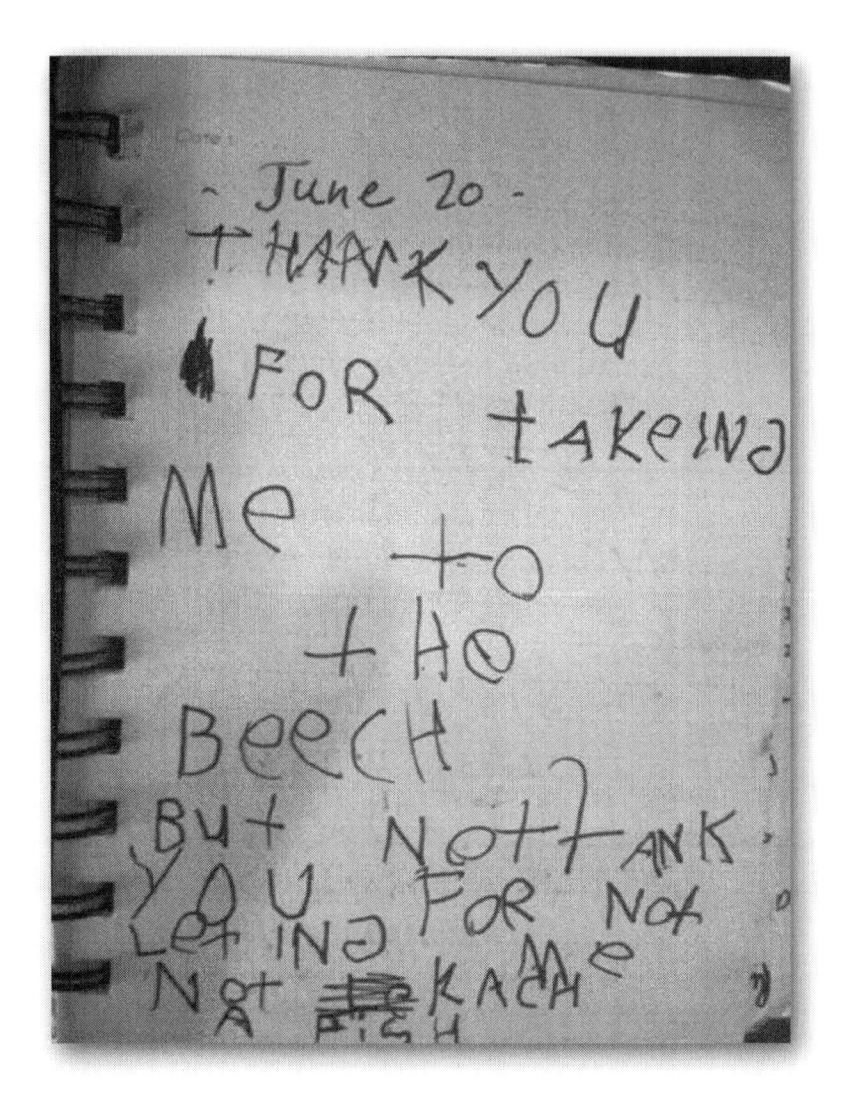

Translation: "Thank you for taking me to the beach, but not thank you for not letting me catch a fish." I'm not sure what this was about but at least he was polite in his disdain.

When we waited for the ferry boat to Morocco, I had my youngest son draw "portraits" of us at a table in a cafe in Tariffa. We laugh about these now. Kids have a way of including every line on your face to the point of a caricature.

A Magic Carpet Ride

Translation: "We road (rode) on donkeys to the castle. That's it."
He was so excited when he discovered these---it's like finding a buried treasure!

Greek Island Musings

AHHHHH.....THE GREEK islands. I've left my heart on those Greek islands. Just saying the words "Greek islands" conjures up visceral feelings of elation, relaxation, euphoria, health.....When I re-read my travel journals, I find excerpts from our lazy days there that remind me how happy and relaxed we were on any Greek island. For example, one excerpt described: *"We drove to a bakery for breakfast tiropites (cheese pies) to tide us over until lunch. We headed straight for the beach and had a great morning/afternoon of complete beach relaxation. The boys played in the sand, tried to catch small fish and collect rocks and walk far out into the water. I read guidebooks of Greece and Rhodes, walked around the strip of shops and found some evil eye bracelets for my girlfriends back home."*

In my opinion, no one can enjoy a Greek island quite like a little boy! Having three boys, I realize this is my reference point....but you learn how to live life all over again through the perspective of a little boy when you parent three of them!

Every two years we took the boys to Greece from 2007-2011 and then the older two sons went on their own for high school graduation trips to a co-ed youth camp for Greek Orthodox kids. Our second son extended his trip with a travel buddy and went to a coastal town for a week where they frolicked and attended a Greek wedding of an acquaintance. The last week of their trip, they stayed at the monasteries of Mount Athos for a most unique experience, completely different from the previous four weeks of adventure, socializing, frolicking and hedonism.

I admire that my sons wanted to continue going back to Greece independently and with friends. The foundation they received seeing Greece with us as a family was a strong one, encompassing everything from family, religion, history, culture and vacation adventures. Going back with peers gave them a chance to experience Greece on their own whims and creativity.

It will be interesting to see what future family trips they plan for their children. What landmarks will they return to and what new ones will they add?

Midnight in a bar in Brussels, Belgium
....and the most medieval square in all of Europe

O<small>N THE WAY</small> back from a Greece trip, we had a connection through Brussels. This was fortuitous because we have a cousin who lives there and we had recently visited with him and his wife when they came to our hometown. We reached out to them before the trip to set up a meeting time for our short connection in Brussels. They were excited to show us their compelling city. Connections are such wonderful opportunities to see another country and really focus on what important landmarks you want to see on your time there. In some ways, it must be like choosing excursions off of a cruise ship. Going over to Greece, we so often connect through London like we did for this particular trip, too. So— England on the way to Greece and Belgium on the return. Perfect!

After we checked into our hotel in Brussels, we met our cousins in the town plaza which is known as the most medieval square in all of Europe for its massive, colossal, awe-inspiring cathedrals and buildings. We took a plethora of photos of the buildings and our cousins regaled us in stories of the buildings' history. For example, there is a story that the architect of one of the towering buildings found a flaw in the structure design and threw himself off of the building in despair. This fascinated our young sons. The drama and intensity of being so passionate about one's art was illustrated so poignantly in this story –and right there before their eyes where they could understand the beauty of these ornate buildings. The Flemish facades on the cobblestone square with massive Gothic, Baroque and Renaissance exteriors from the 17th century Neo-classical era made Brussels a thriving and historic center of commerce.

As we walked through the plaza with our talented, interesting cousin and his boisterous, exotic wife, we absorbed all of the Belgian delights on every corner. Our eight year old son was a perfect taste-tester of Belgian chocolates and Belgian waffles. The sight of him engrossed in a Belgian waffle with whipped cream and strawberries was hedonism at its best. The photos are divine. On one corner, he'd find his sweets and pastries and on the next, we found Belgian beer—another delight! People gathered in the afternoon at the pubs in convivial leisure with their beers and Belgian fare which looked like sports bar food to me.

Our cousins took us back to their fabulously chic apartment. Even the boys perceived its glamour. Our cousin, an important businessman, is also a musician in his free time. Our sons were terribly interested in this fact and all of his instruments in the apartment because they took music lessons. Now they were seeing first hand how some adults actually keep up their talents years after their music lessons. What a great example this was for them. My cousin's wife and I looked through her wedding photo album which was uniquely Greek and unlike anything I had seen in America. It's a unique feeling when you are related to people, yet, because of the different countries you live in, your lifestyle and customs can be so different.

After a good visit at their apartment, they invited us to watch our cousin play in a bar that night. He plays keyboard and guitar and there was no way we were going to miss out on this, no matter how tired we might be from a three week trip in Greece. Later that night, we took a taxi to the restaurant/bar and had dinner before his set which didn't even start until close to midnight. Even though we were very used to eating dinner late in Greece, (like ten p.m.) and staying up late to be part of the nightlife, this was different. We were with an eight, eleven and thirteen year old ….in a bar---at midnight!

What a moment it was! Our Greek cousin, living in Belgium, played his instruments while the skinny, Asian lead singer covered famous nostalgic songs in British Mick Jagger-like style of high kicks and flair. It was an international experience for sure. I had to walk downstairs and out the back door to find a bathroom which is very common in Europe. When I returned to the concert, our eight year old fell asleep in my arms. I found it humorous that my child was asleep in my arms at midnight in a bar as this would never happen back home. But that's why we embraced the experience---it was a foreign moment. The American work ethic back home often prevents people from following their passions to have a second "job" as a musician or artist. But the attitude and philosophy of other countries empowers someone like our cousin to balance his important day job with his hobby as a musician. Viva la difference!

Gypsy Family Travel Evolves

THE GREECE TRIPS were the cornerstone of our family wanderlust. But, really, our globe trotting adventures started in the late 1990's when the older two sons were babies and toddlers going on family vacations to Mexico four times with my husband's big family. Those wonderful trips showed us that you can travel with babies and small children (along with certain circumstances and adjustments). What developed from there was a curiosity to see other places together with the kids.

Between 1996 to 2016, our family went to places in the United States, Mexico, Canada, Greece, Italy, Switzerland, Scotland, Ireland, England, Spain, Belgium, Morocco, Turkey, Dominican Republic, India, Austria, Lichtenstein, Germany, France, Gibraltar, The Vatican. Sometimes it was just two of us going on a trip---like India and Dominican Republic for a wedding and a senior class trip, respectively. The boys reached an age where summer obligations started to require them to stay home and get a job for their high school resume, take ACT prep courses, driver's ed, graduation trips, etc. and it was becoming a time where we needed to save more money for college and not indulge in five member family trips.

Since 2005-2011 was a streak of annual summer trip odysseys to four continents, it definitely filled up our minds and souls with a great basis of wanderlust and nomadic exploration. We took a breather and went to Mexico, Hawaii, and domestic trip destinations. The discoveries that developed from these trips deepened our transformation in global "citizenship" and awareness of the world.....as they do for anyone and everyone who embraces the spirit of travel.

Of course, there are transformative moments in each country we visited but I'm going to highlight a few memorable ones in the upcoming chapters. I am going to digress a little from the descriptive narratives and sensual travel details to outline what we created in our educational component but then I'll continue in following chapters with the more visceral details.

The synergy that emerged with my sons in preparing for these trips was the conception for what became Gypsy Family Travel—my travel and adventure unit that birthed my travel writing. The latter couldn't have happened if I wasn't a primarily at-home mother. The daily summer "routine" included trips to the library and other related field trips that children and parents enjoy together. Being an educator and psychometrist definitely made it easier to guide this process. Making the boys an integral part of the trip itinerary planning was beneficial for my husband and I because it molded the boys' behavior on the trips and kept them engaged and enthusiastic to take ownership of the trip and its purpose. And of course, it was beneficial for the boys because it created their intense metacognitive educational experience on the trips. What we came up with was this......

The "formula" for travel planning with your children can be outlined like this:

Consider your children's personalities and incorporate those characteristics into the itinerary. Are they athletic? scouts? artistic?

Have them each choose a country, state or city they are interested in. You can pick a region of a continent and connect the dots from there.

Have your children research their specific country by checking out books.

Meet together at the dining room table (or kitchen table) and work together daily to keep everyone on track. Leave the materials together in one place for accessibility. Build a bibliography from their favorite books.

Make quizzes for your children to take from their books' information.

Each child is the docent for their specific country so when you tour those countries, treat that child as an actual "docent" by letting them explain monuments, architecture, cuisine, historic facts, etc

When you arrive to that country, let the child/docent who studied that particular country be the first to "step" onto the soil as a a celebratory arrival. You may enter that country by airplane (so let them be the first off the plane), by ferry boat, bus, rental car, etc.

Activities depending on personalities: hiking, rafting, skiing, whale watching, zip lining, camping, art museums...

One year, we bought a live auction trip to Scotland for two. It included a Robert the Bruce tour and other features. We decided to take along our three sons. When they found out we were going to Scotland, our oldest son said, "we always said we would go to Ireland ...." So we thought, "Ireland is close to Scotland; let's do both! Any other places you want to go to?" and our second son said, "Let's go to Spain .....to Valencia--for the tomatina festival" (Because he had studied this tomato-throwing festival in Spanish class). When I heard Spain, I said, 'Let's go to Southern Spain and ferry over to Northern Africa--to Morocco!" and VOILA--our trip itinerary was set--Ireland, Scotland, Spain and Morocco.! Kind of an unusual route but one that fit our family and our interests at that time.

*The suggested reading books I've included on most countries' blog posts are for children and/or parents to read. Some parents have told me that reading a children's book on a country gives gave them a simple "bird's eye view" into what could otherwise be a complicated or complex history in adult versions.

A sample lesson plan for researching and exploring a country can follow this sequence to best integrate the concepts. A lesson can be part of a broad curriculum or it can be as specific as you want it to be. If you are not planning a trip anytime soon, the student can be an *"armchair traveler."*

Sample Lesson Ideas:

Choose a destination-- state or country. Have the student write to the Chamber of Commerce or Tourism Bureau of that destination requesting materials. Some will provide these for free. When the package arrives from the Chamber of Commerce, the student sorts through useful information as they become the "docent" or "travel agent. When I was a teacher in the 90's, my students enthusiastically waited for these packages to arrive. It was the highlight of this unit. *Now the different subjects come in:*

Geography---use Google Maps or a regular atlas to locate the destination.

Social Studies--draw and learn about the country's map symbols and colors.

Science or Art-- make a craft or project depending on the destination you are studying. Example: a volcano project for Santorini, Greece. A paper mache mountain project for The Alps, etc.. Make a poster of your country, showing the highlights.

Cuisine-- make a recipe from that region, serve it for family dinner that night and discuss what you learned about the country you are studying.

Reading- read the books you've checked out about your country and share factoids with your family.

Writing- write a sentence or paragraph on the country (see Quizzes section of this blog)

Language--use an audio translator on the computer to repeat phrases from the various countries. Build a vocabulary word bank of foreign words. (See France on this blog)

Math- create a budget for your travel expenses. Calculate the distance of miles between countries. On the airplane, have the student observe the maps on the TV screens that show the distance and location of the flight route.

Art & Photography: when the trip is over, make a photo book together on iPhoto, Shutterfly, etc.

Integrate the concepts---you use visual, auditory and kinesthetic modalities when you do the following:

visual- learning through images, graphics, sights auditory- hearing kinesthetic- tactile and physical learning

1. Check out books about the destination (ex: Archeology or Sea Life)--- VISUAL
2. check out a related DVD (ex: National Geographic Kids video)--AUDITORY
3. go on a related field trip (ex: visit the city Aquarium, zoo)-- KINESTHETIC

If any of this seems too complicated or overwhelming, even just choosing two ideas will enhance your trip for your children!

Once the latter skills became implemented, I started to think about incorporating high order thinking skills into this "curriculum" of travel planning we were creating together. I remembered Bloom's Taxonomy which was such a significant part of my education training in college. I applied the taxonomy to the creation of our units which was a good way to summarize the integrity and validity of the unit in a simplified way.

Using Bloom's Taxonomy in Travel Planning

BLOOM'S TAXONOMY IS a great tool for travel planning customized to children. I learned this method when in my Education degree. Years later, when creating Gypsy Family Travel, I incorporated it into the units. An easy way to summarize how we applied and implemented our educational components into our travel itineraries is to illustrate how Bloom's Taxonomy streamlines it all. What was created at our dining room table each summer with our library sources reflected this paradigm:

Create- create an outline or plan for where you want to go on your trip. Create a lesson plan, quiz, unit, etc. for your destination.

Evaluate--evaluate your route, logistics, budget.

Analyze- analyze the purpose of your destinations. What are you wanting to accomplish there-- adventure? history? recreation? a combo? Analyze the different geography, customs, languages, religions of each destination.

Apply--apply your knowledge of the newly researched travel unit. Draw a map, a flag from that country or state. Make a quiz of factoids for your family. Make a model or do an experiment or craft relating to that country.

Understand--read your travel guide books. Quiz each other. Complete a quiz. Make flash cards.

Remember--make a photo book when you come home from your trip. Let the kids be involved in this process so they feel ownership of it. Read the photo books frequently. This will keep the memories vivid in their metacognition.

While this taxonomy might seem detailed and structured for many parents, it really doesn't matter which steps are applied and implemented. If a parent wants to tackle even just one or two steps of the structure, it can be successful and practical for children. Whether concrete or abstract, the important part is to take the experiential learning to the next step. From a simple photo album project to a poem, song or art project to symbolize a trip memory, a child's interpretation of a memory or experience is priceless.

Castles and Cathedrals

IF I HAD to summarize the main monuments of our European adventures, I would say castles and cathedrals were our biggest visual memory. The castles and cathedrals of Europe are at the top of our list of favorites and I consider them to be "museums" of royal residences and places of worship.

Walking through each of them for me was like becoming reincarnated into a world I read about, learned about, delved into and envisioned. Many tourists have described their sightseeing into castles and cathedrals as repetitive, redundant....however, I don't see it that way. I placed importance on each specific building and appreciated the specific details of each glorious monument that they are.

Purchasing the guidebooks and taking numerous photos of each place helped our children remember the landmarks; especially because we immediately made photo albums or photo books and documented details. I created the memory *for* my children by having them metacognitively process their experience.

While I wouldn't recommend only touring castles and cathedrals, I definitely would build them into the itinerary as primary points of interest. A developmentally appropriate itinerary for elementary school aged children would strike a balance between cultural sightseeing of museums and monuments with time spent at the beach, children's interactive museums and excursions or theme parks. The latter might even be true for adults! It can be overwhelming to cram in too much intellectual information without a break. You have to give yourself time to process what you've visually experienced. Travel can be tiring and stressful if you don't make time to rehydrate, relax, re-energize.

Sometimes long, relaxing lunches can take care of the latter and give you that extra boost of energy to start touring/sightseeing again. I also viewed our time in the cathedrals as our own spiritual time to reflect and grow closer to God by being among all of the icons or religious artifacts that have honored Him over the centuries.

Cardio Chaos in Canada- Ziplining and Whale Watching

An opportunity to see Canada came about when we visited relatives in Washington State and Idaho. As if Washington and Idaho weren't already ravishing enough and adventurous, adding Canada to the itinerary was a great way to show our sons their third North American country and to revisit Canada for Patrick and me. Driving our rental car from Spokane to Seattle, driving the car onto the ferry boat and connecting to Vancouver was a brilliant way to see so many stunning places. From Vancouver, we went to Victoria in British Columbia. This bright and brilliant city was pulsing with activity and beauty.

The British feel that contributed to Victoria in its architecture and name surely gave it a royal and pristine feel. Victoria originated as a traditional territory of the Lekwuungen People years before the European exploration and settlement occurred. As a tribute to the native people, Signs of Lekwungen is a walkway that is found along the Inner Harbour of Victoria to honor the history and culture of the Lekwungen people. It is said that Captain James Cook was the first explorer to set foot on British Columbia. In later years it was part of the historic Hudson's Bay Company trading post and many years after, it was part of the Gold Rush of 1858 when gold was discovered there.

The plaza of Victoria, right on the sun-dappled bay full of kayaks and boats, was surging with street artists, musicians, shops, restaurants and humanity. The glorious Empress Hotel was the centerpiece to this thriving plaza. The parliament building, all lit up at night, was identical to something you'd see in London. It was all very breathtaking. Our hotel was a nice walk from this gorgeous plaza and we strolled there nightly. The duck pond outside of our hotel was charming and certainly entertaining to our little boys.

There was no relaxation to be had in Victoria because my husband got the idea for us to go, go, go as usual. We signed up for a zip lining excursion in Sooke's National Rainforest which was a bit of a drive away. I was planning on reading a book in the park for the two hours the boys and Patrick would zip line. I was impressed with the lush and "tropical" feel of this rainforest. It seemed like being in a jungle of a tropical location rather than a Canadian rainforest.

I wasn't going to zip line but my family talked me into it and I'm so glad they did!! For an acrophobic, claustrophobic person like me, I did have to overcome some trepidation about various parts of the adventure---but it was WELL WORTH IT!

There was one line called "The Screamer" in which my seven year old son gladly screamed through the whole "ride." The whole experience lasted two hours and it was a good bonding experience for our family as we later discussed all of our different emotions and sensations completing it. The drive back to the hotel was filled with a sense of accomplishment and a nice decrescendo from the adrenalin of the two hour adventure.

Patrick was not ready to call it a day, though. As we drove into town, he saw the boats on the bay and said we should go whale watching, too. "Today?! Right now?" We had just completed an intense and thrilling two hour zip lining course and now he wanted us to go out on Zodiac boats at crazy high speed in the ocean to look for whales. I agreed to this, not realizing the boys were probably exhausted.

Having three Boy Scout sons, a parent is used to high energy and high adventure. But as a mom, we know better that our kids need downtime. On a whim, we suited up in our orange wetsuits and climbed into the Zodiac boats.

What happened next was unexpectedly terrifying and thrilling at the same time. The Zodiac took off at a maximum speed into what seemed like the middle of the sea. We held on for dear life, gripping the bar or strap in front of us and squeezing our seven year old son as close to our bodies as possible. Our hair was whipped back in the wind and the spray of water was in our faces. Our skin flapped in the wind and our bodies took quite a thumping in the waves of the choppy seas. I felt like there was no gravity and that my skeleton inside could not take this much longer. As dangerous as this felt, it was terribly fun and invigorating. Once we slowed down, (thank God), we fortunately saw the whales. This was very relaxing and mesmerizing to see the whales in their habitat and so close to us. I knew we had another high-speed boat ride back to the bay and I had to psyche myself up for it.

Adults and parents feel their own mortality as they get older and when you travel with three young children, you feel it at its peak. Safety is always at the forefront of my mind.

That night, at dinner, our oldest son wept in his dinner plate and didn't know why. I knew it was from joyous exhaustion. There is only so much kids can do and we had two back to back highly cardiovascular and chaotic adventures that day. My husband has great intentions and I love his sense of adventure but it definitely needs some balancing out from me from time to time. I think our son was dehydrated, too and that certainly led to some weakness and tears. We were chapped, tired, dehydrated and positively intoxicated with adventure that day. Canada is a stunning place on this earth and it provided us with natural wonders, landscape and panoramic beauty. Culture, music, drama and fine cuisine awaited us back on the plaza which is a perfect combination to all of the physical activities we enjoyed in Victoria. The plaza's restaurants and shops lured us daily and the street entertainment at night kept us engaged. Steel drum bands, people dancing and the perfect night breeze while we walked to and from our hotel are the memories I'll have of this grand destination.

Creating Gypsy Family Travel

THE FIRST TRUE "Gypsy Family Travel" trip odyssey happened in 2010 for us. I explained earlier how the route evolved; with each of us choosing a destination. The homework we did ahead of time and the fabulous guidance of my travel agent created the combination of an informative itinerary from her expertise and the educational research the boys and I did together through the library and other resources. With Patrick's Boy Scout dad skills and my Cub Scout leader skills, we decided to use backpacks for our trips. This style of luggage has its pros and cons but I have to admit, it gave me an image I'll never forget---the five of us "backpacking" and railing through Europe in a less conventional way than traditional "backpacking" because instead of staying at camp grounds and youth hostels, we were in villas and hotels.

When I look at the photographs of the boys making connections between countries with these big backpacks on their bodies, I realized that I was doing now, as a mother, what many young people do with their peers. The difference was I was "backpacking" through Europe with four males---my husband and three sons. Like a mother koala bear with her cubs clinging to her or me clinging to them, I was directing their discovery and observing their epiphanies; tasting each meal together and digesting each country together. I never wanted to backpack travel as a youth and I had other circumstances and goals going on then but I was enjoying this experience now and enjoying the aspect of control that I could give it.

The trip started off in Shannon, Ireland with a rental car, a map and a desire to see the jubilant country of Ireland with its forty shades of green.

I was the only one jet-lagged because I spent so much of the flight making sure the boys were all comfortable and settled. I've never been able to sleep well on planes but I marveled at how the boys always traveled well on planes. They were always content with the movies and their own entertainment devices. When I wasn't in and out of sleep on this car ride, I noticed my husband's face and gaze. He'd ask me to read to him from the itinerary with its descriptive paragraphs. I realized that while I had familiarized myself and the boys with this itinerary information over the last few weeks, Patrick was new to it. Other than the dinner time discussions we had when we quizzed him about the countries we were traveling to in our units, the elaborate details of the destinations were unfolding to him now. He looked so content driving and exploring but depending on me for the informational part. It reminded me of the partnership we have always had. We craved in each other the fulfilling conversations that we have enjoyed over the decades. We had both been educated at sister and brother Catholic schools in our hometown and we had both grown up in the same Greek Orthodox community of Greek school, Greek Festival dance, catechism, summer camp and youth group. While we weren't always at those events at the same time, there were overlapping years and we had the same focus and priorities in life. We had the same philosophy about life and bringing up a family. The humor, laughter, adventures, infatuation, eros and shared heritage are intensely important components but the intelligence is the sustaining quality and satisfying thread that keeps the banter alive.

    This drive through Ireland was the picture book moment that revealed to me what a fantasy we were living with each other and our precious sons. I looked in the back seat to see our sons content with a Rubik's cube or musical instrument and Patrick and I up front in the car navigating this adventure for them. He looked at me with genuine pride for the part that I contributed to this trip---the planning and education. He kept telling the boys to thank me for all of the preparation I did to make it happen. I had never looked at it that way because I was just so grateful to him for making it happen financially, and taking the time off work to go on this trip. To him, it was a relaxing getaway from the everyday grind and the "familiar."

It was also seeing things come to fruition for him because he bid on this trip auction item and took a chance. He was ready to start investing again in more hedonistic pleasures, maybe, after all these years of paying for school tuition and a mortgage... to this trip. This trip expense originated to be for just the two of us but I upgraded it to take the boys along. The auction item for a trip for two to Scotland was donated by a Scottish Lord who was friends with the philanthropist who chaired the gala we attended.

There was an opportunity to be given a tour of Scottish royalty landmarks by the Scottish Lord and then return to his home, on the sea, for high tea with his Lady. When we won the auction item, my husband was high on romantic feelings of getting away—just the two of us. I was flattered and touched by this gesture but told him, "If I'm going to meet a Lord and a Lady, my kids for sure are going to, also!" He saw the logic in this, being the amazing father that he is and he agreed to this idea. That night, when we returned home from the gala and told the boys about our auction "prize", they were bursting with excitement. My oldest was around fifteen years old at the time and expressed his appreciation that I couldn't meet a Lord and Lady without my kids benefitting from it, too. It touched me that *he* was touched! Already, the maturity and benefits of world travel were rubbing off on the kids. The challenges and sacrifices only make the journey that much richer.

Irresistible Ireland

When the name "Ireland" is spoken, my family instantly lights up with smiles, remembering the colorfulness of this country, its people, architecture, and casual feeling of happy people, Irish music, Irish cuisine and stunning landscape. It's true what they say about the "forty shades of green" and the pastoral view is calming AND intense at the same time.

In my interpretation, the castles are more simple than Scotland or England and the Irish folk have that jubilant spirit whereas, the people of the U.K. seemed more proper and serious. Our itinerary took us to Adare, Limerick, Shannon, Ennistymon, Killarney, Dingle Peninsula, Dublin., etc.. Other places to see are the Ring of Kerry, Galway, Cork, Kilkenny, Aryn Islands but it's not always possible to fit everything into a trip. The nice thing about Ireland is that you won't be disappointed no matter where you visit. The castles and cathedrals were informative and educational and once we were ready for an "intellectual break", there was always a charming tavern to relax in with "fish and chips", salmon, cold beer and lively music. A walk through Adare gave us a chance to snap some photos of the charming cottages. We were very surprised at how colorful the architecture is in Ireland. It was brighter than Mexico, even!

The hotel we stayed at was the Dunraven Arms in Adare. This was a beautiful boutique hotel that celebrities and royals have stayed in and I can totally see why. The decor, garden patio and beautiful hotel rooms were a very nice welcome to this magical, colorful country. Our itinerary in Ireland consisted of: Ennistymon, Dromoland Castle, Rathbaun Farm, Cliffs of Moher, Limerick, St. Mary's Cathedral, King John's Castle, Burnatty Castle (show and dinner included), Rock Shop near Cliffs of

Moher, Muckross House in Killarney, Torc Waterfall, amusement park in Killarney, Dingle Peninsula, Dublin, National Archeological Museum, St. Patrick's Cathedral, Hop On/ Hop Off Bus tour, Christ Church Cathedral, Blarney Inn for dinner and dancing, Dublin Writer's Museum and other places, too, ...but those were the highlights. The beauty of Adare, which looks like something out of a storybook, can be traced to before the Norman Conquest. The 3rd Earl of Dunraven influenced the rebuilding of Adare to include larger thatched houses.

In Killarney, we stayed near Killarney's National Park. Stretching our legs for a good walk along this parkway was lovely. Muckross House was amazing and one of the Ireland highlights we enjoyed the best. The story behind how the homeowners prepared this house for Queen Victoria's visit is astounding and costly. We did not explore the Ring of Kerry but the recommended route for it is: Killorglin, Caragh Lake, Cahirciveen, Wateville, Coomakista Pass and Drrynane. We'll have to go back sometime to do this—gladly! People can leave Killarney to go directly to Dublin like we did or they can explore a scenic route which includes stopping at the Blarney Castle to kiss the stone for good luck.

We chose the direct route so I guess we'll have to go back someday to kiss the Blarney stone and visit Blarney Woolen Mills for some shopping! Kilkenny Castle was recommended to us, too.

In Dublin, we stayed at Cassidy's Hotel which was a boutique hotel. This was in Dublin's city centre. I do remember the sounds of mating sea gulls keeping me awake at night but everything else was glorious! The tour on the Double Decker bus connected us to all of Dublin's attractions. This tour took ninety minutes and we loved every minute of it and could've stayed on for ninety more!: Guinness Storehouse, Dublin Castle, St. Patrick's Cathedral, Phoenix Park and Old Jameson Distillery.

For our first meal in Ireland, I had mussels, my son had lamb stew, my husband had shepherd's pie and the other two sons had fish and chips. It was misty and we wore our rain coats and ponchos. Our oldest son was the "docent" of Ireland for this trip. Because he had researched Ireland, he wanted to see if the Cliffs of Moher had visibility that day because the first time we went, it did not. We made two trips to Cliffs of Moher and both were incredibly foggy. *On our drive afterwards, we found the view charming with its rolling hills, hedges of stone walls, sheep, farmers, shepherds and perfectly maintained cottages with brightly painted homes. We saw sheepdogs, Shetland ponies, wagons and incredible florals.*

At night, we went to the dinner and show at the Bunratty Castle where we were welcomed by a bagpipe player and took a walk up the plank into a hall where they handed us mead. We listened to a harp solo. We entered the Great Hall where we sat with an other American family. The five course meal was delicious and we had to eat it with our hands, Medieval style. Bread, parsnip soup, ribs, veggies, chicken, desserts, wine. This was our first time to try parsnip soup and we loved it so much, I recreated it back home in America.

Dazzling Dingle Peninsula in Ireland

IRELAND IS NON-STOP visual beauty. The people are as colorful as the countryside. From the moment we flew over the forty shades of green pastures, we were in love. Each destination in Ireland we went to was fetching but Dingle Peninsula was mystical. The drive to Dingle was as pleasant for my husband as it was to reach the destination. Arriving there was the kind of experience when every family member getting out of the rental car simply gasped. There's no other way to say it than it takes your breath away. We've never heard waves crash like that. Seagulls were so close to us, they looked us in the eye.

As we explored, I thought about what happened here in history. I could visualize Viking longships sailing across these waters. There is approximately six thousand years of history about Dingle spanning the Mesolithic period to modern times. Reportedly, no Viking remains still exist on the peninsula. However, there are a plethora of archeological monuments there.

Just as I felt at the Cliffs of Moher in Ireland, we were on the edge of the world....the island of the the northeast corner of the European continent. We did not want to stop taking pictures---it was that gorgeous. The panoramic view of sandstone, cliffs, bluest waters and green grass is peaceful but also powerful with the sounds of the crashing waves and the vast sense of a force of nature.

In the nearby town of Dingle, we strolled through the streets of the quaint town and stopped to rest and eat seafood. You cannot go to Ireland without making a day trip to Dingle Peninsula. Being on the edge of the world like that saturates your senses. After enjoying the urban charm of the cities of Ireland, this natural destination provided us with a fulfilling break and treated us to the wonders of Celtic beauty!

We took photo after photo and got up close to a seagull to feed it. It was one of those days when our family enjoyed the landscape and scenery and did not have to learn any correlating history to it. Absorbing the geography of this place and feeling again, the recognition that we are all part of this earth is sometimes the only lesson you need.

Majestic Muckross House in Killarney—A Victorian Mansion

OUR FAVORITE STOP in Killarney, Ireland was Muckross House. This Victorian Mansion is part of the Killarney National Park--the first national park ever created in Ireland. The tour of the house was better than a museum and the grounds were majestic. The history of Muckross House fascinated us. For example, there was a family who lived there at one time who spent an enormous amount of funds and experienced financial difficulties preparing the house for Queen Victoria's visit. The house also was shut for thirty years at the beginning of WWII and later when it was occupied for a while by the Irish Army.

The house is currently preserved so well and the tour guides are very enthusiastic and informative. The blinds and shutters are positioned to restrict a certain amount of light into the house so as to protect the furniture and materials displayed. The decorations and artifacts are stunning and representative of the glory years of the Victorian era. The property was rented out for parties, fishing and hunting. Inside the rooms, you'll see mahogany furniture, Turkish carpets, flocked wallpaper and Italian marble.

A Japanese urn and curtains specially woven are part of the grandeur of the dining room. Wood carved sideboards and fantastic animal head trophies of the hunt boldly stand out in the Main Hall. The rich carvings reminiscent of Victorian style prominently adorn the mansion. The Billiard Room where men enjoyed cigars and bonded had walls decorated with Chinese silk. Twisted balusters on the Upper Landing and grand portraits below a beautiful ceiling molding lend so much formality to the architecture.

The grounds were unbelievable, really. The vivid colors of flowers we couldn't identify were gorgeous and the grounds extended to a beautiful body of water. We literally frolicked through the grounds. The boudoir, children's playroom and impressive kitchen and servant system featured unique details but the room that intrigues my sons still to this day was the Queen's bedroom which served as the bedroom during her visit. The wallpaper, polished limestone chimney-piece, gilded mirrors, finest mahogany and gold silk damask fabric all adorn this stately room.

The room that I liked the best was the kitchen which had bells to correspond to every room in the house. The servants knew who was ordering service and where to deliver the food. The cook had to give permission to anyone wanting to enter the kitchen except for the Lady of the house. And in typical Victorian design, the kitchen is built outside of the main block of the house to restrict the smells from the family and guests. That was one long walk from the kitchen to the dining room for servants carrying food! Queen Victoria's visit was a success as she enjoyed the grounds, the ceremonial reception and party and visited the nearby Torc Waterfall.

Tantalizing Torc Waterfall

THANK GOODNESS KILLARNEY was on our Ireland itinerary. I was enchanted by this city. From the main street atmosphere to an amusement park we found, we enjoyed the variety of entertainment discovered there. From good restaurants to the most fascinating Muckross House and the everlasting beauty of Torc Waterfall, Killarney was scenic and vivid! Torc is an Irish word meaning boar. The significance of this is derived from the legend of Fionn mac Cumhaill, a hero who killed an entranced boar. My husband and Boy Scout sons were overjoyed to find this nature spot right across the way from the Muckross House museum we were scheduled to tour.

We all played in the water, climbed on the rocks and absorbed the beauty of this total gift of nature. The boys hung from tree limbs, balanced on stones and ascended the rocks of the waterfall as they reached for their father to help them cross the streams. The roaring rush of the waterfall behind them was powerful and foreboding, yet, also peaceful because we were in a pocket of wilderness shielded from the street by vines and a thickly forested moss.

Exploring natural landscapes like this is just as important to traveling as sightseeing through historic landmarks. For the kids, especially, it brought opportunities for kinesthetic learning. For us adults, it helps break up the visual processing of sensory overload. In really getting to know a country, I always honor that you have to explore its natural beauty and landscape, too. You have to become part of its vibe and culture if you can. Ireland gave us wonderful opportunities to absorb natural places like Dingle, Cliffs of Moher, and Torc Waterfall in balance to the bustling metropolis of Dublin. We love and crave mass humanity when we travel but the natural places whet one's appetite for the expanse. Dublin was so bursting with people that I compared it to an ant colony with thousands of ants climbing up out of the anthill, one on top of the other.

Yet, ambling through Torc Waterfall was a memorable afternoon of the five of us having a pocket of wilderness all to ourselves in a mossy canopy of exalted Irish greenery and scenery. Torc Waterfall definitely embodies the "forty shades of green" title that Ireland possesses. The clear air and mossy rocks around it are so grand that it is no wonder that Queen Victoria and her ladies in waiting came here to enjoy this Irish gem.

Mohammed, Muslims and Mystical Morocco

———— ꝏ ————

THE DESIRE TO go to Morocco was mine. In the spring of 2010, when we extended the Scotland trip to include Ireland and Spain, I had the inspiration to go to Morocco after the Spain leg of the trip. Looking back, years later, I think the inspiration actually came from a photo I saw in a fashion magazine of all places! I found the magazine many months after the trip and realized that the Moroccan motif of the magazine spread must have lingered in my psyche and eventually influenced this trip route. In addition to the latter, I have always been fascinated with Moroccan and Algerian culture.

The travel agent and I came up with wonderful activities to do on the way there from Spain. She was as excited for me when she described how the Barbary monkeys come up to your car in Gibraltar and eat the hat off your head. She pictured how entertained our sons would be from this sight. We drove to Gibraltar and took pictures in front of the imposing monolithic Rock of Gibraltar. We never saw the monkeys and it was extremely difficult to get into the entry system, so our only experience in Gibraltar was eating an amazing meal at a restaurant at the base. It was the first time we ate Rabo de Toro (tail of the bull).

We left our rental car in Tariffa, Spain and waited at the port for our ferry boat. As we sat in a cafe, our boys drew our portraits in their travel journals and I read to them from a Spanish newspaper. The news was all about the First Lady, Michelle Obama, being in Marbella, Spain. I was pleasantly surprised that I could still read and translate Espanol after all these years. It felt really good to be able to share the information with my family as my sons were currently taking Spanish in school.

Modeling this multilingual skill for them was also a part of the beauty of traveling.

The ferry ride over to Morocco was a sunny morning ride filled with curiosity for another new land. The boys and I wrote in our journals as we sat around a circular table with Patrick, drinking coffee and anticipating the new opportunity in our docent designed gypsy family travel. I was the docent of this country. Luke was the docent of Ireland, Mark was the docent of Spain and John was the docent of Scotland.

When we arrived and completed the immigration process with our passports, we were met by our tour guide. For the sake of anonymity, I'll refer to this wonderful man as Omar. My husband had been hesitant to go to Morocco as he was about going to Turkey. Both countries were heavily Muslim and this was a time, globally, that there was a lot of negativity about the "extremists." I was not as worried for various reasons. I am always cautious and careful when traveling because, after all, I'm a mother. But being ethnic and looking "foreign" myself is a bonus when traveling. There is an acceptance and a way of blending in when you have an international "look." Our oldest two sons are darker in complexion, hair and features and our youngest favors his father more. One of my sons, in particular, is similar to me in features so we can truly blend in more in exotic countries. I also wasn't worried about safety in Morocco because the travel agent guided us well in her expertise. I always leave an itinerary behind with relatives on both sides of the family, too. So with two relatives and a travel agent knowing where we were, I felt comforted that there was a good "trail" on us, so to speak.

Arriving into Morocco was an exotic hustle-bustle of activity. Tangiers Port was our location and it was full of enriching information and experiences. Our guide, Omar, was a gentle spirit; impeccably dressed in linen clothes, crisp pants and nice loafers. He seemed aristocratic, intellectual and genuinely enthusiastic about his job. He spoke about all things Moroccan with such pride. We instantly absorbed his enthusiasm for his country and its culture. As soon as he ushered us into the tour van and the door shut behind us, my husband and I were alert and a bit nervous. Here we were in our first African country with our young children during a globally intense and political time. I had "rehearsed" in my mind that I would always be the last one out of the van because I had this image of my sons being trapped in the van or out of the van without one of his parents. I had seen too many moments on TV shows or movies where a child is kidnapped in a foreign country. Omar introduced us to our private tour van driver and said, "This is Mohammed." Immediately, my husband tensed up and I think his hand clutched my thigh. I patted his hand and stroked it in a soothing way to reassure him that everything will be alright. I had faith in this tour guide duo of Omar and Mohammed.

    I could tell that Mohammed was curious about us as well. He had a job to do that day which was to drive us around on Omar's itinerary as he instructed us all about Morocco. Surely, he could sense that we were nervous. As we asked authentic, sincere questions with deep curiosity and interest in mystical Morocco, it seemed like Mohammed and Omar realized that we were respectful Americans who had traveled far to learn about their country. We had traveled far and at major expense to include this northwestern African country on our list of destinations. They could observe our family dynamic and see that we were a loving family open to other cultures. Their fee was a bargain to us but I knew it was profitable to them. As the day progressed and we asked them questions about their lifestyle and values, I believe that Mohammed and Omar began to see us as equals. We, like them, were parents who loved our children and wanted to educate them. I asked Omar about his family and siblings. I asked him if his sister was allowed to be educated and he said, "My sister is a dentist!" This was enlightening to me because so often in the media we hear about the oppression of females and the discouragement and forbidding of education for them. Of course, this is not prevalent in every country and it was part of the learning process for us to learn what was conventional in this particular culture.

Being the only female in the group of my four male family members and two male tour guides, I respected the Moroccan dress code and wore a short sleeved teeshirt that covered my shoulders and cropped pants and sandals. We sampled everything affably, like cactus pear fruit and the entire delectable Moroccan meal we were served in the restaurant. In the market, I purchased tea leaves that were recommended to me and we drank beverages given to us in the rug factory.

The vocabulary, mythology, history, factoids and cultural lessons we learned that day made our heads spin. The cave of Hercules overlooking the Atlantic ocean and Mediterranean Sea had non-stop visual details. Greek mythology was incorporated in this thrilling cave which also had markets inside of it! My teenage son took a photo inside the Cave of Hercules just as the divers were in action. The shape of this cave opening happens to be the mirror image of Africa with Madagascar next to it! Ironic!!

Omar took us to a restaurant and left us there to enjoy our meal while he went to complete his afternoon prayers. Popeye's Mediterraneo Popular Ristorante was the name of this culinary wonderland. It was tiny and simple. Our Moroccan multi-course meal at the famous restaurant was unforgettable and we still talk about it! Popeye's had a line around the block full of customers waiting to get in. After hours of sightseeing, this meal break was exactly what we needed and it gave our tour guide time for his afternoon prayers. Smoked almonds, salsa, swordfish, figs, dessert with honey, melon and a non-alcoholic fruit drink were just some of the gastronomic spectacle! I recall sitting there at the table with my family anticipating each course with such curiosity and feeling the breeze behind us with the opened window. We realized that we were having a once in a lifetime experience eating this way---with no utensils basically and with no salt or pepper! The beverage was a juice---not a wine or beer that we'd typically have and interestingly enough---from a cauldron that had been boiling for twenty four hours. Our guide, when he returned from his afternoon prayers, showed us the room where Popeye makes his herbal juice. It's a twenty four hour boiling process with fruits, herbs and palmetto in it. Popeye is a world famous herbalist. He came over to our table and patted my oldest son on the head. When we asked our son what Popeye told him, he answered, "He blessed me to be a good cook."

Moroccan food is flavorful and full of spices. We embraced every detail of it! There was a heavenly dessert with honey almonds, sauce and dates. Next course was swordfish and shark, delicious figs, and naan bread. For dessert, there was melon with knives, otherwise— no utensils!

The farmers market taught us so much---we ate cactus pear from the food booth of Berber village women. The Berber women's hats have pompons on them, similar to the South American style; probably due to the traveling of explorers across the continents who bring back styles from foreign places.

The word "Morocco" means "the West" (and it's in Northwestern Africa). Morocco has both Atlantic Ocean and Mediterranean Sea coastlines. The Cave of Hercules that we went into overlooks where the Atlantic and the Mediterranean meet. The cactus pear fruit we ate at the farmers market came right out of a cactus. The Berber women who come down from the mountains worked at the farmers market. Berber people inhabit the Rif Mountains and Atlas Mountains. The official languages in Morocco are Berber, Arabic, Moroccan Arabic and French.

Wherever we went, our tour guide, Omar, and others greeted each other with "Salam Alaikum". It translates to "peace to you." People use it as freely as other cultures use "goodbye", "hello", "Shalom" or "Peace." People respond with "Wa-alaikum salam"-("peace unto you.") We asked Omar, "what is that greeting?". He explained to us in detail about how peace is at the core of his religion. He asked us what our culture's equivalent might be and we answered, "God be with you."

When we passed by mosques, I asked him what the significance of the colored tiles were and he explained that the colors are colors of peace. He also expressed that he believes we are all brothers and sisters in paradise. I asked him if that meant, "all paths lead to God?" He thought so, personally.

When we departed that day on our ferry boat and bid the guide farewell, my husband shook his hand and said, "Salam Alaikum" and he responded, "God be with you." I found this moment transformative for my family, our epiphanies, our journey and our global understanding during this year of 2010 in a time of political turmoil in the world. It was a healing moment for us and good closure to a day that had moments of trepidation for my husband in particular.

Some time later, I looked into my travel journal about our Moroccan experience and found these excerpts which reminded me of specific details we learned. I had recorded the following facts in the next several paragraphs. Several nations had influence over Morocco at one time. Winston Churchill lived there and liked to paint there. Tangiers very hilly-- they call it the "San Francisco of Morocco" or the Rome of Morocco because of the seven hills. Seven is very lucky for them. There are seven entrances to the old town. There are seven stars/points in their star.

We went to a beach area where the Atlantic meets the Mediterranean. Jacques Costeau discovered a fresh spring that exists at that point. We rode camels on a hill overlooking this beach. My youngest son's face was euphoric just standing next to the camel and seeing these creatures for the first time. My husband's reaction was priceless, too. I had ridden camels before but it was still a thrill. There was a four month old baby camel that intrigued us. Many children worked in this area and that made an impression on us. The second language spoken here is French.

Our guide took us to the Cave of Hercules where the legend is that Hercules rested here after he did his seven deeds. Atlas, who held up the world, "named" the Atlantic Ocean and the Atlas Mountains. Tangier was the name of Hercules's wife, therefore the city is named Tangiers. The cave now has shops in it but once, the Berber tribes lived there. There's a spot referred to as "Hercules's chair" where he watched the sunset through a cave hole. There's a natural spring source in the cave from mountain water. We watched the divers doing their tricks against the backdrop silhouette.

After the Berber farmers market, we went to the Old Town Bazaar! Our guide explained the Jewish Ghetto architecture, alleys, doors, nooks, etc. The details --cultural and historic-- and the vocabulary were so in-depth. We learned the meaning of the word "Gibraltar": "Jabal" means mountain. We learned the symbolism of the colors of their Moroccan tiles: Green= peace (Islamic). Blue= came from Phoenicia. In the bazaar, we bought pottery, vases, tablecloths, etc...and looked at amazing rugs while the boys were happily drinking the sodas they were served. So many lessons learned on that tour!

I reflect back to our time in the market place and bazaar. The Moroccan market we went to in Tangiers was exciting! We entered a place that combined Mediterranean, Arabic, Berber and Andalusian flavors. A short ferry ride away from Spain, Morocco was an instant exotic world of its own unique styles, customs, cuisines and history. The Moroccan market was special because of the vivid colors, smells and activity. We learned about a herbal tea mixtures, their own versions of "Moroccan oil", and marveled at the spice market. The hustle bustle of the market was exciting to observe. The meal we had at Popeye's was incredible and it was the first time we had eaten Moroccan food so I was excited to contemplate making Moroccan food once I was back home. Learning about Moroccan spices was brand new information for me. Ras el hanout is a mixture of spices used in many tagine recipes.

Spice markets and farmers markets make me incredibly happy! I think back to the time I was a child and went with my grandfather or dad to the Mecca Coffee shop in my hometown. When we walked in, we were immediately hit with the smell of coffee beans. It was strong, pleasant, pungent and powerful. I feel the same way about spice markets--you walk into a display of amazing products! The Moroccan market had nuts, fruits and vegetables, etc.

Besides the market, there is also the Cave of Hercules, riding camels, shopping at the bazaar, touring the city, seeing the outside of the palace and so much more. Morocco is full of culture, history and fascinating geographical features. The villagers, Berbers, etc...come down from the Rif mountains with their produce. The market we went to was in the port town of Tangiers within walls, paths and buildings. When it was time to depart to the ferry boat at the end of our tour, we were a bit rushed for time.

We had just completed this magical, mystical journey with Omar's guidance and I had just experienced the moment with him---the epiphany---of connecting with someone of the Moslem faith who believed, like me, that "all paths lead to God." He told me that he believed we are all sisters and brothers together in paradise. I understood at that moment that at the core of the Islam faith, there is peace. While this is not true for the "extremists" and the jihadists, there are hypocrisies in other extremist religions which do not spread messages of peace. Having this healing moment between us all, Omar then proposed an idea to us, a solution for getting on the ferry boat in time. He asked us, "do you trust me to take your passports to the front of the immigration line on the ferry boat and expedite your entrance?"

Patrick and I looked at each other knowing this was rule #1 of travel that we were breaking. With trust in our hearts and the assurance that we just *knew*—as humans---not Americans, or as foreigners; as Christians or travelers, that we could trust this human being, we agreed to let him do it. He asked again, "do you *trust* me?" We said, "Yes! We trust you." How could we not? That was a huge leap of faith for Patrick. Not only did he take care of our late departure with this perk of getting us to the front of the line with our passports in his hand and us back at the dock but when we departed, Patrick shook his hand tightly and said, "Omar, salam alaikum!" and Omar answered for the first time that day (and maybe ever), "GOD be with you!."

I witnessed a transformation that day. After the ferry ride, on the ride home in our rental car, everyone was quiet and reflecting on the Moroccan adventure. I mused to the boys, "do you understand now that those little boys in the square selling the wooden camels for two euros, working for their families---they are hungry and poor and they want to believe whatever their parents tell them. They don't know any differently. If their parents tell them to hate Americans, they believe their parents because they love them; just like you love and trust us. All we can do is pray for each other---pray for everyone, pray for the world." My sons understood what I was saying because they had observed little boys showing their pet donkeys in the square for money. They had observed a boy their same age chasing us to sell us wooden camel souvenirs. They saw boys their age helping us with the camel ride we took on the hilltop. They saw this work ethic first hand.

    My husband quietly reflected on this concept, too. The stillness in his peace at that moment softened him even though he eventually back to his ways and beliefs about the world and politics. He not only survived his van ride with a man named Mohammed at which he first recoiled in fear to shaking Omar's hand and saying "Salam Alaikum" at the end of our time together. If traveling and opening up to other cultures achieves even the briefest encounter and revelation like this, then it is worth it. Morocco was exotic, historic, adventurous and mystical.

The Rock of Gibraltar

We went through Gibraltar on our way to Morocco. Gibraltar is a British Overseas territory in southern Spain, known for the famous Rock of Gibraltar. This monolithic limestone promontory on the Iberian Peninsula is the southernmost point of Europe. Barbary monkeys are found there and known to eat the hats off of tourists.

We were hoping to run into these monkeys on our way to Morocco, but getting onto Gibraltar was challenging. We drove around and around looking for the entrance and decided the line of cars was too long but we did get some great photos and ate at a restaurant nearby where our son tried Rabo de Toro for the first time: Tail of the Bull. The restaurant we ate in had a exotic ambience of Moorish tiles and slabs of jamon hanging off the ceilings in the kitchen.

It's fascinating to read about Gibraltar, not just for its geographical features but for its historic significance in battles, caves, Moorish dwellings and fortifications.

Mythology plays a big part in the folklore of this area. Because Gibraltar is a strait which connects the North Atlantic Ocean to the Mediterranean Sea, people have a mythological reference about this called "the pillars of Hercules." It is said that Hercules pulled Africa and Spain apart by hand which formed the Gibraltar and the Moroccan mountain of Jbel Musa.

I was fascinated to learn that several ethnic groups are "Gibraltarian"; which is a mix of Portuguese, Maltese, Genoese and Andalusian descent. The other cultures there are India, Moroccan and British. The main language in Gibraltar is English and the secondary language is Spanish.

I discovered later that John Lennon and Yoko Ono were married at the Rock of Gibraltar because of various reasons. His quote about the destination choice for their marriage is: "We went there and it was beautiful," Lennon said. "It's the 'Pillar of Hercules,' and also symbolically they called it the 'End of the World' at one period. They thought the world outside was a mystery from there, so it was like the Gateway to the World. So, we liked it in the symbolic sense, and the rock foundation of our relationship."

The Alhambra in Granada, Spain

THE HIGHLIGHT FOR me, in all of Spain, was seeing the Alhambra. Having read a book about *Katherine of Aragon*, before seeing her childhood home, the Alhambra, prepared me in a wonderful way! Reading about the descriptiveness of her childhood Moorish home during its finest regalia gave me such a sense of what to appreciate once I arrived there. I recalled the details of the first few chapters of the book when the character of Katherine describes the details of this palace and all of its servants and royalty. You must see the Alhambra in Granada and then drive over to Ronda, Spain. Try not to go when it's hot because you'll be tempted to rush through it.

Something that particularly moved me was that the Alhambra has a connection to me as an American. *This is where King Ferdinand and Queen Isabella commissioned Christopher Columbus to sail to the New World which led us to the discovery of the Americas.* To stand in the room where they all were when this historic moment happened was intense for me. We also found out that Washington Irving had an apartment here.

The *jalis* and calligraphy on this palace was unlike anything we had ever seen. My nine year old son even remarked on it. My architect friend back home pointed out these stylistic treasures to me. Arabic script and white cursive or kufic characters of verses and poems are inscribed onto the backgrounds.

Three vocabulary words that describe the Alhambra are: "alcazaba" which means fortress, "alcazar" which means palace and "medina" which means city.

Another interesting fact about the Alhambra is that it actually takes on three different color tones depending on the light of day reflecting the iron hue of the towers and walls surrounding the hill. It is red but becomes silver at starlight and transforms into gold by sunlight. The words alqala hamra' means red. The changing color tones also happens on the Taj Mahal in India which is another monument I was fortunate enough to visit with my oldest son and sister-in-law. I appreciate so much how these architects incorporated the splendor of the natural sunlight, starlight and moonlight in influencing the color tones of these monuments. Again, it reminds me of the thread throughout my travels of how we share the moon. Whether stargazing on a beach in Greece, staring at the moon longingly on a balcony in Athens or my oppressed Greek ancestors walking by the light of the moon to their hidden cave Greek schools with their teacher, the moon is powerful. The sunsets of Santorini to Manzanillo take on this same power.

This Moorish palace became a Christian court in 1492 under the Catholic monarchs, Ferdinand and Isabella. During the 18th century and part of the 19th century, the Alhambra was neglected and many sections were converted into dungheaps and taverns where thieves and beggars resided. Napoleon's troops used the palace as barracks and towers wiremen and blown apart. But in 1870, protection and restoration turned the Alhambra into national monument, thankfully.

The Alhambra remains one of my favorite trip memories and top three most beautiful monuments or trip destinations I've been honored and privileged to see, experience and behold.

Legendary Loch Ness in Scotland

THE FLAVORS OF Europe ranged for us from Andalusian, Moorish, Grecian, Germanic, so forth.... and the delightfully Celtic flavor. Scotland just left the most majestic and proper stamp on the passport of our hearts. Who hasn't been fascinated with the legend of Loch Ness and its "Loch Ness Monster?" When I was younger, I wanted so badly to believe that this mysterious creature existed. It seemed like there were always updates about possible sightings. It was a tug of war between imagination and scientific fact.....but it kept the Loch Ness monster in the media for all those years.

There was no way I was going to go to Scotland and miss seeing the lake, Loch Ness! On a misty day, we drove to the breathtaking area of the Scottish Highlands of Inverness. The lake was vast and water was calm. I was standing at Loch Ness as an adult ---but remembering the curiosity I had a a child about this place.

My kids played along with me and pretended to be looking for "Nessie" as the Scots call her. For those who like cold and misty weather, they'll LOVE Scotland! My husband and sons love this kind of weather. I prefer the sun but the brisk weather in Scotland keeps you on your toes and lends itself to the feeling of crisp and proper.

As we gazed at Loch Ness lake and played games pretending to find "Nessie", we met some charming Scottish children who were fishing. They were the quintessential Scots---flaming carrot top red hair, greenish eyes and freckles. We asked to take their photos and we conversed with them briefly, enjoying their accents. On the walk back to town to observe the boat locks and how they work, I found a path that led us to a magnificent abbey. This abbey had a life size chess board outside in the courtyard so the boys stopped to "play chess". We explored through the abbey, marveling at its architecture. We were free to just roam the grounds and when I looked it up later on the internet, it looked like you can stay there for lodging. How I wish I would've known about this place when I was planning the trip!

However, it's enchanting to find discoveries by accident on your travels and it made for a special moment. We walked on a while more, stopping to eat mulberries off the trees and then enjoying a Scottish lunch in the town at The Lock Inn. My husband explained the lock system to us and how the boats change locks to go upstream. This was such an authentic Scottish feature that engrossed us since we live in such a landlocked area of the United States. In this small village atmosphere, I smelled the Scottish food from the tavern while I looked out onto the cooperative spirit of the villagers working on the lock system. I noticed details about people that I did not notice in the crowds of Edinburgh, filled with inevitable tourists.

At Loch Ness, while we gazed through the telescope and marveled at the quiet and vast expanse of the lake, I noticed the two Scottish siblings fishing next to us. Every freckle on their faces and their flaming red hair were details that made the moment feel so Scottish to me. We conversed with them briefly and gained a sense of their lifestyle in this charming village.

All those decades ago when I daydreamed about the Loch Ness monster, I tried to envision what the shore and landscape looked like around the lake. In the fake photos of the mythological sea creature, it always showed it as a murky lake with this long necked beast in the shadows. Now as a psychometrist, I realize that I was distracting myself as a child in elementary school with this myth as a coping mechanism of dealing with the unknown—the unknown of my mother's illness. I was controlling the unknown by pondering the unknown. Going there all those decades later to see Loch Ness gave me answers. It, in fact, did not look like what I had pictured. But there was something reassuring about just finding my answers. It gave me closure. I was satisfied somehow to appreciate what Loch Ness looked like to me when I found it. It was a quiet moment, again with my sons and husband, absorbing it and appreciating being on the other side of the world. The legend of the Loch Ness monster described how this sea creature came up from another body of water, possibly China, and landed in this lagoon or something like that. It has always been fascinating to me that various cultures all over the world have similar mythological themes to explain their natural phenomena. Storytelling has always been a need that sustained the generations. Again, our cosmos share this need; a need to resolve our doubts.

Saturated by Scotland

THE LANDSCAPE OF Scotland is a kaleidoscope of beauty and rich history. It has a sophistication to it that is unlike neighboring Ireland which is alluring in its own way. Scotland and England have a certain "aura" that evokes warriors and history to me; royalty and structure.

A custom we noticed that was unique to Scotland was how they seated families at restaurants. Upon seeing our three sons, we were always ushered to the back of a restaurant. Once seated, you still had to often order at the counter. The customer service is different of course, all over the world. Their restaurants also closed much earlier than what we were used to in the Mediterranean countries where the nightlife gets going much later in the night.

It was fine to "cocoon" back in our grand manors of lodging since our brains were swimming with so much information from the day's sightseeing of castles, cathedrals, torture museums, optical illusion museums, Ghost and Ghouls tours and the royal tour from the Scottish Lord. The manor we stayed at (called Cromlix House) had been visited by celebrities and was everything you'd expect in a Scottish estate…. and more! The entry room of Cromlix House had an intoxicating scent of star gazer lilies in the plaid-decorated den. A tiny chapel was attached to the side of the entry room and we found out that people had been married in this tiny chapel through the years. The different floors and wings of the house had turrets in them. Our bedroom had its own turret and I climbed out onto it through the window as my husband took photos of me from below in the garden. The vanity in this huge bedroom had intricate combs and brushes next to an elegant silver plated mirror. A fireplace mantel and interesting portraits adorned the room. I read the book <u>The Constant Princess</u> by Philippa Gregory while lying on this grand bed. The book, about Katherine, Queen of Aragon, was an appropriate book for me to re-read on this trip since we visited her childhood palace, the Alhambra, when we went to Spain directly after Scotland. It made me feel connected to the imagery of Katherine and her ladies in waiting tending to her in her massive royal bedroom chambers. It's fun to fantasize.

When I explored the house, I found my sons playing chess in a study which looked like it came right out of the game "Clue". There was a greenhouse dining room for our meals and so many other rooms like conservatories and studies. Outside, on the acreage, we saw herds of sheep every morning when we took our walks in the misty Scottish weather. Our favorite part of Cromlix House were the grounds in the back. I referred to them as the "secret gardens" and we explored deep into them with our sons.

Thickly forested trees along paths and trails enticed us to go deeper into the grounds until we reached the fence line. I loved those morning explorations. They were unscripted and not part of our itinerary but they were spontaneous, random discoveries.

The Royal Mile of Edinburgh kept us engaged for hours each day. From Edinburgh Castle to Holyrood Palace and everything in between this mile, we were saturated by all the wonderfully Scottish details and nuances. Camera Obscura and Torture Museums were fun diversions for the boys. St. Giles Cathedral, whiskey distilleries, street artists and musicians and the Ghosts and Ghouls tour of the underground life showed us so much of Edinburgh's historic tapestry. The Witchery Restaurant and the musical show of dancers, bagpipes and haggis were fine nights of dining. Tenets Beer and Smithwicks Beer were enjoyed at Scottish taverns as well as Jameson Whiskey.

Our upcoming itinerary led us to St. Andrew's—the birthplace of golf and the University that Prince William and Kate Middleton attended.

(Although, at the time in 2010, we did not know about Kate, now the Duchess of Cambridge, yet.) Nothing could prepare us for the day we were about to embark upon in the Highlands...

The Highlands of Scotland

AFTER SPENDING TIME in Edinburgh and Stirling, we devoted a day of driving up north for the unforgettable monster of all days trips. The misted glens of the Highlands moved me to tears. Standing there, taking it in, it was unexpected to find myself tearing up. It may be one of the top three most beautiful places upon which I've laid my eyes. Because I love history, I envisioned what it must've been like when the massacre occurred between the enemies; the Campbells and the MacDonalds.

We spent time just exploring the hills and taking photos. Within seconds, our youngest son had taken off down a hill, surrounded by an electrifying "sea" of green! They say the Highlands are not that tall in actuality---it was surreal. The grandeur of these hills was imposing, majestic, and transported us to and from history to present time.

Ben Nevis, Britain's highest mountain and the shadows of imposing mountains in the Glencoe area just did not seem real to us. We had to stop, get out of the rental car and take photos frequently because we needed proof later that what we saw was true. The enthralling Scottish countryside is a mixture of greenest pastures and illuminated skies, dotted with Highland cows and herds of sheep. Although the horizon of sun in Greece is the most beautiful in the world to me, the sun's rays against the clouds in Scotland are unparalleled in terms of storybook beauty. The word "fantastic" has never been truer when describing Glencoe's sun-rayed horizon because that is what it is---a *fantasy!*

We ended the day in a village tavern eating Scottish food and watching our sons play pool among the locals. It was probably the locals' equivalent to a "sports bar" and it was a memorable way for us to absorb the simple vibe compared to the luxurious Cromlix House lodging.

While the rest of Scotland was riveting for us, especially with the haunting legacy left on Edinburgh's Old Town, the time spent in the Highlands, Loch Ness and Glencoe will always be the core of our spellbinding visuals and memories.

Rambling Las Ramblas

Because Spain is a very big European country, people tend to pick cardinal point regions to visit so they can concentrate on the area. We chose mostly Southern Spain but also went to Barcelona. Seville, Granada, Ronda, Malaga, Marbella, Tariffa, Estepona (and Gibraltar; its own "country" within a country) were the cities we went to and from what I've heard Northern Spain has its own beauty worth exploring. The history of Spain is so rich and having tour guides or tour buses in Barcelona and Seville was very important in order to fully appreciate all of the details. The tour bus in Barcelona was an extensive way to see such a busy, fast-paced city. Barcelona is known for its modernity; and Seville for its antiquity.

My youngest son was most excited about the boqueria in Barcelona. A boqueria is a farmers market so extensive it was like walking through a food museum! Fresh smoothies were a favorite of his daily walk out onto Las Ramblas. Las Ramblas is the most famous street in Barcelona because of the mass humanity that walks there daily. Jamon, the Spanish word for ham, hung in the boquerias, with its raw and pungent aroma and you could buy slices of it. Entering the boqueria was like finding a smorgasbord of food fantasy. Row after row of the most succulent fruits, vegetables and produce, huge legs of jamon and even fresh fruit smoothies were beautifully displayed. My youngest son's eyes were popping out of his head, practically because we have nothing this vast and lush back home in terms of produce! Our landlocked state back home has pretty sad produce, actually. We could spend so much time in the boqueria enjoying all the fresh foods and commerce! This was a delicious (pun intended) cultural custom for us to observe because in our opinion, no farmer's market in any other country compares to the Spanish boqueria. Swiss, Mexican, Greek or even Moroccan---none were as seductive and flirtatious as the boqueria of Barcelona! Like the pride of the chic Italian fashion or the staggering beauty of Greek island architecture, different countries reign supreme for their specialties but Spain wins the prize for their boquerias and tapas!

Spain was one of the top destination choices for our sons because of their familiarity with the country and the language from their Spanish class at school. Being a large country, we had to choose which regions we could visit. We had nine days to see Spain and we chose the southern side. Malaga, Marbella, Tariffa, Barcelona, Seville, Granada, Ronda, etc.. Barcelona had the modern experiences and Seville had the antiquity and history. A flamenco show in Barcelona was on our itinerary and our curiosity was peaked.

If you had a Flamenco dancer doll like I did as a child, you will know what it felt like to see this image come to life as the real thing! My Flamenco dancer doll had a red dress, black hair, lace and the fan. Supposedly, our uncle bought it for us during a trip to Spain. It was part of my bedroom decorations for years. When I found out decades later that we'd be seeing a Flamenco show in Spain, it delighted me! There was so much emotion, music and "storytelling" in the show and it was interesting to watch my husband and sons focus on the details while trying to interpret the performance.

This electrifying evening happened at the Tablao Flamenco El Cordobes located in the Las Ramblas area in the city center. Reportedly, the best Granada artists have made it become one of the most important Flamenco spots in Spain. It was exciting for us to attend a performance that has gained international prestige.

Being as stunned by the Flamenco dancing as we were, I later studied its origin as an art form. The dance is a combination of six musical talents; cante (singing), toque, (guitar), baile (dance), jaleo (vocalizations), palmas (hand clapping) and pito (finger snapping.) Originally, it only involved the voice part which focused on a primal chant accompanied by rhythm. It was fascinating for me to learn that many historians theorize that flamenco was the invention of the gypsies who arrived to Andalusia from India in 1425, approximately. The gypsies in Spain were persecuted by the Catholic inquisition and the Moors were also forced to convert to Christianity. Gypsies were forced to stop wearing their traditional dress and to stop speaking their language, called Romany. They were commanded to stop their wandering and methods of labor. This detail about gypsies is coincidental to me to incorporate into my creation of the Gypsy Family Travel unit. The flamenco show was a wonderfully Spanish feature to experience along with all of the other activities we experienced.

    Our rented apartment around the corner of the famous Las Ramblas street was so accessible to all of the activities we did there. The boqueria, the Flamenco Show, the buses or ten block walk to the incredible museums in the area were right at our fingertips. One particular day on Las Ramblas, we saw more than we would have ever wanted to see. I was walking ahead with my sons and my husband was a few feet behind us. We were in throngs of mass humanity on this street as it's the most populated street in all of Spain. As we walked past the masses, something came across my vision that just registered as WRONG. I perceived it faster than I comprehended it and then when I realized it was a totally naked man I turned my boys in a semi-circular huddle to distract them from this inappropriateness. We were not on a nude beach; we were on a street in the city-center. People are not supposed to be nude on the street. The signs say no public urination but they don't say anything about public nudity! As soon as I turned the boys around, our youngest popped out of the huddle and said, "There's a naked man! What the heck?" We started laughing uncontrollably with tears rolling down our cheeks. We were nervously amused and shocked as we watched other people's reactions, too. My son continued with his comments, "He has enough money to have a cell phone but he doesn't have clothes?!?" I couldn't believe he captured this detail but it was true---the man was walking down the street naked but holding a cell phone and wearing flip flops to protect his feet from the heat.

Suddenly, I saw my husband chasing the man down the street, it appeared. I thought, "Oh, how chivalrous,...Patrick is going to go tell that man he is being inappropriate." But I was mistaken, he was running to catch up with him to take his picture! This was a strange sight as the man was older, portly and very hairy all over his body. We had a good laugh over that strange scene for quite some time.

What is it about Barcelona and these lively men? Walking into our apartment for the first time, we struggled with the key and the lock. An intoxicated older man stumbled over to me and kept pawing at me which startled my husband and sons. Patrick, in his attempt to speak Espanol, started yelling at the man "Vamoose, you %*%**!" (wanting to say "Vamos") The man kept inching towards us. Patrick yelled it again and the boys started yelling back to their dad, "Dad, Dad! You're telling him, "*Come* with me, you $$**$**," you're not telling him to *go away*! The poor man looked confused and flustered and we eventually got safely inside our apartment building. The boys squealed with delight at their dad's mistake and his temper. We giggled at the thought of their Spanish language expertise in this moment. The mishaps in travel can be as entertaining as they are frustrating and the look on the man's face was one of the most hilarious memories we have of Spain. Those "lost in translation" moments are part of the adventure.

The Splendor of Seville

AFTER TIME ALL over the south of Spain with its sophistication and swagger, Seville was an important spot on our route. It gave us the feeling for antiquity and history that we crave. Seville is the fourth largest city in Spain and considered to be the cultural center of the area. The Plaza de Espana resides there with its unique semi-circular shape and ceramic-tiled structures. The Seville Cathedral and La Giralda with the orange tree courtyard are all part of Seville's splendid charm. The Santa Cruz quarter is a labyrinth of small alleyways and Moorish style courtyards and white houses known for their florals and orange trees. The history of this province dates back more than 2,000 years consisting of the influence of Romans, Vandals, Visigoths and Moors I could really appreciate the antiquity of this city and it had an compelling Spanish authenticity to it.

The most memorable experience for us there was our time spent in the Seville Cathedral. Items in the Sevilla Cathedral were so inspiring and gave me such an understanding of Catholicism at its grandeur. While Greek Orthodoxy (and Eastern Orthodoxy) has its magnificence, it tends to be spread out among its places of worship. I had never seen so much grandeur in one building alone, however, like I experienced at the Seville Cathedral. There was an altar of pure gold brought in from the Incas. It is said to be the most valuable altar in the world. Sevilla Cathedral is the largest Gothic cathedral and the third largest cathedral in the world. Christopher Columbus's tomb is in this cathedral. Although, it is also said that his tomb is elsewhere.

We saw the port in Seville where his fleet embarked from for the famous voyage to the New Word. It's the farthest inland port which means it's not on the ocean, but a river. Our bus tour guide was fine but it was our time spent alone at our Seville Dona Maria Hotel and rooftop pool that was very special for us. Usually, we do not spend a lot of time at our hotels on trips. This particular historic hotel was irresistible because of its thoroughly Spanish furnishings and ambience. It was directly across from the Cathedral right on the impeccable cobblestoned plaza. Horse drawn carriages and lanterns and lamplights aglow on the plaza with this illuminated Cathedral behind it all was magnetic. We strolled nearby for tapas and incredible shopping in what felt like the essence of Spain for me.

While Spain was full of wonderful moments of tapas, rooftop pools at our hotel, incredible cathedrals, posh stores, flamenco shows and exciting beaches, there were moments of frustration of course. Ordering a simple Cafe Americano at the coffee shops was…well, not so simple! I used my limited Espanol to make this happen. Every morning I'd order a Cafe Americano. I'd ask for leche (milk) and the barista would tell me that it didn't come with cream or that they didn't have cream. I could tell he or she was messing with me, almost enjoying my frustration or thinking I was helpless.

But little did they know, that nothing would deter me from lunging over the counter and grabbing a milk carton and saying, "CON LECHE!". Other times, I'd order my coffee and anxious to stay on schedule to tour the sights with our guides while my family waited on me. I'd order my coffee and THEN the barista would tell me that the coffee was not actually ready in the vat and that it would take four minutes to brew. The first time this happened, I let it go. The next few times, I knew better to ask ahead of time, "Is your coffee ready?" (Listo cafe?) The time I waited for the coffee to brew became problematic for us because we were so late getting to the airport because we couldn't maneuver our rental van through the tiny corridors between the buildings. Our van was practically physically stuck between buildings. The boys were fascinated by this and my husband was very nervous trying to navigate this. We were late to the airport because of the coffee and the tiny alleyways trapping our rental van and unfortunately, we had to take a later flight (eight hours later) between cities. Our boys played cards or napped in the airport and we went with the flow. I never took American coffee for granted again.

It was August and the Spaniards were getting tired of all their tourists, I could tell. June and July are months they embrace the tourism (like many other southern European countries, too) but by August, they feel tired and overwhelmed with accommodating tourists. One example of this that I observed was a day on the beach in Barcelona when I walked to the storefront to find a restroom. There was no signage, so I walked up to a waiter and asked him "Donde es el baño?"(Where is the bathroom?) He waved me off and said, "No tenemos baño". (we don't have a bathroom) and he did not indicate or offer that beach-goers could use the restaurant bathroom inside (which I already assumed.) I walked several feet around this strip mall/storefront and eventually found a public bathroom. I was so irritated that the snarky (but handsome) waiter blew me off and told me he didn't know where the bathroom was so I marched up to him after my restroom break and told him emphatically, "El baño esta AQUI!" (the bathroom is over there!) and pointed to it dramatically. He smirked at me and answered, "No sabe." (I didn't know.) Baloney ---he knew. I assumed this was just an example of how the locals eventually get tired of the tourists' requests.

I wasn't going to let it taint my memories of Spain overall. I am sure Greece and other countries (especially France, reportedly) have a reputation for moments like this and it's just part of the travel experience.

In the nine days we were in Spain and the nine cities we saw, The Alhambra was the most powerful historic place we saw and the flamenco show was the most powerfully, vivid artistic event we saw.

Barcelona is also the city where I had an epiphany about how we are stewards of the earth and society. I thought of how Gaudi created the Sagrada Familia which is the Gothic cathedral he designed that has been worked on continuously for a century. While we stared at this massive sanctuary, I asked myself, "what is *my* gift to the world of art, civilization, society?" Gaudi's gift to the world is his art and this Sagrada Familia cathedral which means "sacred family." I whispered the words again, "sagrada familia.....sacred family" and I was instantly illumined with the realization that my "sacred family" is my community that I contribute to or hope to build with my service and passion. I am passionate about mentoring the youth in my church and had presently been a youth director in my church community. Volunteering and guiding them was a work in progress at all times and while it was not a cathedral or work of art, it was my *"sacred family"*. Just as Gaudi inevitably languished and toiled over challenges with his artistic structures, we, too, experience challenges with our passions and activist endeavors. How we feel about something and what we give to it does not have to be measured by bricks, mortar, steeples, stained-glass windows or a century worth of work and scaffolds. It can be just as significant to your community to be a good steward and consistently work towards a goal. In fact, in some ways, my sagrada familia would continue through the generations as more and more of our families and loved ones bring their progeny to our church and teach them traditions and service. Artists and architects influence the world for the ages but us everyday people can influence, guide, help or serve our smaller microcosm for the ages, too. Perhaps that it was I was called to do---just be a good steward and hone my craft which is to guide and volunteer. We are not all called to use the same talents. Furthermore, not everyone is called to be passionate about their purpose either. When we do know our passion, it is a responsibility to examine it and put it in action.

In that moment, in Barcelona, I was fulfilled to discover that I was fulfilling my passion and I was serving my society---in my treasure, time and talents with my sagrada familia which was my church's ministries, youth group and families. Thank you, Gaudi, for helping me realize that by appreciating your art and not envying it; by being inspired by it and not overwhelmed or frustrated by it.

Planning the next Odyssey

THE NEXT YEAR, my husband and I were at a fundraiser gala for the Alzheimer's Association where they were auctioning off a trip for two to Switzerland for a week of sightseeing by a tour guide. The tour guide happened to be a friend of ours who donated this trip package. The winner of the auction item could choose whether to go in the winter for skiing the Alps or the summer. No one was really bidding due to the fear of international travel at this time in 2011. We won the item and upgraded it to take along our three sons, knowing we'd add Greece for sure to the itinerary and then come up with the rest of the route with the boys on my docent-designed research units. That night, when we told the boys we won another auction trip, our oldest son was emotional and overjoyed. They are so worth it! We didn't even know at the time how many countries we'd actually see on this trip---until we got there. But, we knew Italy and Greece would be a major part of the trip so my travel agent and I started building the itinerary.

While the previous year I was inspired to tack on an African country, this year I was inspired to take a cooking class in Italy and stay at an organic farm. I had friends who had taken a cooking class in France many years before this and that always interested me since my husband and I love to cook.

I started vigorously searching the internet for organic farm experiences like the one we enjoyed so much in Crete, Greece. There were days I felt like I could go cross-eyed from spending so much time looking at my computer. I'd print off reams of paper to incorporate into my paperwork from the travel agent. There were certain legs of the trip that she'd leave up to me. This seemed like the perfect arrangement of travel planning because travel agents endorse the companies and excursions that have affiliations with and I could augment the trip with places off the beaten path. It was a perfect marriage!

During this time, I had read *North of Ithaka* by Eleni N. Gage and had become engrossed in the information about an area of Greece called Epirus. Eleni Gage is the daughter of the famed writer, Nicholas Gage who wrote the novel which inspired the movie *ELENI*. While *ELENI* describes the life story of Nicholas Gage's mother and her murder, *North of Ithaka* describes his daughter Eleni's (named after his mother) experience with overseeing the rebuilding of her ancestors' home. The project was about restoration and closure of their ancestry, so to speak.

When the book *ELENI* came out in the early 1980's, my sister received a hardback, autographed copy of the book from an in law. Mom's cancer was in remission at the time and I remember this as a somewhat happy, peaceful season, with decreased anxiety in the home. I remember lounging with mom on my parents' king sized bed late at night and reading books together while she waited for my dad to come home from the late shift. My mother, brother, sister and I were voracious readers and we inherited this skill from our mother. She was such an intelligent person who had skipped a grade in school and she had a lifelong love of learning, reading and traveling.

My father used to humorously remark at the way we'd all be reading enormous novels in the airports and airplanes on our trips. This kept us occupied on long layovers as non-revenue, stand by, American Airlines employee passengers. My dad asked my brother one time, "How many pages are in that book?"

George replied, "a thousand." My dad remarked, "My goodness, I don't think I've read a thousand pages in my whole life!" I was a preteen at the time when I heard this exchange and realized that my blue-collar father had such a different childhood than us. He was trying to survive war-torn Greece and eventually support his family when his father died. There was no university for my dad. His opportunity came in the form of the Merchant Marines. The education he received, though, could fill numerous thousand page books! What we might be reading in novels, Daddy had lived.

So, as I laid there with Mom reading books, I'd peek over at her copy of *ELENI*. I was literally reading over her shoulder but she didn't seem to mind. Maybe this was our way of being close—a literary cuddle. Inside the next bedroom was my sister who loved to stay in bed, reading and sleeping so much that I jokingly called her a narcoleptic. Somehow, she caught wind of the content of *ELENI*, too and before we knew it, we were all sharing the same copy of the book. Probably, when Mom was cleaning the house, we must've grabbed her copy at different times of the day and started catching up before Mom's reading time. It became such a joke between us that we made a game out of it. My sister cracked up when she opened her closet door and found me crouched inside with the light on, stealing my reading time of *ELENI*. It is such a sweet memory to me, now. Mom died a year later. Nowadays, the solution would be for us to each have a copy but the paperback edition had probably not come out yet.

The book *ELENI* describes features of Greece that makes one long to go back there. We had just been to Greece in 1982 for a month as a family. Reading the book, however, had us returning there, mentally. Nicholas Gage wrote about a time decades before this when his family was enduring struggles and tragedy but it was the nuances he included that touched my mother. She read excerpts to us, saying "…...he described the taste of the mulberries being picked off the vine…..and the essence of the village……only someone who has *been there* can understand this." I derived such pleasure knowing my mom was intellectually satisfied from the power of Nicholas Gage's words. I didn't always get along with my mother but we were close. I once heard a friend say this extrapolation about someone and it made sense to me. You can be close to someone without getting along all the time. It was the way my mother said things--- with the lilt in her voice and the sureness of knowing who she was and what she stood for that I respected. She was tough as nails and soft at the same time. Mom made an impact on everyone she encountered and her legacy endures.

So my journey down the path of *ELENI* and *North of Ithaka*, decades apart, drove me to taking my sons to this area of Greece by way of the nearby island of Lefkada. The route makes sense to me in my mind! Epirus is close to the Ionian side of Greece and I started to connect the dots that we could go to the island of Lefkada but be near Epirus if we decide to do activities on the mainland. Then, I remembered we have Greek-American friends who vacation there every summer. I contacted my friend to see if they would be in Lefkada the same time we were there and after some back and forth emails, we scheduled a day to meet up there.

Another book that inspired my idea for the cooking class location was the satisfying read of *Living in a Foreign Language* by Michael Tucker. The author, (an actor from the television show L.A. Law) and his actress wife Jill Eikenberry chronicle their delightful journey into making a home in Italy and absorbing and adopting the lifestyle and culture of la dolce vita. So, two books led me to my itinerary of 2011: *North of Ithaka* and *Living in a Foreign Language.* I was kind of proud about this development. It felt like a "bucket list" activity for me or a "reading list" adventure of following up good books with a "field trip."

Going to the island of Lefkada was also fulfilling another bucket list goal for me because I knew the nearby islet of Skorpios was accessible via ferry boat tours. Skorpios had been the private island of Aristotle Onassis. I have always been fascinated with Onassis and especially his second wife, Jacqueline Kennedy Onassis. I believe I've read every biography out there about Jackie. I'm also fascinated with his long time love, Maria Callas. Maria Callas and Ari Onassis were the two most famous Greeks in the world at one time and their passionate love affair is legendary. Skorpios was his private island and also the interior design project of Jackie Onassis when she became his wife. On the internet, I found information about possible excursions to Skorpios and I was becoming ecstatic about this possibility. Skorpios was up for sale at this time as

Onassis's only grandchild and heir did not want it. It was rumored that Bill Gates and Madonna were interested in purchasing it.

So although Switzerland, Italy and Greece were the core countries of this trip itinerary of 2011, we ended up having adventures in England, Austria, Lichtenstein, France and Germany, too because of connections, layovers and bordering countries. With the backpack mentality of my husband and his desire to often be in a different country per day, we embraced his spirit and indulged his desires to use our rental car as our magic carpet. Aladdin, Jasmine, Abu, the Genie and the Sultan were off for more magic carpet rides.

Getting here, we experienced some crazy luck on this trip as we departed on our flight from New York to Zurich. On the runway, our pilot informed us about a wing malfunction which caused smoke to come out. They needed to fix the situation so they asked us to disembark the plane for a few hours while they made arrangements. Inside the airport terminal, we were lined up to receive airport vouchers to restaurants while we waited for the situation to be resolved. Each passenger was granted vouchers up to a certain amount. My husband told us to go through the line again and request more because at this point, no one was really paying attention to "repeat customers". We racked up several hundreds of dollars of vouchers and darted off to the best steakhouse in the airport. In our excitement, we ordered nachos, burgers, steaks, calamari rings, etc. and feasted on this free food extravaganza. We recognized a fellow passenger at the adjacent table. We laughed with him about our good fortune and perks. We lingered for some time enjoying the plentiful dinner, not even worried about getting to our new gate for the re-routed flight. I'm usually always on top of this but this particular evening we felt like we were alright within our time frame. All of a sudden, our fellow passenger from the restaurant, came up to us and said, "You need to hurry! Our flight is boarding at the gate!" We thanked him profusely and scrambled to get up to the gate in time to board our flight to Zurich. Breathless and panting, we boarded the flight and felt very lucky in many ways. Our bellies were pleasantly full and we were relieved to be on a plane that did not have a malfunction. The valuable vouchers were a bonus!

Ironically, on the way back from this trip in 2011, when we departed from London to America, we experienced more airport perks. At the ticket counter, we checked in and the clerk had a serious expression on his face. He said, "This flight is full and I'm going to be honest with you---it doesn't look like you're going to get on it. We can offer you a deal to take a later flight and we'll credit you money or issue you new flights that leave much later." This concerned us because we had hotel reservations for our layover in Boston and we didn't want to prolong all of our traveling after twenty three days in Europe. We calmly asked the clerk, "how long of a delay until the next flight and what's the credit amount?" He said, "You'd be waiting until the 7:00 p.m. flight in two hours and we can either give you $1500 of airport voucher credits or credit it back to your credit card." I looked at him calmly and slyly and said, "O-kay, I guess we'll wait for the 7:00 p.m flight". (a mere two hour wait!) I told my husband that I'd love to buy him an Hermes tie from the airport shop with some of that voucher credit but he smartly decided we should credit it back to our Visa card. After all, it was the cost of one flight over here! Reimbursed! Another lucky airport arrangement perk!

The Alps, Alpine Slide and the "Willy Wonka" wonder of Switzerland

SWITZERLAND WAS THE first country on the 2011 itinerary of our European odyssey. Zurich and Chur were our primary destinations. In the Alps, there's a city called Churwalden. We found an Alpine slide....the longest one in the world, reportedly. This was another one of those terrifying activities my family talked me into. I have to admit, it was thrilling and another activity I only participated in because my sons were experiencing it. Like zip lining with the boys in Canada, I had to overcome my fear of heights to ride the chair lift up in the summer---when there would be no thick snow to fall onto if the cable broke. At the top of the lift, my husband and the alpine slide operator instructed me how to maneuver the brakes and car down this rail. All for one and one for all, like everything else we did on our adventurous trips, I joined in on the fun! I was tentative but determined.

On the chair lift ride up to the departure point for the alpine ride, I shared a lift with my ten year old and my husband. I marveled at the way my youngest son trusted and welcomed each new adventure. Of course, he was the youngest child so he had the examples and leadership of his older brothers to pave the way for him but I still found it admirable that he was a confident risk-taker. This was another opportunity for me to either join them or get left behind. If my ten year old son could do it, I should at least try! Since he was the youngest, he wasn't always old enough to participate in some of the activities we had done over the years; swimming with the dolphins, doing a zipline alone or driving this alpine car alone.

He had to tandem zipline and he had to ride in the alpine car with my husband. He couldn't scuba dive, yet, because he wasn't old enough to be certified so he hung out with me on those days when the others were off on their excursions. He couldn't ascend the volcano in Santorini because he was only six years old at the time and we thought it was smarter for him to go part of the way and then wait for his oldest brother and dad to come down. But he had steered a sailboat and a motor boat in Greece on two occasions!

Here I was, an adult with no age or weight restrictions---so I felt like I had to say "yes" and participate in this activity. I was hesitant, especially as the instructor told me the directions for the brakes and controls. But, I wasn't going to miss out on riding on the longest alpine ride in the world so I went for it! It was exciting and worthwhile but once was enough for me. Thanks to my boys, I tried another thrilling travel adventure and stretched my wings!

Just hiking through the Alps is worth the trip to Switzerland. The scenery and the feather light air carries your spirit into the heavens. We would stop just to gasp at the view. The other treasures of Switzerland are the swiss chocolates, Zurich, Lake Lucerne and being in a "neutral" country that borders five other countries: Italy, Germany, France, Austria, Lichtenstein. There is no "national" language there as you hear many different ones. (Same thing with the cuisine.) We drove into the bordering countries through the "roundabouts". Merely driving a few blocks into a new country, the flavor and architecture instantly changed! France had its own flavor, Germany, Italy, Austria, etc....My husband described it like the Willy Wonka movie---each "room" being a different motif.

Of course, Zurich, Geneva, Basel, Bern and other cities are highlights too, and we enjoyed three other cities but my sons would say Chur and Churwalden were their favorites; hiking and sliding in the Alps and strolling through an Alpine village on their own--I can see why!

Our time spent in Zurich was extraordinary because our tour guide was our hometown friend who lives there now and donated the auction item package of a one week stay in her Churwalden condo in the alps and the tour of Zurich. She showed us all of the sights for the entire day on foot and on bus. We ate authentic Swiss meals with her on the lake, shopped at a farmer's market, saw landmarks, had a happy hour in a vegan bar and a formal meal at night in The Armory. We shopped, laughed, talked, learned and delighted in the appeal of Zurich. We learned a custom by watching a bachelorette party in action and how it's done differently there and we visited her chic apartment. Our tour guide friend explained to us how bachelorette parties are done. When a woman gets married in Switzerland, she has a "hen party" which is a type of bachelorette party where the females and males often sell things on the streets like alcohol shots, kisses or women's undergarments to raise money to pay for the drinks of the guests of their party. The bachelor or bachelorette are always responsible to pay for the evening's festivities.

On the bus tour, our boys saw another unusual European street scene---a woman in a Gothic cape walking her half-naked boyfriend on a leash. He was only wearing leather short shorts and boots with a collar around his neck while being led on a leash. It's all part of the escapades of traveling. If we hadn't had the boys with us, this scene would probably not be as humorous to us. Watching the boys' reaction to this reminded us what a trip odyssey we were on, being in another part of the world where social differences in lifestyle stand out to us. The global awareness you gain includes the differences in social mores and this was certainly one of them. What wouldn't be common back home in our conservative part of the United States is accepted in other parts of the world. Our sons learned this from a young age as I did, too, by experiencing world travel.

A Trance in France

France...oui oui! We drove into France from Basel, Switzerland. One of the highlights of visiting Switzerland was the ease of traveling into all of the bordering countries. The fun memory of France was that my son, a high school freshman at the time, was going to impress us by ordering our meal in French (mistakes and all). The waitress just looked at us with impatience and we giggled throughout the meal, anyway! The French earn their reputation for coming across as aloof but the snug and toasty intimacy of this French cafe made up for it. We studied the terms of the menu on the blackboard above us as we tried to translate it. We observed the tables of duos and groups around us. The dark wood of this tavern cafe with the drizzling raindrops down the window subsumed us into our afternoon trance. The food was fine but the ambience was exceptional.

Driving into France from our tour of bordering countries to Switzerland, gave us that thrill of entering new architecture, new language and new cuisine all within a few miles of other countries! ---the beauty and magic of the European continent is that it's so diverse! These French food terms (oooh la laa!) : *Pomme frites, quiche, charcuterie, baguettes, crepes, eclairs, mousse au chocholat, tourte, tarte, escargot and croissant* came to life during our jaunt into France. A dreary, drizzly day could not dampen our mood to see all things Francais!

I have a goal to celebrate my fiftieth birthday in Paris. I want to connect to my roots by visiting where some of my Greek relatives lived and worked. My Francophile mother named me Eugenie Marie after all, and she insisted on keeping me in "very French" pixie haircuts when I was a child. I may have protested then but now I understand her affinity for all things French. I remember us shopping in a children's specialty dress shop in Tulsa when I was a child. She searched through the clearance racks to find me dresses we could afford. One particular long sleeved white dress with pleats, gold buttons and navy blue piping caught her eye. After I put on the dress and looked at it in the mirror, Mom exclaimed, "EUGENIE MARIE! You look SO French!" I realize now how much fun this was for my mother---dressing her youngest daughter up like a doll. My older sister was more tomboyish for several years so Mom enjoyed this bond with me. I could sense, even as a ten year old, that this moment made my mom happy. I didn't fully understand it until I grew up. I think the moment shaped my later avid interest in clothes, style and just glamour in general. Not having daughters in my all-sons family, I appreciate now that I had this mother-daughter bonding activity at least in my childhood.

Going to Paris someday will allow me to look up the street where my great uncles and great aunts lived. As a girl, I used to address the airmail envelopes that my grandfather sent to his brothers. Papou liked my cursive handwriting and each month he diligently mailed his brothers a letter. I remember writing out "Rue de Frederique" and thinking it was interesting how the French say "street." What a fortuitous lesson this ended up being for an elementary school child to have a hands on way to be involved in the correspondence between her American citizen and French citizen relatives.

Flash forward several decades to when I created Gypsy Family Travel, I have been thinking of ways to include pen pal information on my website so my blog readers could possibly communicate with people in different countries. Chamber of Commerce and Department of Tourism addresses were resources that my third grade students used when we researched various destinations. Once I do include it in my blog site, it will feel like another full circle moment for me from my childhood activity of addressing Papou's airmail envelopes to France!

A Vineyard in Germany

IN AND OUT of the bordering countries of Switzerland, we drove into charming Germany. While Munich and Frankfurt are the big cities I've been to in Germany as a teenager, we found a little town in Germany during our "Willy Wonka" style drive through the bordering countries of Switzerland. My husband compared these bordering countries architectural differences as being in the Willy Wonka movie and going into wildly different themed rooms of confections.

In this German town, I remember being impressed by the greenery and the architecture of course. The city life at night made me interested in going back for a longer trip someday and making my way through all the *burgs and schlosses*.

We went to a bakery for some pastries and we drove past a vineyard which we were not expecting in Germany of all places! I went into the bakery with a son or two and began trying to communicate with the employee. I do not speak any German at all, so there was a lot of hand gestures going on to describe the shape and identity of the pastry I was salivating for in the glass case.

Decades before, in 1986, I had strolled through the streets of Munich with my father and new stepmother on a layover back to America from Greece and here I was twenty five years later, strolling through the streets with my sons, looking for pastries.

As we drove out of the tiny town we were in with our pastries, we happened upon a lush green vineyard! We tend to think of Spain, Italy and Greece as countries with vineyards but of course, there are vineyards all over the world. We shot some photos of this unexpected surprise vista and traveled on down the road with our newfound geographical knowledge.

Castles and cathedrals seem to be the pride of Germany sightseeing. I'm interested in returning to Germany and seeing the following: Neuschwanstein Bavaria---the inspiration for Disney's Sleeping Beauty castle and Cathedral of Cologne- one of the tallest cathedrals in the world. Loving Gothic architecture as I do, the Cathedral intrigues me. Other landmarks I hope to visit in Germany are the Black Forest, the Christmas Market in Nuremberg and the Heidelberg Castle.

"Al-lo in Austria and Lichtenstein

WE DROVE INTO Austria and Lichtenstein in our rental car while staying in Switzerland. Strolling around a town in Austria (Schlossberg, I think), shopping and eating was relaxing after spending energetic days on the Alps, hiking and doing the alpine ride. We had quite a bit of schnitzel in Switzerland and the boys were ready for some other cuisine. I think we even had sushi in one of those countries which seemed funny to us, too. Schnitzel is a boneless meat that is tenderized, breaded and fried. The pastries and bakeries were a welcome sight when we craved a snack and energy boost from all the adventure and hiking! Walking through the Austrian city we were in provided us with one of our most hilarious memories of Europe.

Our youngest son, ten years old at the time, mistakenly walked into a dressing room of a shop and was greeted by a very loud "A-llo!" from a portly old woman who was dressing. He ran out of there embarrassed and entertained at such a scene. His imitation, even still today, of this lady saying "Allo!" characterized our memories of Austria.

The distinctive memory and visual of Austria and Lichtenstein is, of course, the Alps. The view of the Alps is really that grand and the air is so clean and crisp, you get mesmerized taking it all in. I didn't realize, until this trip, that *the Alps are the highest mountain range covering the large area all entirely within Europe.* The Alps border the following eight countries: Lichtenstein, Austria, Slovenia, France, Germany, Italy, Monaco and Switzerland. The geographic importance of the mountain range is because it represents so much of Europe's surface, thus greatly influencing the climate. Historically, the Alps are significant because they were a barrier for human migration and trade. I learned that the Alps exist because the continents of Africa and Europe are colliding after hundreds of millions of years of pressure pushing the terrain above sea level.

Another interesting fact about the Alps is that many people died of cold and starvation during the crusades while they were trying to reach the Mediterranean by crossing over the Alps. Another historic fact about this mountain range revealed that Hannibal, one of the greatest military commanders in history, reportedly crossed the Alps with a herd of elephants and lost them. Man vs nature does not always work. The word "alpine" is now used to describe a climate at which trees do not grow because of their altitude.

Driving from Austria to Lichtenstein, my husband pulled the car over and stopped to park. He told us to get out of the car and stand on the mountainside to enjoy the vistas of Lichtenstein. A tiny country, Lichtenstein embodies the Alpine beauty and all of its splendor. It was a brief moment of adding another country to our collection and will always remind me of how much I admire my husband's sense of adventure as the rental car navigator of our family!

Magnificent Milano

Milan was an anticipated destination for me! The fashion, frenzy, food, and glamour......the very feminine trip highlight for me in my all-boy family. Right after Zurich, we railed down to Milan for a day of shopping. This was not without complication, however. In leaving Zurich to find the rail station, we got so lost and confused on the roundabouts and could not always understand every international driving sign. I knew we were becoming dangerously late in making our connection. I held back the tears and sobs that I could feel bubbling up in my throat. My husband was apprehensive for me as well because he knew how much I was looking forward to my first true "chick day" on this trip. Everything else up until Milan was male-driven activity. I carved out a few female-friendly days for myself on this trip----the shopping in Milan and the cooking class in Orvieto, Italy. By the time we reached the rail station, it was a mad dash of scrambling around to get to our station. With Olympian skills, we maneuvered and stood there gasping and sighing with relief that we made it.

The woes of traveling can be many. It's not for the faint-hearted.

Once off the Eurail in Milan, we took a taxi to the hotel and The Milan Sheraton Diana could not have been more glamorous! We had two hotel rooms because there were five of us. We pampered ourselves right away in all the fun luxury items; bathrobes and rose petals on the bed! The hotel breakfast dining hall was even glamorous! I still have the vision of sipping cappuccinos in large white mugs under dazzling chandeliers on white leather banquettes. After all the drama of getting to Milan, the peacefulness of lounging and drinking Italian coffee amidst this white and black decorated backdrop was picture perfect for me in my red dress, black sweater, and ornate gold jewelry. I was ready to take on Milano (and the rest of Italy) in a stylish way. Every day was a chic day of aviator sunglasses, manicured fingernails, chic black, white and red outfits and a budget I had saved for a year. This was going to be my special shopping spree trip and I promised myself I would buy classic European staple items. I'm happy to say that I accomplished that. When I went shopping, I packed a favorite pair of stylish high heeled shoes in my tote because I knew I wanted at least one photo dressed up in Milano from head to toe (and not with my walking shoes on!). My husband took the photo and I put the heels back in the tote. It was just for cheeky fun and I put the photo in my closet back home as a reminder of the day in the style capital of Europa!

Milan has been a fashion center since the Middle Ages and Renaissance time. The industry of luxury goods and fashion was so significant in the 16th century, that the term "milaner" or "millaner" (associated with Milan) was designated to the fineries of clothing, jewelry, hats and other luxurious items. Later, in the 19th century, the term "millenery" came to mean "one who made or sold hats." The Milanese fashion consciousness really emerged in the 1880's and late 19th century and then in the 1970's, Milan became the main capital for ready to wear, "pret-a-porte" female and male fashion.

The boys all went to the Duomo which they found impressive because of the fascinating architecture and also because it housed "preserved hierarchs" as my son said. While they did that, I spent time alone walking through the many streets of stores. The Piazza del Duomo and the Quadrilatero della Moda, with the Via Montenapoleone street was where I focused my shopping. I wanted time alone there and then later time with my family so we could experience it together. I jokingly call the high-end boutiques "clothing museums". It wasn't a joke, though, entirely, because Via Montenapoleone is one of the most expensive shopping streets in the world. The boys became part of the action, too, for a while because they had heard so much about Milan from me ahead of time so, naturally, they were curious....even if they didn't buy anything! After dinner, we shopped some more to make sure we didn't miss anything! I don't have any daughters to share this experience with but I do love my sons for trying to join in my fun and excitement! They are troopers and my husband is amazing for teaching them patience while a woman shops. This is a life skill if you ask me!

Mambo Italiano

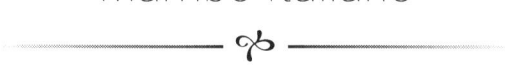

A ZIGZAG TOUR of Italy is the convenient way to traverse the country. Starting in Milan and working our way back and forth through (Umbria and Tuscany) Venice, Orvieto, Todi, Spoletto, Sienna, San Gimignano, Florence, Rome, Bari (on this trip with our sons)....was our route this trip. On other trips, I've done other cities that I recommend, like Sorrento. The fortress style of Orvieto, Todi, Spoletto, San Gimignano was picturesque but the grandness of Rome and Florence with all of the historical sites was significant. All over Italy, the customer service was impeccable and it was apparent to me why it ranks as the most visited country destination. I was impressed by the professionalism of the employees everywhere who greeted me with "Bongiourno!, Prego, Signora!" etc. whenever they dealt with your accommodations in their three piece suits no matter that it was a summer day.

    Tour guides at the major cities and time built in to shop and sightsee was a perfect combination. As we walked around the important sightseeing spots, it fascinated me how my sons knew other details that I hadn't taught them in our research units. For example, my youngest son knew many details from watching the movie Roman Holiday which I had recorded for us to watch but didn't expect him to stay up and finish. The rest of the details they knew from their video game! --They knew specific details about the Medici family (when we arrived in Florence and toured there.) When we went to the Pantheon, they read an inscription and said, "Marcus Agrippa for the third time." and they knew another inscription/emblem, SPQR, that was an acronym for "Senate and people of Rome".

They saw this emblem everywhere. My husband and I found this funny---that video games can be educational too I guess. When I went to Rome as a ten year old, I knew a lot of details from watching Masterpiece Theater's I Claudius series with my big brother. Times have changed I guess.

The Colosseum, the Roman Forum, temples, basilicas, stadiums, Circus Maximus, The Pantheon... so much to see and research ahead of time---or to leave up to the tour guide. But I recommend preparing ahead of time--as an educator but mostly as a mother because it *holds the kids' attention better if they are engaged and looking for the right answer or something familiar in the information.* If they are just listening to a tour guide ramble on about unfamiliar details, children can tune them out.

There was a moment in the Pantheon when I stood there watching my sons study the details and recalling my own first time in the Pantheon, thirty two years before, watching my mom standing there in her trench coat saying, *"Absorb this. Are you ABSORBING this??"* It was a defining moment for me as a child to see the intensity with which my mother was imparting her values and wanderlust to us but also her influential motherly ways of pushing us to understand the significance of this opportunity. I think really for me, my inspiration for Gypsy Family Travel began with the moment of watching my mother proclaim, *"Absorb! Absorb this!"*

Divinely, later I went through thousands of photos from that trip and found the most spiritual and poignant photos of the sun pouring into the Pantheon and St. Peter's Basilica, illuminating these places of pagan and Christian worship, respectively. I'm choosing to take it a sign that mom was celebrating me *absorbing* with my children.

The Vatican

EVERY CITY IN Italy was a supreme adventure into history, art, fashion, cuisine and splendor. The Vatican, however, holds its own historic value in a category all by itself. The Vatican, located in Rome, is also referred to as The Holy See. Located within this enclave of Rome are the following religious and cultural structures: St. Peter's Basilica, Sistine Chapel, and Vatican Museum. Our sons were fascinated that there are Popes laid to rest in the Vatican. When I went there as a ten-eleven year old, I remember being fascinated by the sculpture of the Pieta. There is so much emotion shown in the body language of the Virgin Mary cradling Jesus in her arms.

A big surprise for us as a family (when I went there as a child in 1979) was that the Pope was visiting the Vatican that day!! We had no idea this was going to happen. It was the newly elected Pope John Paul II. A crowd was gathering and I remember the excitement in my mother's voice when she told us what was about to transpire. My tall twenty year old brother put me on top of his shoulders so that I could see the entrance of the cardinals and Pope. Our 1979 photo is very blurry and our waving hand was in the way! Since I was the highest of all the spectators, the Pope saw me and I waved to him! It is an *unforgettable memory* for me.

Recently, my sister found this newspaper clipping my mother saved for us regarding Pope John Paul II around that time we saw him. He agreed to officiate at the wedding of a janitor's daughter! Read this poignant article to learn about his kindness and generosity. The clipping was so yellowed and aged, I will cite it here.

Pope to Officiate At Wedding in Rare Ceremony (1979)

"Vatican City- Just because she asked him, Pope John Paul II will officiate Sunday at the wedding of Vittoria Janni, a 22-year old garbage collector's daughter. The tradition-breaking pope will be bestowing a privilege rarely accorded even to royal couples when he performs the wedding rite for Miss Janni and Mario Maltese, 24, an employee of a burglar alarm company in the Vatican's richly frescoed Pauline Chapel. The Polish-born pope was visiting a Nativity scene set up in a sanitation center near the Vatican Jan. 6 when Miss Janni walked up to him and said: "Your Holiness, I would like to tell you a thing. I would like you to marry me." His Holiness nodded again and walked a few steps away. Then he turned and asked, "But how old are you?" I must have seemed very young to him, perhaps my dress made me look like a little girl."

Seeing a pontiff, who is now a saint (Pope John Paul II) and a monarch (Queen Elizabeth) were memorable high points of visiting Europe.

Vividly Venice

OUR ITALY ITINERARY was full of tourism details determined to define the most complete of all Italian adventures. Naturally, Venice had to be included in order to achieve a complete and successful Italian extravaganza. Venice was visually stunning! The water taxi to the hotel was already an adventure in itself. It was hard to imagine how much more exciting the gondola would be! The pastels of the buildings were like something out of a fairy tale. The architecture was breathtaking, romantic and majestic. The gelato, meals and gondola ride were the icing on the tiramisu. St. Mark's square and the Doges Palace were historically edifying and our tour guide was wonderful.

We stayed at the Venice Kette Hotel and met our private guide in St. Mark's square to learn the history of the famous landmarks: the Basilica and its Byzantine heritage, the Doge's Palace and its adjoining prisons, to learn how the city built on swamps became such a city of enlightenment, to discover the labyrinthine passageways, alleys and canals of Venice, to learn about famous Venetians; Casanova and Marco Polo and to take a gondola ride.

The gondola is such an interesting vessel and the progression of them involved many unique facts and details. The "felze" or small cabin used to have louvered shutters to protect the passengers from the elements of weather but also to provide privacy from spectators. The shutters were the original "Venetian blinds" that became popular window coverings in later years. Eventually, the shutters were discouraged and the gondolas became more open and exposed. While in previous centuries, gondolas could be various colors, eventually a law in Venice required that the gondolas should be painted black. Every detail on the gondola itself has symbolisms from its dol fin prow head needed to balance the weight of the gondolier at the stern and its S shape symbolizing the twisting Grand Canal.

The vivid colors of Venetian buildings and the famous Murano glass were like jewels along the canal. The displays in the shops stunned and the gelato stands around various corners added to the luxuriated feelings of impulsivity and indulgence in Venice. After all, you pay approximately one hundred dollars for a gondola ride, steered by a man in a striking costume of black, white and red. The romantic ride with its background music and allure in the glossy, black, grand vessel is one of those supremely Italiano moments.

Our dinner exposed my husband to one of his most delicious, foreign meals ----spaghetti in squid ink. For dessert, we had tiramisu and espresso, which is my favorite dessert combination ever. The sumptuous meal took place in a romantically-lit restaurant with chic Italian interiors which seemed so perfectly appropriate in this legendary city. The day was packed with history, luxury, glamorous shopping, romance and delicious food. It is said that Venice will eventually be under water. Time is of the essence in seeing this legendary city.

Organic Farm in Orvieto

OUR TOUR THROUGH Italy zigzagged back and forth through the narrow country to hit the major provinces and regions. Umbria is one of those regions that called to me and tugged at my heart when I looked for a farm villa and cooking class experience. Agriturismo was a major focal point for me in planning our trip to Italy. The organic farm we stayed at in Orvieto offered a cooking class. I signed up for this while our sons enjoyed the pool and grounds. This class was the highlight of our stay at the organic farm scheduled between day trips to the neighboring towns of San Gimignano, Sienna, Florence and other towns.

The quaint and picturesque towns were medieval fortifications filled with incredible architecture and ambience. Every studio, gallery and shop inside the walled cities beckoned to us. My husband enjoyed watching me being drawn to the fashions and accessories. Unbeknownst to me, he had a surprise in store for me later. Back at the organic farm villa, before we took the cooking class, we showered and changed before the class and dinner. Before we headed downstairs to the kitchen, my husband stopped me and said, "Wait. I have something for you." He handed me a tiny velvet bag with a big grin on his handsome face with his romantic brown eyes. I asked, "What is this?!" and he answered, "I got it for you today and thought it would look great on you." He had tucked away into a jewelry store in Orvieto when I wasn't looking while we shopped around. I opened the velvet drawstring bag and found an incredibly unique cocktail ring with an unusual massive brown stone on a gold band. It was stylishly Italian, perfectly romantic and an exceptionally loving memento and symbol of our relationship and chemistry. Patrick and I always aim to spoil each other and he wanted to celebrate the moment with a romantic gesture. Every time I wear the ring, I think of that romantic evening as we walked off to our cooking class, intoxicated with Italian vacation glamour and culture. The evening was about to be topped off with a most educational and informative cooking experience in our rustic and grand farm villa with an underground cave wine cellar.

My husband "audited" the cooking class and took notes so I could be more hands-on with the recipes. We made a variety of Italian dishes and the chefs served us all later in a large dining room where the guests of the organic farm hotel all sat together at a long dining table. We conversed with people from all over the world while enjoying the meal that I helped make! Very satisfying event! The class lasted for a few hours as we made several courses. This was another agritourismo experience that we could add to our "travel resume."

Agritourismo is the new buzz word for agricultural tourism and organic farm villas-- a special concept in traveling. We've done it several times now and it is one of the ways I incorporated my sons' interests into our travel itineraries.

Being an outdoorsy family with an agricultural flair back home, we especially enjoy getting a taste of this on our trips. One of my sons in particular has always loved animals and nature more than most kids. Enjoying nature, animals and plants in foreign environments and climates is educational and adventurous because you get to learn new recipes and engage into the cultural life of that area. I highly recommend it!

Hawaii Hedonism

After several trips to Europe, it was time to slow down. A lucky raffle ticket purchased by my husband turned into a trip for two to Hawaii. When they called my husband's name at another auction, we simply could not believe our luck. We turned the trip for two into a trip for five and took the boys to see America's fiftieth state. Going to Hawaii over Thanksgiving Break in 2012--six days total was fast but doable. I had been before as a kid but I don't know for how long. The eight hour flight, not counting our connection from our hometown to California, was as long as some flights to Europe but it wasn't hard to get on track once we arrived because of the amenities of Hawaii being one of the United States--same language, internet, no international phone plan needed, etc.

    The flight started off in a relaxing way when my husband and I ordered a bottle of wine and snacks. We toasted to our next adventure and we were nestled into our seat belts and blankets. I even took out my contacts and wore my eyeglasses to prepare for some napping and movie watching. This relaxation did not last long when all of a sudden a passenger next to us collapsed in the aisle shortly after take-off. My husband took off his seatbelt, jumped up and administered CPR to the gentleman until the flight attendant could find a medical professional to intervene. The passenger had blood pressure issues and was dehydrated which caused his collapse. Patrick's Boy Scout dad skills came in handy!

    This trip had some rest and relaxation perks that my sons found to be a welcoming atmosphere for brotherly bonding. Because there was less sightseeing to do (except on Pearl Harbor), the boys enjoyed playing pool in the billiards room of the hotel, watching the dolphins, scuba diving, watching the native women weave ti leaves, build sand castles, etc. At our hotel in Maui, our youngest son discovered a most unusual contraption called "the Fishpipe" which was a large rotating barrel ride. An interior ball is suspended by air and gallons of water. The person inside the Fish Pipe gets to "ride" and bounce inside this barrel which imitates the feeling of a waterslide but one that rotates instead. I watched and photographed my son on this ride enjoying it vicariously through him. A boy of his age naturally finds not only the Fish Pipe ride thrilling but also the tiny plane ride over the ocean the day after this stay in Maui. We went to Maui, Lanai and Pearl Harbor. The Four Seasons Lanai had two locations--an ocean side location Manele Bay and a mountain top location, Koele Lodge.

Lanai had a remote feel to it. It was basically a private island until 2012. It was known as the pineapple island because of its plantation. Except for the only real settlement of Lanai City, the rest of the island was just natural tranquility. Arriving on Lanai and driving to the hotel was a surreal experience as the landscape was barren in spots. I felt like we were in a jeep on the moon's surface. The topographical view from the tiny plane we flew in from Maui to Lanai was mind-blowing. Scenes from Jurassic Park were filmed here in Hawaii and I can see why! Thankfully, I looked at these vistas after looking away from the airplane windows in the first twenty minutes of our flight. Being as terribly claustrophobic as I am, the plane ride in the tiny eight seater plane had unnerved me to the point of quiet weeping. It is such an involuntary reaction when claustrophobic crying bubbles up in me and it's very difficult to control. My husband massaged my neck to keep me calm and with his soothing words he encouraged me to look out the window in the last few minutes of the flight. Again, knowing my sons could handle and enjoy this, I was motivated to attempt this. Like the zip lining, alpine sliding and so many other physical adventures we embarked on together, this was one more opportunity to spread my wings. I looked out and marveled at the splendorous view. God's Earth is a miraculous creation and instantly, I was elated to experience it at this height. I survived the fear of the tiny airplane ride and I was almost looking forward to the flight back to see the views again.

All of the tranquility was perfect for Thanksgiving Break....a time where your kids already need a break in the semester. For us, it was a break from college applications for one son, the start of high school for another son and one last frolic in the tropical sunshine and beach before returning home to the hectic Christmas season.

Our oldest two sons went scuba diving with my husband since they are all certified. Mark experienced some anxiety with his equipment but dealt with it and moved forward---like his mama who overcame her claustrophobic tiny airplane ride. We were gaining skills and expanding our horizons---on actual horizons of sea and sky! My youngest son was still young and curious enough to be interested in doing a craft with ti leaves with the Hawaiian native lady in the hotel. It was precious to watch him being surrounded by the bodacious Hawaiian women with their crafts and tools. Our son is wonderfully sensitive and receptive to art and it was heart warming to watch his appreciation of another cultural and foreign art form. He is the one that appreciated the jalis and calligraphy of the Alhambra Palace in Spain and the walking sticks he'd find in Scotland (which he nicknamed "Shalalays"). Now, he was adding Hawaiian ti leaves weaving and leis to his international art appreciation.

Our teenage sons taught our youngest son how to play pool in the hotel arcade every night and they cherished this boy-time together as "rec" rooms were not pervasive on our Europe trips. Big frozen virgin drinks from the arcade bar were other highlights for our sons relaxing after an intense season of high school and a most exciting but exhausting family celebration of Eagle Scout rank for our oldest son.

Hawaii was "just what the doctor ordered" for us. We were in much need of rest, relaxation and the surrounding of complete natural beauty! Watching the spinner dolphins come to our beach on Manele Bay to rest up after feeding is a view I'll never forget. Doing yoga on the beach, stretching and breathing in the clean air and viewing the endless sky was perfect enough. On top of that, the view of majestic dolphins jumping and circling each other right off the shore enhanced our yoga session.

Having this take place before or after a breakfast of exotic star fruits, melons, berries, etc, we definitely incorporated the mind/body/spirit theme of yoga. Following up yoga with hiking through the gardens of Koehle Lodge, playing miniature golf, scuba diving and weaving ti leaves was just more of the Hawaii hedonism that we savored every day. A purely recreational vacation like this was such a departure for us compared to our elaborate educational and historic itineraries of other trips. The only "sightseeing" we did was in Honolulu at Pearl Harbor exhibits and museums as well as meeting a veteran in his nineties. From Waikiki Beach to the busy streets of Honolulu's shops, we immersed again into an urban vibe after our very secluded retreat in Lanai.

The Menagerie of Mexico

Off an on through the years, we retreated to the "playground of North America"---and enjoyed several Mexican vacations. Mexico is a destination which has been full of good memories for us both as a couple and a family. The accessibility of traveling to Mexico from our hometown makes it a good vacation because of the ease of getting there, not changing time zones drastically, and recovering quickly when returning to the states. Mexican resorts are affordable and have the amenities of the all-inclusive environment. The kids loved the excursions on land....like all terrain vehicles in the sand dunes.

Deep sea fishing was a new adventure for the boys...and quite a male bonding experience. The sunsets in Manzanillo were extraordinary and a great way to unwind after so much activity. We made an event out of going to a seaside restaurant one night just to take in the sunset. We had been staying in a villa in a gated community so driving into town gave us an opportunity for a change of pace.

Many years prior to this Mexico trip, we had gone several times as a family to Puerto Vallarta, Los Cabos, Playa del Carmen, Riviera Maya and as a couple to Acapulco, Puerto Vallarta, Cancun, and a few times in our youth. The dolphin experience we had in Puerto Aventuras in 2005 was a truly palpable bonding activity for me and my two oldest sons. Since our youngest was not old enough to participate, he watched with my husband from the shore. Swimming with the dolphins is a stimulating lesson in how humans and animals interact.

In Puerto Aventuras, we did the Dolphin Discovery excursion, swimming and interacting with dolphins. It was an adventurous excursion involving animals, nature and science. We sat through a brief video training first and then literally immersed ourselves into this experience! We went through a rotation of getting to touch the dolphins and get more comfortable with each other. I did this activity with my two elementary aged sons. The younger son wasn't quite big enough (weight wise) to do the dolphin ride successfully because the dolphins have to be comfortable with the size of child. After several attempts, he "supermanned" ! It was a really unique experience to interact so closely with these special animals. Touching them, riding them, being pushed up into the air in the stream. It was a leap of faith! We ordered photos and a video of our experience through the company. We also walked through an aviary of tropical birds and got to hold those as well!

Describing all of the menagerie of activities we've done on various Mexico trips would require several travel essays or chapters. Mexico is America's travel playground; a quick getaway. It is a treasured destination for so many people because of the way it recharges your batteries. Sun, sand, music, frozen drinks---and in much less complicated flight connections than going overseas.

A recent favorite memory of mine about recharging in Mexico happened in the fall of 2014. Patrick and I and a couple of our dearest friends went to Puerto Vallarta for a four day weekend. A weekend of typical all-inclusive resort relaxation was "just what the doctor ordered." One particular night, we strolled on the beach at midnight after a decadent dinner and dancing in a tiny disco. With our shoes off, we went up and down the beach and ended up on four chaise lounges under a sky full of stars. With beers in our hands, reclined on our chaise lounges we watched a mariachi band nearby. They had retired for the evening but decided to keep on singing ---just to each other. They stood close to the water's edge of the shore and as the waves lapped up to us, they sang their hearts out. Their instruments played the melody of the songs and their voices sang the tunes but it was their hearts on display that night. The joy and camaraderie from their hearts as they all huddled together smiling and singing with each other and to each other was the showcase of their ensemble. My friend commented, "look at them singing to each other…they don't notice anything around them….they are just singing to sing." I was happy she reflected this out loud to us because it really froze us in the moment. We knew we were there on the beach, relaxing together and gazing at the stars celebrating our friendship and a break from our family and careers back home. But knowing these local Mexican musicians also took this midnight moment to celebrate each other, be in the moment and freeze time made us all the same in that moment. We were not employees and resort guests; not Mexicans and Americans –but humans under a sky of stars at midnight loving life and each other. Those stars, that moon, —-how they follow me around.

A Sunset Cruise Gone Awry

More Mexico trips were in store for us and at another auction, we purchased a Mexico trip with relatives. Manzanillo, Mexico was perfect for a group of us residing together in a staffed, private villa.

Deep sea fishing, riding all terrain vehicles, a rooftop birthday party with pinatas, a beachside formal dinner, jet skis and many other activities were part of the week's festivities. Late night card games, ping pong, games in the pool, tennis and a visit to the farmer's market bonded us and our extended family in happy memories. But the stand-out memory we all have of this trip is of the sunset cruise that almost became disastrous.

We purchased a peaceful sunset cruise which was supposed to take us around the coves of ostentatious villas while watching the sun set. We boarded the boat, sat on the bow and the first mate served us drinks while we lounged and reclined. Despite the rainy weather that started to form, we decided impulsively to forge ahead with our cruise rather than reschedule it. Sprinkling rain would not have been a problem, however, it did not remain as sprinkling rain. Before we knew it, thunder and lightning ripped through the sky, the horizon became dark and the sea became choppy. The first mate warned us to head inside the boat. We jumped up and helped each other angle back single-filed onto the side of the boat to enter the interior.

My youngest son, twelve years old at the time, was on the opposite side of the boat and that frightened me to not be able to reach for him to descend into the man hole, safely. Instinctively, my adult niece next to him saw the fear in my eyes and guided him along. She became protective for him in my place knowing I was helpless on the other side of this chaos going on. One by one, I saw our sons safely reach the interior of the boat and I sat anxiously next to my husband wondering what was in store for us. I didn't want to put a damper on the cruise with my concerns. I sat, anxiously looking out the window at the storm hoping we could turn around and go back to shore. In an effort to distract ourselves, we started to dance to some eighties' tunes on the sound system. The boat tossed us from side to side. Furniture was sliding around and we were falling into the banquettes as we laughed nervously.

After several minutes of this, our brother in law approached us with the latest report from the captain. The storm was getting worse. It was time to decide what to do. My brother in law and husband simultaneously said, "Let's turn back!" and they gave the captain our preference. I was so relieved upon hearing this because all I could envision were my parents interrogating me how I could allow any danger to happen to their grandsons, God forbid any of them went man overboard!

As soon as we started returning to the port, I accepted a tequila shot from the first mate. Meanwhile, different family members were climbing the ladder to the top of the boat for a view. Every one of them came back with the same report. "You have to go up there to see our Captain!! He has a bandana on his head, a gold tooth, looks like a Pirates of the Caribbean character and acts like he has the best job in the world!! He's crazy!!"

Captain was asking my seasick sister in law who was up on the top deck with him, "Isn't this bee-yoooo-ti-ful??" about the crazy storm and chaotic skies tossing our little boat around. Had the moon turned the tide? What was supposed to be a peaceful sunset cruise became a terrorizing, hilarious memory for us. As my relative helped me steady up the ladder to see this cartoon-like Captain, he called out to his wife, "Look, Gina is drinking tequila at a time like this!" My relative turned around to see what he was talking about and as soon as she did, she quickly became sick.

Soaking wet, we left the port and went to the nearest restaurant to eat dinner and celebrate our survival. Nervous laughter, sea sickness, bodies tossed around a tiny boat, tequila shots and one crazy captain was the outcome of our "peaceful sunset cruise". Like so many other adventures in traveling, this will remain one of those memories we still laugh about today.

"Mother and Son Reunions... are only a ticket away" Dominican Republic

MOTHER-SON TRIPS ARE important, especially since my sons each get to take a couple of father-son trips in Boy Scouts. I cherish and appreciate how special these trips are for them with their dad and it definitely inspires me to continue to take mother-son trips with them. Three particular trips that we took were San Francisco, Dominican Republic and India. My oldest son and I went to Dominican Republic for his senior class spring break trip and two years later to India for a wedding. My middle son and I went to San Francisco and still talk about that trip all the time. I'm not sure where my youngest and I will go but I have a feeling it will be through the National Geographic Expeditions as he is our most adventurous son.

Dominican Republic was a Spring Break destination for my high school senior. It was a mother-son trip in Punta Cana and we were looking forward to the rest and relaxation after a productive high school career. "D.R" as we called it was a gorgeous beach resort trip for us and I'll always remember how surprisingly warm the water was for March….you could walk right into it! Barcelo Bavarro Palace Deluxe was the hotel we stayed at in Punta Cana.

This particular trip kept us at the resort instead of venturing off since we were herding teenagers and concerned about safety but we did pick up some cultural nuances. We learned about larimar, the unique stone of Dominican Republic and its healing effects. The gorgeous color of larimar blue was featured in all of the jewelry stores at the resort so naturally, this peaked my curiosity.

Larimar is an active chakra crystal whose vibration is said to assist with clear communication by helping people express their emotions. It was discovered in 1974 by a man named Miguel Mendez who named the stone after his daughter. He took the first three letters of her name, "Larissa" (Lar) and the local word for "the sea" which is "Mar". The combination of the two words makes the word "Larimar" and this blue stone is only found in the Dominican Republic. When the stone is closely examined, the colors in it reflect the sea and sky and boasts a strong feminine energy conveying harmony. It attracts spiritual feelings and its higher heart chakra (thymus) is said to yield a vibration that assists people with forgiving others and purging deep emotional pain. Resentment and fear are some of the emotions that larimar is supposed to aid as well. One recommendation is for people to hold a piece of larimar stone close to the area where they are experiencing pain. The energy from doing so helps it work at its highest potential.

There are beliefs that the larimar stone can be helpful in relating and activating a kundalini energy for calming and soothing. Kundalini is an energy which moves up the spine from the base to the crown and it's associated with "enlightenment." What I found particularly fascinating is that the latter is associated with the serpent that legend says dwells at the base of the spine. The serpent is wrapped three and a half times around the sacrum until it's provoked or awakened. The latter moved me because I found coincidental symbolism with myself. When it referenced the "three and a half," I thought of my sons. I had three and "a half" pregnancies since I bore three sons but had a miscarriage before the first son. (Not quite a half pregnancy but metaphorical). When it referenced the sacrum, I thought of the sacroiliac joint I damaged by carrying my three sons around on my hip; lifting them in high chairs, cribs, car seats and strollers. Years of chiropractic and physical therapy treated my sacroiliac joint and bulged disk. Yoga and other physical fitness strengthened this injured area but on this particular trip, I was suffering from a terrible and painful eye infection that caused me to miss out on much of the fun with everyone. Luke and I bickered in our frustration of a delayed flight connection on the way here and other mishaps in reaching all the others at the resort. Healing any kind of physical or emotional pain was much needed on this trip of temporary discomfort.

One of the sweetest memories I'll always hold dear is when Luke bought me a larimar necklace and earring set at a beach bazaar in the hopes to cheer me up as I was dealing with an eye infection on this trip. At the time, neither of us knew all of the symbolisms of the larimar stone but now, learning how it is used to aid in effective communication, resolving pain and celebrating feminine energy it is very meaningful and poignant to me that he was expressing his love for me with this larimar jewelry gift set. In his effort to comfort me and let me know he was thinking of me, he spent some of his souvenir money to bestow this gift to me. It reminded me of the way his father always chivalrously and romantically presented me with jewelry over the years on our various trips. I wear it with motherly pride when I think of the subliminal message and symbolisms of it.

Dealing with sickness, injuries and infirmaries on vacation is the ultimate inconvenience and very stressful. Going with the flow on vacation sometimes brings about interesting and bittersweet alternatives. While the group of twenty seniors and their mothers went on a day cruise of snorkeling and dancing, I skipped it in the hopes to let my eye rest and not be caught out on the sea all day, trapped with no relief from pain. Fortunately, I found two other mothers who decided to stay at the resort and out of the sun. We sat under a beach umbrella, sipping alcoholic beverages and having an intimate chat about so many topics relevant to women our age. We were three mothers celebrating our children in their senior year who were leaving for college soon. While it would have been fun to be with the other fifteen or so moms and twenty kids, I cherish that memory of the three of us friends, bonding on the beach into the shimmering Dominican sunset. The unexpected surprises you find on travels create the sweetest memories.

"Yes, I know how to operate a catamaran"
Aruba, Bahamas, Curacao, Puerto Rico

Dominican Republic in the Caribbean reminded me of so many tropical vacations in my past. The getaway trips of island countries from my childhood and adulthood trips provided the usual tropical environments that people seek for these types of vacations. Finding cultural flair on various islands is always a bonus and we enjoyed immersing ourselves into the cuisines or musical styles.

Aruba was becoming more well known in the early eighties and the white sand beaches and clear green Caribbean water thrilled us. I remember people horseback riding on the beach, my parents going to the hotel casinos, and all of us shopping in the town center. Beautiful embroideries and wooden sculpture souvenirs were some of the specialties. A fun fact about Aruba that we learned while we were there, is that it's only seventeen miles from Venezuela. We could see Venezuela from our resort in Aruba.

A unique detail about Aruba was that it was a small country with three official languages: English, Spanish and Dutch because it had been settled by Dutch. Aruba is a Dutch word and both Aruba and other nearby islands were *referred to as the Dutch Caribbean*. I'd like to go back with the kids next time as the boys are so adventurous.

Scuba diving is a popular activity to do in beautiful Aruba. I specifically remember the water being so crystal clear that I could see little schools of fish swimming around my feet. Bahamas became the new getaway trip location! As newlyweds, it was a popular destination during the nineties and we went twice. Both times, we enjoyed one of our favorite Bahamian traditions---conch; conch fritters, conch salad and cracked conch. The Poop Deck (crazy name) was a romantic restaurant setting for us after a long day of being on the beach. It was nice to anticipate dressing up and go into town and dining in candlelight.

The casinos were a definite draw and highlight of our getaway as was the music of the steel drum bands everywhere. I got a little swept up in all of the gambling at the resorts. I was on a roll and I was hooked! While my husband and relatives relaxed on the beach, I disappeared one afternoon to go back into the casinos. My relatives wanted to know where I went and my cousin had a hunch that I was inside the hotel casino. Sure enough, she found me at a table with senior citizens playing blackjack. I did so well gambling on that trip, that I decided to spend my winnings on a gorgeous Gucci watch in the hotel jewelry store. I would not have been able to afford an expensive watch like that as a young newlywed teacher so this was quite a splurge! On another day of gambling earnings, I took a bus by myself into the town forty five minutes away to shop for trendy clothes and stylish shoes. It was unusual for me to go by myself without my husband but I was proud of my independence, too. On other nights, we all went to dinner together or we split off as a couple for a romantic dinner for two.

We walked the streets and met some darling Bahamian children who sold us fruits similar to bananas or plantains. The Bahamian people are so nice and we are glad we interacted with them and observed the local flavor of the towns and not just the resorts.

One adventure my husband and I tried was taking out a catamaran. We didn't really have the experience required to do this on our own and it was risky. We got caught far out on the water and nervously tried to make our way back. At the time, luckily, I did not know my husband, "the captain" was nervous and I just sat and enjoyed the sea breeze. To this day, it is still a story he tells with trepidation. If you are going to do the catamaran, know what you are getting into!

On our second trip there, we did a banana boat--a fun water ride that five people can fit on--a long tube that looks like a banana pulled by a speedboat. That was exhilarating, too, and much safer than the catamaran. The Booze Cruise was a tale in itself and glass bottom boats are a great way to enjoy the view and relax. Getting ON the water is something I'll always recommend.

Puerto Rico is another wonderful Caribbean island that holds good memories of Pina Coladas, pottery, flora and fauna and lovely hotels and resorts. Lately, there seems to be a renewed interest in Puerto Rico. I had not heard much about people traveling there for vacations but we did in the late seventies or early eighties, approximately. I specifically remember one snafu when my mom booked the trip--the ticket agent on the phone (nothing was online back then) confused San Juan for Santa Domingo. Nevertheless, it worked out that we went to San Juan, Puerto Rico. Now, I am curious about Santa Domingo as I write about this snafu. The markets were very authentic in Puerto Rico at that time. We mostly spent time at the resort.

A convenient thing about Puerto Rico is that you don't need a passport to get there as it's part of the United States. This has been a quick trip idea for friends of mine who did not have updated passports. Puerto Rico, which mean "rich port" was definitely that—rich in culture, music, food and people which are all part of the vivid details of this Caribbean gem.

The First Baby Chick Leaves the Nest

After the Spring Break vacation in Dominican Republic, my oldest son took a trip to Greece that summer before going off to his freshmen year in college. Three weeks at a co-ed summer excursion camp for Greek Orthodox youth was his graduation gift from us. He saw Greece with his peers for the first time instead of his family as in the past several times he went there. When he returned from Greece, we had a few sun-filled weeks together sunbathing at our pool, talking about his trip adventures and walking up to the neighborhood farmer's market together with my husband and our dog.

Luke knew there were only a few weeks left at home to squeeze in all the family bonding he could before heading off to the independence of college life. We shopped together for his dorm room and we gave him several going away parties or dinners to make it a positive send-off.

Knowing that it would be me who would have the hardest time of all with this good-bye, I carefully planned out the college move-in transition with everyone's needs in mind. I knew that a one-day drop off would be stressful with all the parents and students crammed into dorm elevators and hallways having to face a tearful goodbye and then drive home sobbing. I decided to make it a three day event for us and my plan worked out well. We drove up early and on the first day, moved him in and stayed overnight in Lawrence, Kansas. Luke came back to our hotel for a nap while Patrick and I went to happy hour on Massachusetts street. We went to dinner and then dropped Luke off to his dorm where he spent the night alone since his roommate had to go back to his hometown for an event. Being in a hotel nearby his college, he knew we were still there and we didn't have to face our tearful goodbye, yet, which was smart since move-in day is already stressful. The next morning, we met him for breakfast on Massachusetts street. We asked him about his suite mates and the comfort of his dorm room. He confidently told us that he was going to check out the "lay of the land" to find the buildings of his classes. We thought that was a great idea and he already knew that Patrick and I were going into Kansas City for the next two days. So---we still did not have to say good-bye, yet. He met us in Kansas City that night for dinner at our favorite Greek taverna. He spent the night with us at our hotel, knowing tomorrow would be the real good-bye. The following morning, we did some more of our favorite Kansas City activities by going to the farmer's market and having dessert in the cafe of the beautiful Nelson-Atkins Museum at the plaza. I held back tears the best I could during that dessert time. I knew what was coming ahead and I tried to be brave and positive for him.

On our ride to Lawrence to finally drop Luke off and say good-bye, Patrick drove our car and I rode with Luke in his car. The thirty to forty minute ride, approximately, was surreal. I remember it being sunny because it was August. I remember small talk and happy chatter. Mostly, I remember feeling like being in a tunnel. I thought of the scene in the movie, Love Story, when Jenny is watching Oliver ice skate. They are smiling and being brave for each other. At that moment, she knew she was dying. At the coffee shop overlooking the skating rink, she asks him to take her to the hospital. That's exactly how I felt---I was in a tunnel, watching Luke leave us and feeling like it was the end of something. It was the end of his childhood and his dependence on us. It was the end of our family of five being together under our roof. It was the beginning, however, of a great new chapter for him—college. Being the mom, I knew I needed to be positive and cheerful for him. I had spent two years weeping occasional tears anyway, preparing for this day, whenever I thought about the eventual college drop off.

At the dorm, we asked him if he wanted us to hug him there in the parking lot or up in his dorm room. His face went pale and we knew the answer---he wanted to say good-bye in the privacy of his dorm. We went up there and said some parting words and gave hugs. I told him "these are going to be the best years of your life and the worst years of your life." (The best of times and the worst of times as in *A Tale of Two Cities*.) My husband nodded his head and pointed to me and told Luke, "She's absolutely right." We gave him encouragement and reminded him that we'd see him in week for Labor Day. I instantly became strong for Luke because I knew we were switching places. I had been emotional for two years thinking about this day but for him (and Patrick), it was a brand new emotion.

After we hugged and embraced in a huddle and prepared to walk off, I noticed it was Patrick now who was emotional. He looked at me through tears and motioned with his hands, "one more hug". So, we embraced again. At this point, my posture toughened up and I took on a whole new strength because both my son and my husband were softening. I had given myself two years to process these emotions and now I had to be strong for them.

On the drive home, Patrick and I were silent and numb. It had been a good three day send-off filled with activity and bonding. An hour into our drive, Luke called and asked how he should handle the dorm Luau Welcome Party at the pool. He had the right outfit, liked his roommate, but now needed to make small talk with new people. I told him something assertive and encouraging. I had ripped the "bandage" off and I had to heal now. When we arrived home to Tulsa that evening, our sons sat with us under the grapevine pergola and told us, "We didn't have enough time to say good-bye to Luke this morning when we left for school. Can we call him?" It was very sweet and we called him for a Face Time conversation. The parents had their closure but the brothers needed theirs. It was an adjustment for all of us. We reunited five days later for Labor Day weekend and all was fine.

Why am I including this in a travel book? *This was a journey, too*. It is a journey to raise a child, love them, care for them, provide them shelter and guidance. They take you to places you never knew you could experience emotionally. Then, the goal is to raise them to be independent and forge ahead in their own life. Leaving for college is a trip; a journey. We experienced ours in a three day event, mostly for my own emotional needs. I had not gone away to college (out of town) as my husband did because I went to a local college. This was new for me and I knew what I needed to do to "survive" it.

Little did I know at the time, that the next summer Luke and I would be traveling to India together for a family wedding. Traveling the longest distance to date, to a third world country would find us in an adventure of an Indian wedding, dance performances and an immersion in culture. India was another mother-son trip for Luke and I after our first year apart and it was a great bonding experience that brought us even closer.

A Journey Within

THE YEAR THAT Luke went to college was a year of transitions and challenges for me. I spent the first several weeks of his absence getting used to changes like less laundry and cooking. I marveled at how much laundry I used to have to do for a family of five. It seemed so much easier for me just having one less person in the home. I watched a lot of depressing or intense television movies when I wasn't working and I think I just co-cooned in my time of adjustment. The emotional intensity of ripping the bandage off to have your first child leave the nest was strong and I was smart this time to let myself take it easy. I had not felt the transition very realistically or therapeutically when my mother died and although this closure was not a death---it was still an ending to something.

The rest of the year was interesting. My father underwent two surgeries and naturally, it is difficult for any children to watch their parents age or suffer. After spending so much time in hospitals for mom's cancer treatment, many of my family members experienced a visceral reaction when they entered a hospital. The smell of the hospital where she died used to make me gag for years and years after her death. Smells are so powerful. Going back there for Daddy's consecutive knee surgeries was a little depressing. We all kept up with taking turns to keep him company in his recovery and there were some intense days that even involved the emergency room when he had a strange reaction to pain medications. I was with him at home when I noticed my father hallucinating and not being able to open his eyes. On a phone call to my sister, we decided to call the ambulance and the first responders came to assist. That night in the emergency room, (due to hallucinations) my father told my husband and I some emotional details and memories which scared me even more.

During this time of his recovery, I was dealing with an office move which was going to require me having to organize and move decades of files to another office. After years of having an office with a good window view, I moved to room with no windows at the new location. For me, as a claustrophobic person, I thought this might be a deal-breaker and an end to my job at this office. I knew my threshold and I was not excited to make this adjustment. I had to think long and hard about whether I could deal with the loss of income, though.

Back and forth to the hospital to see Daddy, I contemplated this change. After speaking to my sister about it, she reminded me that I wasn't in the office physically that much more than three hours at a time evaluating a client. She encouraged me to hang mirrors to reflect light and give the illusion of windows and space. I accepted this challenge and thought I should at least give it a try before quitting.

Around this same time, my husband and I invested in a property as a twenty fifth anniversary present to each other. While this was exciting, it required signing hundreds of pages of documents with the bankers and realtor. Back and forth I drove from the hospital to the notary office to complete paperwork. Naturally, complications arose with the paperwork and we had to re-do everything. More trips back and forth. At this same time, my sister-in-law and I were meeting with a travel agent to plan our India trip for the summer. The India trip was no easy task. Not only did we have to order Indian garments and learn dances for the wedding but we also had to complete several forms for a visa to enter India. I didn't know how I was going to juggle all these important demands. I had work, family, hospital visits, realtor forms, office move, visa forms and on top of all of that, I had to plan a ceremony for my son's Boy Scout Eagle Rank ceremony AND a baptism for a new precious Goddaughter. I studied website after website for ways to remodel the investment project and website after website for Indian clothing. Decorating is not something I like to do so this was a new frontier for me. We had to make a movie of photos for the Eagle Scout ceremony and that took several attempts. A long biography had to be written about my son for the Eagle program and many items had to be ordered for the baptism. It felt like I was constantly on the computer. The distraction of planning the India trip reminded me that this was a fantasy trip for many people. I was not going to let this opportunity pass me by.

Spiritually, my psyche was telling me to rise to the challenges and prepare myself physically and emotionally for the best possible achievement for all of these challenges. I was overcoming so many doubts and concerns anyway to go on the longest flight ever for me on a trip. Jogging, weight training, vitamins, juices, a three day cleanse and yoga/meditation converged together to get me in the best shape I could be in to prepare for the journey to India. I even decreased my coffee intake to prepare for any withdrawals I might have from not being near a Starbucks frequently.

I survived the office move and after several days in my new room with no windows, I organized, sorted and filed decades of client files into new file cabinets. The Eagle Ceremony and baptism on back to back weekends were joyful celebrations and a good way to spend the Lenten season before Easter.

Flight anxiety and office claustrophobia were overcome. The investment project was completed and I actually was content with my decorating project outcome. Sometimes you don't have to go far to experience a journey or transformation. I stretched myself far and I learned to reprogram some of my thoughts and concerns. I looked back on this year and realized it was a journey within.

Intensely India

THE LAST YEAR had presented me with so many incredible challenges that all became very rewarding and good lessons. The opportunity to go to India for a family wedding was an incredible turning point for me, personally. The Golden Triangle of Dehli-Agra-Jaipur was the sightseeing route for us in 2015 that exposed us to temples, forts, landscapes, mass humanity and culture.

After the Golden Triangle, we were fortunate enough to travel to Udaipur for an Indian wedding of a relative of ours. This experience was the icing on the cake because we were engaged in three days of customs, mind-blowing visuals, music, decorations, food and all of the special effects that come with an Indian wedding. The family roles, the choreographed dances, the elephant at the Baraat and the camel rides were only some of the attractions! Haldi turmeric body polishing of the bride and groom, the Mehndi henna tattoos, the performance artists, the Sangeet dances, the water splashing ritual and the unforgettable Baraat procession of dancing while the groom rode down a hill on the elephant. Not to be outdone---next came the bride's procession to meet the groom---entering with fireworks, rose petal explosions, marigold leis, incense, and more intense music.

The trip started off with the Golden Triangle itinerary of Dehli-Agra-Jaipur. It was a fast pace of sightseeing, temples, tombs and forts. We were squeezing a lot in nine days for various reasons. I'd suggest breaking up the trip by staying overnight a day or two in Dubai and doing a desert experience there. The latter was an option for us but we chose to keep traveling so that we wouldn't have to unpack and get transportation back to the airport, etc. Another suggestion I'd make is to spend a bit more time in each city if possible---not so much for the sightseeing, but to enjoy the luxury hotels and to catch up on sleep due to the time difference and any jet lag from the twenty hour flight.

We flew into Dehli, full of mass humanity and interesting architecture in Old Dehl, specifically. We saw Jama Masjid; the *great mosque of Old Dehli* which is the largest in India and the last architectural magnificence of Shah Jahan and learned that the minarets constructed of vertical stripes of red sandstone and white marble created the optical illusion of leaning away. Next, we drove past the Red Fort and then saw the Qutub Minar which is a high tower dating back to 13th century Islamic culture. India Gate was the last stop which revealed a 42 m high stone arch of triumph standing at the eastern end of the Rajpath. We saw the President's House, Rashtrapati Bhawan, which is a palatial building that blends Mughal and western architecture and was completed in 1929.

Agra was the second day of our sightseeing. We woke up at 4:00 am. to catch the 5:30 a.m. sunrise setting of the Taj Mahal. This mausoleum of Empress Mumtaz Mahal, the beloved spouse of Shah Jahan, is everything you think it will be...and more. Depending on the light of day, the white marble takes on different tones. From a distance, you see an all-white or opalescent tone but as you get up to it, you notice the jewel inlay. Our guide shined a light up to the carnelian and it glowed!

The hotel welcomed us with a *bindi dot of saffron and a marigold lei*. You could see the Taj Mahal in the background of our hotel. When we returned from the Taj Mahal, we noticed that an orange was taken from our fruit bowl and a monkey must have peeled it apart and eaten it! The monkey left the evidence on our balcony! Our hotel pool was a perfect spot for dining. We skipped dinner at the hotel restaurant and decided to dine poolside so we could enjoy the view as long as possible.

The colors of India were even brighter than the doors of Dublin or any city in Mexico, which until then and been the most colorful places I had seen. Men working in the fields, cities or praying at the mosques were often seen taking naps in the shade when they could. Driving down the streets, we'd see cows among the cars but we also saw monkeys, boars, camel carts and more. Monkeys climbed along the roofs of buildings and forts and one even jumped on our tour van!

Jaipur was our next stop on the Golden Triangle and probably my favorite! We saw the Amber Fort, City Palace and Jantar Mantar Observatory. There were several beggars around which is always emotional. There are many opportunities to give them money. You just need to be prepared that this continues for a while and it can be difficult on a tour. We also tried to ask people if it was alright to take pictures of people (or with them) with at least a gesture or body language. Most people said yes.

The Indian people had a joy and peace about them. The men were gentlemanly and the women were feminine, colorful and graceful.

As we drove through miles upon miles of Indian highways between the impoverished towns, my son was concerned about the population and conditions of the people. He asked me why many of the Indian people continue to populate at such a rate, knowing that they live in poverty. I told him that I remember reading that family is a source of pride for the Indian male. I followed this concept up with our tour guide in the van and he confirmed this and elaborated by telling us, "They believe that they will come back in other lives. Therefore, this is just one of their lives." This belief of reincarnation seemed to explain to me the inspiration for the Indian people's joy. They make the best of their lives because they believe they will be reincarnated. Having observed this joy, I understand why people return from India trips enlightened by what they've learned and appreciated.

An Indian Wedding Extravaganza

THE OPPORTUNITY TO be part of a wedding in India was a high point for us. The *wedding events* in India far surpassed even sightseeing in India, for me. Becoming part of the culture for three straight days in the wedding extravaganza will be an unforgettable visual memory for us; one that we are still visually and auditorily processing! The events included: Haldi, Mehndi, Sangeet, water ritual and Baraat. The music at the Haldi breakfast started my Indian wedding experience off in a joyful, musical way. The Mehndi, at lunchtime, was a whirlwind of activities: *henna decorations, bangle making, a palm reader, performance artists, signature drink cocktails and buffet, a hair salon, the bride and groom entering in a decorated bicycle buggy* encrusted with flowers and lots of dancing!---all started off with a camel ride outside! Getting the henna "tattoo" was an exotic and flamboyant expression of art and culture and definitely one of my favorite activities in India. The ink lasted for a week, probably, and made me feel like such a part of the culture there. I was marked and it was a perfect complement to our intricate Indian traditional dress.

I looked up some video and content on these rituals before I went to the wedding but I'm glad that I didn't over research it like I usually do because it was more visually exciting to not know what to expect as I entered these incredibly joyful events! As someone who usually over researches a country and studying it with my sons before a trip, I recommend sometimes not doing that.

This particular trip was one of those times that I left it up to be surprised; partly because I wasn't traveling with my whole family (just my oldest son) and partly because our schedules did not allow this pre-planning. My nineteen year old son was excited to see India for musical inspiration (as India did for the Beatles' White Album). My pre-planning for this trip consisted of a itinerary planned out with my travel agent and sister-in-law, ordering Indian clothing to wear (and learning all about the different kinds and styles) and rehearsing a dance we had to perform for the bride and groom at the Sangeet. I also prepared for this trip with increased yoga and mediation practice and consuming more turmeric and curry to get into the spirit of things. I discovered a "turmeric juice cleanse".

Turmeric "Juice" Cleanse
Juice of 1 lemon and pinch of honey
1/4 - 1/2 teaspoon turmeric powder
1/4 teaspoon red chile powder or cayenne (boosts metabolism)
1 1/2 cups water

The Sangeet : This event featured traditional dances presented to the bride and groom by various groups of family and friends. We presented our choreographed dance on an amphitheater stage with lasers and lights. I was so mesmerized by the performances, that I didn't want to take my eyes off of the stage for a minute to take pictures. My son wore a Kurta Pajama and I wore an Anarkali. This event felt like what a "rehearsal dinner" is back home in the states. For us, in the groom's family, it was a highlight because we performed the dances we rehearsed so much in preparation for the wedding. This was our chance to prove we could immerse in the Indian culture. It was also the event where we wore our most formal dresses. At the end of all of the dance presentations, we all went on stage to dance spontaneously, not choreographed. Our circle grew and grew---as a family should. Both sides of the family joyously danced to the drumbeats of the Indian music. An elderly woman on the bride's side of the family grabbed me and hugged me, as she did to the other new relatives. I was moved by this even though it is so familiar to me in our own circle dancing on stage at the Greek Festival back home with friends and loved ones. Here, I was experiencing it with new relatives ---on another continent on the other side of the world in exotic garments that were not of my heritage. I was a global citizen. We all were in this weekend.

One of the most meaningful epiphanies I experienced in India happened at this Sangeet performance. My son and I danced on the front line of the group dance. My son, being a musician and a true stage "ham", was like a "Bollywood John Travolta" in these dance moments. At nineteen years old and in his colorful Kurta Pajama costume, he owned the stage that night in all of his uninhibited teenage glory. I looked over at him and realized something huge. Through my childhood, I ate, slept and breathed dance since I was a student of classical ballet, tap, jazz and acrobatics. I fantasized about having a daughter someday to also grow up with a "ballet box" which would store her ballet "toe" (pointe) shoes and dance shoes of all kinds and wear the royal blue leotard and pink tights. I would be her biggest cheerleader while not being a "stage mom". Although this dream did not exactly come to fruition like that, I had three boys who still inherited a love of dance from their parents and became vivacious Greek dance performers at our local Greek festival. But in this moment in India, doing our choreographed wedding dances, I looked over at my son and realized, "How unique is this? I am dancing on a stage with lights and lasers in India with my son!! And we are on the front row together." This doesn't happen often and we embraced this opportunity with joy, rehearsals and celebration. It far surpassed any fantasy I had of watching a daughter dance on some stage back at home.

One of my favorite memories of going on this journey to India was selecting traditional Indian dresses to buy and take over there. My sister-in-law and I sat for hours in front of the computer perusing thousands of resplendent costumes and garments on Indian fashion websites. We jokingly referred to our addiction as "IFAA": Indian Fashion Addicts Anonymous. We ordered three outfits for the events and with each costume requirement, we learned more about the different traditions and textiles. Between the costumes and the dances, we learned so much terminology. We were in the "India zone." I fondly reflect on this time because I feel like my sister-in-law and I have a unique connection in this regard; we have a "carpe diem" attitude about travel and adventure. There is probably no one else in my family or circle of friends who would prioritize a journey like this and also get into all of the emphasis on the fashion of it. We just truly enjoyed embracing the lavish details of the Indian wedding extravaganza and knowing what wisdom was to be gained from this experience. The expense and preparation to make a trip like this happen is what usually deters other people from international travel and I understand that ---but I don't subscribe to that.

In general, the obstacles I needed to overcome to accomplish this trip were part of my own spiritual journey. I prefer to travel with my husband so going without him was a big step. I also have some flight anxiety after decades of growing up jetting around. The latter came during my thirties, probably due to being a mother. I also had to save up the money to go on this trip as it was not in our budget. My husband and I had invested in something special for our 25th wedding anniversary and biting off two big expenses at once was not practical. I happily proposed to pay for my share of the trip on my own and doing so made me appreciate the trip even more. Deciding to take my nineteen year old son with us was both for practicality and for bonding. I felt like my sister-in-law and I needed a tall, protective male with us because we were two American women going to a third world country. I also thought it would be a very enriching trip for him in his college years. Luke is our musician and upon hearing he was going to India, he immediately thought of the Beatles and their White Album which was inspired by their travels to India.

Other preparations for this trip that made me grow spiritually, were to increase my yoga and meditation practice. I am not consistent with yoga—at all. I am hyper and gravitate more to cardio and training with weights. To slow down and do yoga means I have to, well, uh....*slow* down. This goes against my modus operandi which is to get things done! Cross things off my list! However, I thought it would be good for me to push myself since I was pushing myself in so many other areas for this trip: independence, overcoming fears, saving scrupulously, etc. I increased the yoga and I also increased my health habits. When I ordered the costumes from India, I had to be measured for them. This was uncomfortable and humbling. I was used to it from my days as a student of dance but here I was, turning forty seven years old (on the day we left for India) getting measured by my husband for costumes that have no zippers or buttons. The costumes just pull over your head and you squeeze in to them. Yikes! This was so different from our usual clothes, that my sister-in-law and I had to coach each other through this process. I practiced at home and gave her some advice. "You pull it over your head, push your boobs up, pull the dress down,...." Both of us got trapped in our dresses and had to ask our husbands for help to get them off for fear of suffocation....and fear of ripping the dress.

So increased jogging was added to my list. It helped. Yoga, jogging, weights, meditation, turmeric "juice" to gain that Indian "glow" and lastly---a three day cleanse. The cleanse was not for weight loss but rather to cleanse your system of any cravings and purify a bit. I was hoping to eliminate my caffeine intake because I am addicted to Starbucks coffee and I knew it wouldn't be accessible to me on my jet lagged traveling days. So, I even cut back on coffee. This was HUGE! I was ready for India in every way possible. We had done the reading and research, ordered costumes, rehearsed our new dances, gotten in shape and prepared ourselves spiritually and culturally.

Luke was going to be looking for sitars in India. I was going to focus on the philosophy and spirituality to incorporate into my writing and my sister-in-law was going to focus on her photography. We were an artistic trio in this regard and our easy traveling habits made us the "dream team," as my sister-in- law named us.

The next morning was the water ritual. The bride told me it isn't an actual ritual but they decided to include something fun for that morning- a casual event. When you arrived to breakfast, you were given a white kurta to wear with your leggings. The people who joined in grabbed buckets and water guns and filled them up with the nearby pool water and SPLASHED each other ---all set to music. People clutched each other to make each other wet which I interpreted to be a bonding gesture. (much like the turmeric body polishing ritual).

That night, was the climax of all of the events: the Baraat, which is the bridegroom's wedding procession (on an elephant or horse) accompanied by bands, dancers and sometimes fireworks as it reaches the meeting point between the two families. The groom is given the marigold garland (like a lei) as are some of the family members. The marigold garland, reminiscent of a Hawaiian lei, (which is also presented at times of welcome), is a symbol associated with the vibrancy of the sun. The marigold is also referred to as the "herb of the sun" representing passion and creativity. In terms of the wedding celebration, the marigold is used as a love charm and a sign of a new beginning. It is also considered a sign of purity in Hindu festivals and worship ceremonies. When it's presented as a welcome gesture at homes or hotels, it is used as a sign of respect and honor. I felt this symbol of honor when I saw the marigold leis bestowed upon the families joining together in the wedding ceremony as the Baraat procession was completing and entering into another ceremony.

As all of this transpired outside on a decorated lawn with guests joyfully milling about, I looked at all the guests in the crowd. A sea of colors and hues from pastels and jewel tones to electrifying shades of chartreuse and lime---the saris, anarkalis, lehenga cholis, salwar kameez and so many more varieties of Indian dress decorated the landscape like ornamental jewels. I had a wedding "moment" when I looked over at a striking and exotic Indian female guest and mouthed the words "I looooove your dress!" Almost simultaneously, she mouthed back "I love yours!" I felt blissful about the realization that all the guests shared in common the pleasure of dressing formally for the wedding occasions to participate in the grandeur *with* the bride and groom. While the bride and groom were the centerpiece of the event and dressed royally beyond comparison, the guests' grandeur fell right into place with the feel and look of the wedding landscape and tone. It was all worth it!--the measuring of custom made costumes, the long flights and layovers to get to India, the details, logistics and fatigue. I felt like I was in a movie, worried that I'd forget the best scenes. I knew all I could do was take it in, absorb (like my mother always told us to do) and take photos to study once back at home.

As fireworks shot off above us in the sky and rose petals shot out of a tube, I looked over at my son and sister-in-law and said, *"What is happening to us??....Is this really happening? Are we ever going to be able to internalize all of this??"* They wistfully understood the incredulousness of these rhetorical questions.

The wedding music was joyful, haunting and spine-tingling. The food and drink never stopped circulating to us as we sat outside on banquettes and cushions that were set up around a platform where the bride, groom and their parents sat with the wedding officiator and lots of incense. My son and I sat together and absorbed the visuals. It was interesting to see people talking, laughing and milling about. Indian weddings are not uptight and overly structured like other weddings. I appreciated this casual quality.

You could watch several movies about Indian weddings but until you experience one in person, there is no way to describe the elation, celebration and sensual riches that happen and how it mixes inside you like a chemical reaction. We were transformed.

The Pulse of India

THERE WAS AN active pace to touring India. Our minds were racing with all the visual stimuli. On one hand, there were moments of peaceful reflection and on another hand, there was an intensity to the touristic learning process. Because we didn't know what to expect, really, it made the journey very captivating. Being the second most populated country in the world, it is no wonder the pulse of this land would be so intense. The vivid imagery might have "hit our retinas" initially, but it felt like we had to delay what we felt and comprehended later on in the day. Our tour guide pointed out nuances about the Indian lifestyle and we were so relieved that he did because as we drove past something, we could've missed some details--because there was so much to look at!

An outdoor "barber shop" happening in the middle of a fruit stand market was priceless. I admired how the Indian people embraced the outdoors. It seemed like everyone was outside most of the time which stood out to me because in America, it seems like we are indoors so much. Sometimes it was hard to decipher the activity among the scenery. It was challenging for me to avoid looking at the pollution and debris. Although I have seen it before in other countries, it was very much a part of some landscapes here. When we discussed the situation of poverty with our Indian tour guide, he told us that the Indian people are not emotionally burdened by their life of poverty because they believe in their next life, they will be reincarnated in different and better circumstances perhaps. Their current situation is just for the present time.

Another detail that stood out to me was the multigenerational quality to the Indian lifestyle. Like many other cultures, the old and young are together frequently. This is very common to me since I grew up in a multigenerational household. The adults and children worked together. I observed the children learning from the adults, yet, still playing with their peers and siblings. As someone who evaluates children and young adults for psychoeducational reasons, I think about this cooperative environment and have so many questions about it. I think about their "outdoor classroom" and what emotional stability it must provide. Washing a cow with their peers is a hands-on learning activity that American students would have to go on a field trip to experience! (unless, of course, they live on a farm).

The women's work was so physical! I admired their strength and grace. I might have known, factually, that millions of women carry things on their heads but to see it in person is really stunning. Physical labor in dresses! Another detail we don't see back home.

Physical labor, feminine dressing and graceful smiles, no matter what the load is that they carry! We saw this "pulse of India" on the Golden Triangle tour of Dehli-Agra- Jaipur and then on down to Udaipur. I am still processing what we envisioned in India. It is what makes India a journey and not just a trip. The heartbeat and pulse of this exotic country is truly unique!

India is an exotic land with its architectural imagery, history, religion and cuisine. The people in India stood out to me for their lovely skin and silky hair. The children with their spry bodies and colorful spirits stood out to me for their curiosity and innocence. Out of 1.25 billion people, approximately 440 million of the population are children. This is a staggering statistic to me. From what I've read, the children are enrolled in school but approximately half drop out of school to work and help their families. The street children in India are unsupervised children who work independently. Because of the risk of having their earnings taken, they immediately use them for food. Most families are multigenerational (as in many cultures) and they follow the joint family system where many families live together in one household.

A Magic Carpet Ride

The recreational games that Indian children play consist of Parcheesi (the national game of India), kite flying, hockey, cricket, chess and soccer. Because India is known for their festivals, many Indian children attend the following festivals: Diwali, Holi and Rakhi are a few of the many festivals they celebrate. In their daily greetings, the children and adults greet each other with "Namaste" which means "I bow to you" or *"I bow to your true self."* It is beautiful how faith and family are valued in this culture.

The Spectacular Taj Mahal

THE TAJ MAHAL is one of the most recognized monuments in the world. Its grandeur is powerful-it is everything you expect and more. The intensely romantic symbolism behind the Taj Mahal is historic and poetic. Shah Jahan had this mausoleum built in honor of his Empress Mumtaz Mahal after her death. It is said that 20,000 people and 1,000 elephants were involved in building it for twenty two years.

Leading up to the mausoleum is a Mughal garden with canals and fountains. The dome supposedly symbolizes the female form (breast) and the Taj Mahal is a perfectly proportionate marble building with rich details, carvings, inlaid jewels and an opalescent lighting to it. The other buildings surrounding the Taj Mahal are there for balance.

What was particularly moving to me was the story of the Shah Jahan's imprisonment by his own son in the fort overlooking the Taj Mahal. He was eventually buried in the mausoleum next to his beloved Empress. He was referred to as one of the greatest Mughals. What impressed my son the most was the fact that the entire building, which seems so massive as you approach it, was all basically built to house a tomb!

What impressed me the most was the ornate and intricate carving on the building and how it is full of colorful details. Our tour guide shined a light up to it which revealed a glow of jewels like carnelian and other jewels and colors.

My teenage son was also very happy to find out later that George Harrison, the Beatle, took a photo in front of the Taj Mahal when he was in his early twenties. It was a special memory to share with my son after his first year away from home at college.

A Magic Carpet Ride

Our time in Agra was an unquenchable, powerful series of feelings. Late at night, although we were always tired and running on empty, I asked my sister-in-law to join me on the hotel room balcony for a glass of wine. Our hotel room had a view of the Taj Mahal and a view of the grounds of the most magnificent hotel either of us had ever been to in all of our extensive traveling. I bought the bottle even though I knew we'd only be able to drink one glass in our exhaustion. It was a sumptuous moment for us as we were intoxicated by the night view of the most romantic monument in the entire world. The wine was pungent and the view was ethereal.

What especially stood out to us what that we realized and appreciated that the Taj Mahal is not lit up at night. It is simply there in its somber state as a meaningful monument and not an attraction to be overly commercialized. It will probably sound dramatic, but I can't help reflect now that the two of us could appreciate this monument in our special way because we not only share the love of world travel but also we have in common the love of great husbands whom we've known since childhood. While we don't have a tragic story like Shah Jahan and his beloved, Mumtaz Mahal, we honor her memory.

A moment of Namaste in India: Udaipur

ONE GOAL I had for my time in India was to do yoga there. It didn't matter to me if it was in a true yoga class setting or just me alone with my yoga DVD that I adore. In the fast pace of our touring and all of its scheduled appointments with tour guides and van pick ups, it appeared that it was not going to transpire for me. But one early morning during the wedding weekend extravaganza, when I could not sleep in, I went out on the hotel balcony to gaze at the mountains of Udaipur. The dark and ominous sky on this quiet, still morning felt like when night meets day as it was still not dawn. Basically, I was out on my balcony while my son slept with nothing to do but absorb this stillness on the other side of the world; again.... "sharing the same moon." I made tea as quietly as I could and took a book out there but couldn't really read it since I wasn't going to turn on the light and disturb my nineteen year old sleeping son.

Instantly, I got the idea of what to do in the quiet stillness and dark! I didn't have a yoga mat but I did have my yoga dvd and laptop so I put it on mute and spread out a long hotel bath towel and with my balcony doors thrown open, I stretched and meditated to the Udaipur sky as the dawn emerged. I can't say I had a kundalini moment but I did have the awakening and bliss that are components of kundalini. I was probably too exhausted from all of the wedding energy and I wasn't really anticipating a rigorous yoga session this morning. But I love and cherish that it came to me to have a namaste moment there in this country. Namaste, meaning "I bow to your true self", is exactly what I was feeling at that moment---a respect for this country and culture and a respect for what my body was telling me to do and feel at that moment. My "true self" was physically tired from this intense traveling but my emotions were somber and enlightened by the transformation taking place in this Indian experience. Yoga is mind, body, spirit and at that moment, my mind, body, spirit welcomed this yoga experience communing with the Udaipur mountain range better than it could have experienced in a yoga class in the hotel somewhere. Doing it quietly out of respect for my son's slumber was also a component of the spirit because it demonstrated self sacrifice and courtesy.

Elephant Rides and Snake Charmers

Jaipur was my favorite city in India for many reasons. The "pink city" as it's often referred to seems to reflect that welcoming tone and hue that it was painted in to prepare for the welcoming arrival of Prince Albert. One of the sights we visited was the majestic Amber Fort. This imposing and stately palace and fort was filled with splendor everywhere we looked. Ascending to the Amber Fort on elephants was chaotic and thrilling. My son and I shared an elephant and my sister-in-law rode solo on her elephant. As we tried to take photos and absorb all of the intense visuals, my son became distracted and alarmed by the chaos of the salesmen running alongside us to sell us souvenirs. I told him to focus on the scenery and ignore the chaos or else he'd missed the moment. In his effort to protect me, he kept responding to the salesmen and declining their aggressive offers and sales pitches. They threw items at us: hats, scarves, umbrellas.....etc., and Luke would toss them right back. It was quite a scene. When we reached the top, it was peaceful and they lined the elephants back up along the wall for their rest and descent.

While touring the Amber Fort in Jaipur, we encountered a snake charming duo of brothers. We not only watched their performance but we also were able to sit and interact with the cobra whose fangs and venom were removed. Snake charming is a ritual that involves pretending to hypnotize a snake by playing an instrument. Reportedly, snakes actually are responding to the movement in the performance, rather than the sound. Snake charming performances happen in other countries other than just India.

The practice is also performed in Morocco, Egypt, Tunisia, Pakistan, Sri Lanka and other countries. The performance symbolized the snake charmer showing heroism by controlling the evil (or devil) in the snake. There are other interpretations of what snake charming symbolizes. This practice has died out overall but now can be seen at festivals and markets---or in our case, at the Amber Fort in Jaipur. Since the fangs and venom are removed from the cobra, I didn't feel in danger of the snake.

This particular pair of snake charmers was a man and his younger, teenage brother. I was not expecting to see this ritual along the path of the majestic Amber Fort but I'm so thrilled we did! --especially since my son is a musician and could appreciate the instrumental part of this ancient tradition! We each sat with the duo and took pictures with the snake. I got especially daring and kissed the snake once I found out the venom and fangs were removed. Still, this was a daring move and it shocked my son and others back home who saw my photographs. That's living on the edge for me.

As we meandered down the winding stone paths of the Amber Fort, we stopped for a moment to catch our breath (physically and mentally) and absorb some more details. Two Indian ladies dressed in clothes with incredible colors and patterns were sweeping the paths and resting in a nook of a wall. I asked them if I could take their picture. During the duration of this trip, I had become sensitive to the Indian people being photographed so much and so randomly as if they were zoo animals. It felt like people were gawking and snapping them like papparazzi. Yet, I know it's out of curiosity and admiration for such an exotic country that tourists want to capture each visual with photographs. The ladies nodded yes to my question and one of them motioned me over to her and indicated by rubbing her fingers together that she wanted a tip for the photo. I was happy to tip them and got in middle of them to pose for a photograph taken by my son. Just as he was ready to shoot the photo, the one lady leaned in and embraced my arm made the peace sign with her fingers and coyly smiled as if we were lifelong friends. We all chuckled.

While it is probably so perfunctory for those local ladies to pose with tourists, for me that was a defining moment in travel. I looked at the photo in the camera and later when it was uploaded to my computer and I'm always stunned by what I see. Three women, all ethnic, smiling boldly at a palace. We were from different worlds, different sides of the world and "commoners" but posed in a royal place. The vivid colors of their authentic Indian dress and the vivid colors of my American summer clothes jump off the screen. It's a sea of color. There's a broom nearby in the photo because they were doing manual labor. I am the tourist wearing a tourist style purse and accessories. I have a sari-type scarf around my shoulders in order to respect the dress code of tourists in India.

Somehow the sari type scarf is the common thread that ties us together in the photo uniting the "East meets West" clothing. When I analyze the emotions in the photo, I feel bonded to these women regardless of our places in life. We appear to be from the same age group but we walk such different paths in life. But in that moment, what is common in the photo is our smiles. The magnitude of each smile is what bonds us. It doesn't matter where we come from ---what mattered at that moment was that we were enjoying a sunny day at a palace fort, appreciating history and what it provides to everyone there. The ladies were provided with tips and employment. I was provided with knowledge and history. My son was provided with a photographic opportunity watching his mother interact with locals. The ladies were providing a service and taking their earnings back home to their children, most likely. I was providing a service and education to *my* child, too. They went home with tips and earnings and I went home with a photo that I will always treasure, not only for its exotic tone and memory but also for the pride I have in my son who took the photo.

Blogs, Guest Blogging and Magazine Travel Writing

Returning from India was as impassioned as preparing to go there. My son and I had incredible jet lag as we traveled back for twenty two hours plus a five hour layover in Dehli and Dubai and a twelve hour layover in Udaipur. We basically traveled for two days back to the states. I had come down with a terrible cough from the dryness and germs of the airplane ride and after a week of medications interrupting my sleep, I spent another week overcoming jet lag. My son and I found each other at 1:00 a.m. in the den for insomniac "movie dates." I will always remember that as a special time with him. It is funny how you respond to movies when you're not that lucid.

Before India, I had started experimenting with a blog. I barely knew how to move the cursor or load the images to the template. I had a desire to create something I could put in the universe for other mothers and educators. Since so many people had asked me how I create my trip itineraries with my sons, I wanted to "pay it forward" and give them the information. I agonized over how it would be perceived. I wanted to make sure the intention matched the perception. I hid it from the public and occasionally loaded it to Pinterest to see if there were any followers. I sent samples to friends I trusted to get their reaction. I tested it on two homeschool families to see if their children liked it as an armchair traveler "series." The input was positive and it gave me some encouragement to continue.

Coming up with the name and logo later for the blog/website reminded me of a very inspirational mentor in my life who happened to be a true half-cast gypsy. I met her because of piano lessons I was taking from her mother. Being proud of her heritage, she wore authentic gypsy clothing which was quite unusual in our homogenous and landlocked home town. She lived in a house almost big enough to be a mansion with her elderly mother who was my piano teacher. I can vividly remember the living room where I took piano lessons. There was antique furniture, a grand piano on one side and an upright piano on the other side. Outside of the grand French doors, going into this art deco style parlor, was a long hallway leading back to the kitchen and den where my gypsy friend collaborated with me on my original poetry. The den was cozy and full of books. I could tell, even at a very young age, that this was a house with a creative spirit; music, poetry, literature and art. In fact, out of all the stately imagery in this significant house, it was a small 4 x 4 piece of framed art that was the most powerful image for me. The granddaughter of my piano teacher had painted a clown when she was a child. She was probably around Kindergarten age when she made this artwork. She grew up to be what I considered a hippie but I don't know if I even met her more than twice. Someone framed her childhood clown picture and hung it on the wall with all of the fancy art and antique furniture in that room. It prominently stood out to me---as small as it was physically, it was HUGE to me, symbolically. Every woman in that house---a hippie, a gyspy and a Victorian grandmother all so diverse, valued her childhood art; her picture of a clown. They found a prominent place to display it and in this house of the creative spirit, the childhood art was depicted with such value. Now, her gypsy mother was nurturing *my* art—my original poetry— and telling me that it was good enough to try to publish in a children's magazine. I know that experience influenced me later as a mom to display my sons' artwork throughout the house in professional framing and to help them submit their artwork to Highlights Magazine and other contests.

A Magic Carpet Ride

My gypsy friend, who was a painter, mentored me in my childhood poetry writing and even helped me get my poem published in a children's magazine. I marveled at her enthusiasm and her faith in me. While I wasn't mastering my piano lessons and not as interested in it anyway, my gypsy friend and mentor saw my passion for poetry and worked with me. My mother found this to be very thoughtful of her and appreciated the interest she took in me. I think my gypsy friend knew I needed a little more attention and diversion in something I felt confident in since my mother was battling cancer throughout my childhood and since I was struggling with practicing piano, too. She helped shine a bright light onto a hobby I loved and was trying to express. I now think of her whenever I recite that published poem to my kids or whenever I look at a painting she gave us.

Flash forward to 2015, stories poured out of me after that India trip. Conquering many fears I had to go on this journey gave me a feeling of independence and success which in turn, motivated me to express my creative side after all of these decades in a scientific career. I wrote and wrote and wrote that summer, especially after the re immersion from India. India is not just a country—it's a soul transformation.

October rolled around and something happened that made my website almost crash permanently. After spending money and hours on the phone to salvage the site, I thought, "This is nuts. I better share this blog and launch it immediately or else all of this work was for nought." So, that night after maybe seven hours of struggling to revive the blog site, I made it public by sharing it on social media.

When I woke up, I discovered that it had received hundreds of views over the wee hours of midnight to morning. I received wonderful feedback and encouraging comments and even one very special phone call that meant so much to me. Gypsy Family Travel was born and she was announcing her birthday that October day!

Shortly after, a writer friend sent the blog link to an editor at a parenting magazine and they found the content very useful for their audience so they put me on their online magazine as a guest blog. It was originally supposed to be for two weeks but it turned into one month. I was happy to have the exposure and saw some traffic to my site because of it. I had interviewed my writer friend about her immersion trip to a "Blue Zone" island in Greece for my blog and she had so much fun collaborating with me editing her story and photos that she encouraged me to keep up the writing hobby. She referred to me as a "fellow writer" and this took me by surprise because I wasn't thinking of myself in this way. I was a dedicated psychometrist and educator working in my scientific field and writing statistical reports and evaluations about students' information-processing functions and remediation plans. To think of myself as a "writer" encouraged me to "raise the bar" for myself and elevate my style and effort to meet her "expectations."

Another friend encouraged me to share it with her friend who is the publisher of a magazine. The publisher had seen my India photos on social media and asked me questions about the trip. She and her senior editor looked through the material and asked me to meet them for an appointment. I became the travel writer for a local magazine and could not have been more thrilled for this opportunity! The synergy of that first meeting and the way they embraced creative concepts gave me such a respect for this team. I was given two assignments straight out of the gate and entered a world of deadlines and drop boxes; word counts, bylines and photo credits. Staff titles like "graphics manager" and "managing editor" were new to me.

Being a psychometrist, I had my own world of reports, statistics, conferences, deadlines, letterhead, and terminology. This creative world of magazine publishing was a new horizon for me and just the balance I needed. The "scientist" in me was fulfilled in my psychometry career and now the "artist" in me was getting fulfilled as a travel writer.

Three years away from the empty nest, I embraced this opportunity and paced myself to still focus on my youngest son and his needs before jumping into too much. I know some absolutes to be true: "If you bungle raising your children; nothing else you do matters much." (Jackie Onassis, one of my idols said something to that effect.) The other quote that motivates and grounds me is, "The days are long but the years are short." I was not going to look back and regret not spending quantity time with my sons as a trade off for more career time. I had the balance I needed and my sons and husband needed- or at least kept trying to keep that balance. I was always driven by several parenting mantras that structured and guided my parenting skills and philosophies. If I didn't have that synchronous and synergistic vibe with my sons, I would not have created Gypsy Family Travel. It was the *quantity* time with them, especially every summer that helped this evolve. I watched them grow and delve into discoveries in an educational way and in play.

Years before, we researched together and we played Top Secret Adventure: a hilarious board game about the world. Every month a book and package arrived that had travel props that enriched your understanding of a country and each country was represented on the board game. Those memories and activities built up to the creation of Gypsy Family Travel.

The empty nest was going to be alright because of the quantity time I had raising the boys. One of my best friends made a comment once saying, *"I look forward to the empty nest...don't you??"* At first I looked at her like she had two heads. What was she *saying*? She is raising three daughters and I am raising three sons. Aren't we supposed to be sad to let them go? How is she saying this? Then, I thought about her statement. She was not saying she is ready to get rid of them. She and her husband have been as engrossed in their family as Patrick and I have been. They go to basketball games every week, attend family camps with their daughters, do youth group activities with them, similar to what we do with youth group, Boy Scouts and school activities. We live in different states but often met them to watch our kids compete in diocesan youth group regional speech contests out of state. We were crazy proud of each other's kids and we jointly held them up to the same standards in which she and I were raised. Not only did she and I walk the same walk as first generation Greek daughters but we also were sorority sisters (same sorority; different colleges). We both married half-Greek husbands and we both experienced fulfilling marriages with husbands we adored and admired. So, of course, she is looking forward to the empty nest.

The pace of family life like this was fast paced and rigorous, like climbing a mountain......no wonder she was looking forward to the empty nest. Maybe it represents the end of a race. A triumph?

She was simply expressing that she looks forward to the uninterrupted, less hectic pace with her husband. I realized how conditioned we are as mothers to think we must be mostly defined and fulfilled by our nest, constantly fluffed with our baby birds. Her statement was very liberating to me because by understanding it, I gave myself permission to start proclaiming that I, too, was looking forward to the empty nest. This is the same best friend who wisely told me decades before this, when our kids were toddlers and preschoolers, *"Legos are meant to be dumped on the floor!"* She was right about that, too. Homes with children are not supposed to be sterile environments with perfectly straightened up rooms and décor. The legos are there for touching, building, experimenting and discovering. As we all find out, the legos are eventually picked up and put back into the basket or tub. Out of the way. Forever. Enjoy the kids and the long days. The days are long but the years are short.

My Sons' Global Awareness

When I created the travel blog, I interviewed my three sons about their knowledge and experiences from our trips. I wanted the blog to have their voice in it as much as mine. My oldest son shared his perspective in this interview I conducted with him.

What did you learn through traveling?
"Traveling showed me what life outside of America is like. There are cultures very different from our own. Traveling gave me the best memories of being with my family. In Spain and the Mediterranean, they have siestas---which is taking a break out of the day. Americans are about "work, work work" so this siesta was different. There were no restaurants open to go to. It showed me that some countries prioritize leisure and family time more."

What were the pros and cons of traveling?
"I realized America has certain conveniences like twenty four hour grocery stores. Our roads and parking are better in America. Our van practically got stuck between buildings in Seville."

What was your favorite trip?
"I think my favorite trip itinerary was: Switzerland, Italy, Austria, Lichtenstein, France, Germany and Greece a few years ago because I like being in the Mediterranean and close to the sea. Greece is my favorite country and that was our last stop on this trip."

What was the most exotic trip you've taken?
"India was the most exotic trip I took because it's a total 180 from America. There wasn't a lot of English spoken and we didn't eat the street food. It was definitely a third world country."

What people skills did you acquire through traveling?
"I learned patience and understanding since there is a language barrier when you're traveling. Each side has to understand what the other is saying. I don't focus on the negatives because there's too many good things that happen."

What advice do you have about long flights?
"My advice about long flights is watch movies, take good music and sleep."

(This son went on a trip to Ireland with his college ruby team to play in a 10-day tour. They raised their own funds for most of the travel expenses and then stayed in youth hostels. He mountain biked, played guitar in a pub at night and played on an Irish rugby team for one of the games.)

My middle son shared this information about his perspective on travel. I interviewed my eighteen year old to see how he summarizes our family travel experiences. This is what he shared with me:

"Traveling gave me a better understanding of different cultures....the bigger picture of the world. It opens you up, shows you, makes you aware of the world--not the bubble of America. *I liked the bus tours even better than some of the museums* because someone is speaking to you and it's more interactive." (On most of the museums, cathedrals, castles, etc...we had a private tour guide so he's referring to museums where we may not have had a guide.)

Meeting relatives in Greece for the first time, learning in interactive children' museums and trying new experiences in foreign environments are highlights of his experience.

Now, at eighteen years old, he set off on his first independent trip. He went to Greece for five weeks; three weeks at a camp and two weeks on his own with a friend. He stayed at the monastery, Mount Athos, for six days and wrote about his experience in a journal.....a tradition we started when he was a little boy traveling with the family. He presented us with this idea of independent travel a year earlier. It took some faith on our part and a lot of meticulous planning but entrusting him with responsibility on this journey was worth it. It turned out to be a successful trip and a huge learning experience!

My son's visit to Mount Athos, Greece

MY GREGARIOUS EIGHTEEN year old son visited Mount Athos---the most significant collection of monasteries in Greece. Women are not allowed on Mount Athos. To visit there, you must go through an application process that has to be approved. He and his friend from the U.S. were traveling through Greece together during the summer and Mount Athos was the final destination on their trip. I asked him to keep a journal while he was there. His journal exceeded my expectations! I'm so happy he will have these memories and details recorded for posterity.

Their adventure started when they had to take several forms of transportation just to arrive to this most holy place! It was planes, trains, automobiles, and ferries! They had just enjoyed three weeks at a co-ed youth camp in Greece and another eight days of freedom, adventure and a Greek wedding celebration in the coastal town of Nafpaktos. Now they were ending their five week trip at Mount Athos for six days. I urged my son to keep a travel journal about this special experience he was about to embark upon. I had taught him, when he was in elementary school, how to do this on our family trips. His older brother urged him to keep a journal as well, because he had not done it on his solo trip to Greece, and he regretted it. My son took our advice and diligently wrote daily in his journal. I'll always save that little black journal for him. Here is his story....

Mount Athos : Day One 7-20-2015
I'd by lying if I said I wasn't terrified. Only one week left, yet July 28th seems so far away. Here I am, laying in my cot at Philotheo,

with bats flying overhead throughout the hallways and no air-conditioning system to ease me into a much desired sleep. This is my first impression of the Holy Mountain, a site in which thousands of pilgrims travel to and from all around the world each year. Just nine hours in, and yet there's nothing quite like the experience. A 9:45 a.m. ferry ride turned into a two and a half hour mind trip. As expected, there was no means of accessing wi-fi aboard the boat, so I had the duration of the trip to keep to my thoughts and ponder how exactly the week would unfold! (Mom had watched a documentary on Mt. Athos years ago and told me the monks pick peaches, make wine and pray all day. She said it was a fascinating documentary but she was concerned about what two eighteen year olds would do there.)

Upon arrival in Dafne, it was made abundantly clear that I'd be continuing my self-reflection for an indefinite period of time. No wifi, no English-speakers, and no girls anywhere. We boarded the bus to Kerya, the capital of Athos, and arrived around 45 minutes later.

From Kerya, we located the shuttle to Philotheo, one of the many monasteries in which we'll be staying during our trip. On the way to the monastery, our shuttle hit a rough patch of gravel, which led to an emergency tire change as the air-conditioning system was beginning to give out. Sweaty, tired, and curious, we finally arrived at Philotheo around 2:00ish pm.

After checking in our names and information, we were directed to our room by a young, Greek monk. We were given three hours of free time, which was used for sleeping and reading, and we headed towards the chapel for 5:00 evening vespers. By this time, I was so overwhelmed by homesickness and a change of culture that I began a repetition of Jesus Prayers in my head. By the end of the service, I had probably reached 1500+repetitions. I struggled greatly with the language barrier. I read and write Greek but do not speak it fluently. After vespers, the group of pilgrims and visitors— around twenty five-- headed into the dining hall. Here, I was served lentils, garbanzo beans, bread, and you guessed it---peaches! Naturally, I ate three peaches as the group feasted in silence. Here, during meals, it is customary to eat in a quiet manner, for a monk is chanting the epistle all throughout the meal. After dinner, the group was directed back into the church for a second prayer service. Upon dismissal, we were led into the inner sanctum, where, spread out upon a table, lay five different relics: a piece of Christ's cross, part of the skull of St. Mammas, and various body parts from Sts. John Chrysostom, Marina, and another one I can't remember.

After venerating these relics, as well as the miraculous icon of the Virgin Mary, we were allowed free time for the remainder of the evening. So, here I am, writing the first of many journal entries during this extended period of time at Mount Athos. It has been a humbling and intimidating experience thus far, but I am interested to see where this trip takes me over the next five days. I've never missed home so much in my life, but I know that I'll most likely never get this experience again, so I just have to make the most of my time upon the mountain.-End of Day One

Mount Athos: Day Two 7-21-2015
It has been exactly one month since I left Tulsa to embark on my journey in Greece. Although I can't say that I missed home too much while I was at (Ionian Village) camp, it is now one full week until I'm back in the U.S., and I couldn't be more anxious to return home. The past two days at Athos have seemed like an eternity. This morning, we woke up at 4:00 a.m for a four-hour church service. Between the snores of monks and my own little naps, I found myself praying more thoroughly than I have ever before in my life. During this time, I prayed for as many individuals I could think of. The prayer helped me reflect on my life and relationships with

these individuals, as well as making the service seem shorter than it actually was.

After the service, we headed towards the dining hall for breakfast, where we were served pasta, bread, salad and, once again, peaches. After another silent breakfast came and went, we were allowed to return to our rooms for mid-morning siesta. After napping for four hours, we packed our backpacks, filled up our water bottles, and headed for the monastery, Karakalo. Originally, planned to be a thirty minute hike, we got sidetracked and thrown off course, thanks to a bit of off roading. Upon arrival in Karakalo, we were greeted by a pair of monks who offered us coffee, ouzo, water and Turkish Delight. We lounged in the monastery grounds for 2-3 hours before evening vespers began. Vespers lasted around 1.5 hours, and afterwards, we were fed a meal of rice and zuchini, bread, feta, wine and water.

After the meal, we headed back into the chapel for another small compline service and the opportunity to venerate several more relics. Here, we were allowed to look upon another fragment of the Holy Cross, the right hand of Saint John the Baptist, the skulls of Sts. Christopher and Bartholomew, pieces of the bodies of Sts. Peter and Paul, the right arm of St. Theodoro, and parts of newer, non-Orthodox saints' bodies, as well as a bone from the martyr Gideon, who was a 17th century monk of Karakalo.

After venerating these relics, we exited the monastery and headed back towards Philotheo. By this time of the day, my clothes had all been soiled by dirt and sweat, but we fortunately made it back to the monastery before the gates closed for the night. So, here I am once again, spilling my thoughts and reflections into this little book from Oklahoma. Not a lot of conversing is done on the mountain; even my conversations with Ian are kept to a brief minimum words. I find myself most at peace with my surrounding when I have a book in my hand. Already, I have finished <u>Game of Thrones</u>, and I am about to begin <u>Crime and Punishment.</u>

As beautiful and interesting as this journey has been, I can definitely see why very few are called to live the monastic life. As a teenager living in the 21st century, so much of my life and everyday routine involves instant gratification on top of an always busy schedule. Here, you pray, sleep and eat peaches; it's not exactly for the faint-hearted, such as myself. Although I am not quite as homesick as I was yesterday, I still find myself fretting about my return on a regular basis. I am very curious to see where the next three days take me, and I am excited for my return in only one week from the day.--End of Day Two

Mount Athos: Day Three 7-22-2015
Today was my birthday. By far and large, it was definitely the most unique of the 18 birthdays I have celebrated throughout my life. Unlike the previous 17 "celebrations" that I have experienced, there was no such party or festivities to honor the day. Similar to the previous morning, I was woken up to the continued pounding of metal, which, in my opinion, serves as a highly effective alarm clock. An additional hour-and-a-half's rest led to a 5:30 a.m. Entrance into the Monastery's chapel for morning services. After a long 2.5 hours came and went, we were ushered into the dining hall where we ate a meal of bread, marmalade, more peaches, and water. If hunger truly bares its teeth at you upon Mount Athos, then Wednesdays and Fridays are a challenge unlike no other. I have trained my stomach to allow my body to get by on only a few portions of food per day.

Going to bed hungry and waking up in the same fashion is no longer a foreign feeling to me. After pocketing a peach, I headed back to my room to pack and get ready for the travel to Dafne, where we would be boarding a ferry to St. Anna's monastery. After an hour's travel, we arrived in Dafne to the comforting sight of civilization (in this case, more than 20 individuals). With the absence of outside communication greatly affecting my well-being over the previous two days, I began a frantic search for wifi or any means to contact any family from back home. After drawing much ridicule on my first attempts to ask for wifi/telephone usage, I finally met a store owner who allowed me to purchase a phone card that was valid for five minutes.

    Although I knew the time difference was too great to expect a response, I nonetheless placed a call for my home. I wanted to leave a message for my parents so they knew I was doing well on my birthday, but the lack of response only prompted me to believe that maybe my call didn't go through. After five more calls later that day, I was finally able to briefly speak to my grandmother, Yiayia Artemis. It was very comforting to hear a familiar voice, especially on a day where I've grown accustomed to a mass influx of notifications wishing me a happy birthday. As mentioned greatly throughout this journal, being in a situation like mine—not knowing much of the language, being cut off from communication, having a complete change in culture—it all makes you realize how comforting home is, wherever that may be. I can only recall another incident where I truly missed home to the point of near-sickness, and that was five years ago at Camp Hale, which is, in fact, in Oklahoma. Back then, as a small twelve year old, I was lucky enough to have my dad come drive in for the rescue and my mom to talk to over the phone every night. Here, I have nobody, and although I may now be an official "adult", I wish I had my parents to come fly in for another glorious rescue. Regardless, I still have another two days without communication so I will have to make due with the few conversations I share with Ian. After placing the initial phone call, I was tasked with the issue of having to find a storage unit for my mammoth of a suitcase. This proved to be a real challenge, considering how limited my Greek is. It's not like I was ready and willing to just drop my bag off with some stranger at the port, either.

Our itinerary called for an hour and a half's walk from St. Anna's monastery to St. Paul's. This hike would take place on Friday, and between today (Wednesday) and then, Ian would be summiting the actual Mt. Athos. One look at that mountain told me that there was no possible way that I'd make it to the peak and back in a 24 hour period, so now I was facing the issue of having to separate from Ian for nearly a day and a half. Reluctantly, I agreed to the proposition, and fortunately, found a store owner who would hold my bag for me. However, five minutes after leaving my bag, I knew that there was no way that I'd be willing to make that big of a risk. Ian and I decided on a sudden change in the itinerary, one that wouldn't require many transportations of my suitcase, and one that didn't involve Ian making the hike to the peak and back. We boarded a small ferry and made our way towards St. Dionysios monastery, which is built into the side of the mountain. If you google search "Mount Athos", you will most likely come up with a picture of this particular monastery. It's a massive structure, split into four quadrants, and at all times of the day, you can hear/feel massive waves of wind flooding the grounds of the monastery.

We made our way up to the gates, found our room, and took a three-hour nap before evening services began. After the service, we were treated to a meal of an unknown bean soup, a watermelon rind, baby pears and bread. A man gave me a slice of watermelon, and I almost reached across the table to hug him. After dinner, we headed back to the room, prepared for bed and stayed up for a couple of hours talking about random topics. Now, as an end to one of the most interesting birthdays I've ever experienced, I'm here in my small, creaky bed getting ready for another short night's sleep; it's quite the far cry from a typical hometown birthday, but hey, not many people can say they celebrated their birthday by living as a monastic for a day. - End of Day Three

P.S. Compline this evening introduced us to several new relics, including body parts from St. John the Baptist, St. George, St. Nymphon, the Theotokos as well as another piece of the Holy Cross, along with an icon made from beeswax that is said to have floated all the way back to the monastery after being stolen by the Turks. (it's myrrh streaming too, so that's pretty unique)

Mt. Athos: Day Four 7-23-2015
"CLANG! CLANG!" "KNOCK, KNOCK, KNOCK". My fourth morning on Mount Athos began in a fashion much similar to the previous days spent at Philotheo. The homemade alarm system seems to be a popular fix amongst all of the monasteries here on the mountain. Instead of jumping out of bed and trudging over towards the chapel, however, we decided to take an additional few minutes to nap and get some extra rest in. Well, five minutes turned into seven hours, and by 11:00 am., we were finally well-rested for the first time in nearly a week. After gathering our bags and eating what little snacks we had left over (we missed breakfast), we made our way down the monastery (St. Dionysios) and waited for the ferry for two hours. A ten minute ferry ride took us to the St. Paul's monastery, which too is built into the side of the mountain. After a monk's greetings and a complimentary tray of water, tsiporo ouzo and Turkish Delight, we settled into our room at around 2:00 pm where we napped for four hours until evening services come around. Upon arriving at the chapel, which was far larger than the previous three I had entered during my time on the mountain, I realized how architecturally different each monastery had been. Philotheo was modest and plain, much like its monks, Karakalo was characterized by its tall, white tower. St. Dionysios was a behemoth of a mountainside structure and heavily reminiscent of Lord of the Rings and St. Paul's was a lavish, built-up structure with massive walls and a grand church.

An hour-long service led to dinner at 7:00 pm which consisted of wine, squash and fish, bread, water and wait for it-- MORE PEACHES! After only eating a few bites of the meal (my stomach has shrunk significantly) I exited the dining hall with my hands behind my back. A monk corrected me and told me not to walk with my hands behind my back. After venerating the relics, which I wasn't quite able to make out (regarding names), we headed back towards our room to check in for the night. Today was a short day compared to the previous days spent here, and it was also the first day where I haven't felt extremely homesick. I think getting closer and closer to returning to Ouranoupoli has wiped away all of my worries about missing home and outside communication, and I'm sure tomorrow---my last day on the mountain- will be the most enjoyable day that I'll have during this pilgrimage. Until then, I'm hopping in bed, popping in my headphones, and going to sleep. Peace out, reader. – End of Day Four

Mount Athos: Day Five 7-24-2015
Today was my last full day on Mount Athos. As I stated way back on day one, *there's really nothing that can compare to the experience.* Though I started out my journey as a scared, homesick traveler, I've grown accustomed to the complete change in culture. A few nibbles on a peach can tide me over for nearly a full day, a four-hour prayer service is a walk in the park, and cold showers are as common as breathing or blinking your eyes. Still, as ordinary as my surroundings may seem, I will never come to embrace the nightly struggle of falling asleep in a furnace. My sleeping schedule is completely out of whack, and with as few hours of sleep I may get per day, I can never ease my way into slumber on the mountain. That being said, I am extremely excited to make the ferry back to Ouranoupoli in a few short hours. *Solitude and deep contemplation really allow you to embrace the small things*

in life, such as talking to your family, eating a full meal, or sleeping in your own bed.

The excitement began this morning after another four-hour morning Orthros and Liturgy, followed by a feast of bread and marmalade. A 45-minute nap session quickly turned into a full blown sprint to the ferry, which we very nearly missed. A ten minute boat ride took us from St. Paul's monastery to St. Gregory's, where we currently are right at this moment. After napping for a few hours (this time, in a room with one fellow American from Maine), we headed up a very steep hill for evening services, a dinner of fruits and more unknown soup, and veneration of the relics, which included body parts from St. Gregory, St. Anastasia, St. Damian, the Samaritan Woman's cranium, St. Dionysios of Athen's cranium, and another piece of the Holy Cross.

After this collection of events ended, we met up with our roommate (whose name I don't quite remember) and headed back towards our quarters. I had the most entertaining conversation over the past week or so with this random stranger. No shock, it was all about professional basketball. So finally, for the last time, I'm recording the final words into this journal, which I hope will inform whoever is reading this about the overall experience that Mount Athos has been for me over the past week. I'll try to add some closing remarks on the ferry tomorrow, but if I don't get around to doing so, I hope you enjoyed hearing my tale on the Holy Mountain, and I can't wait to be back home.-- End of Day Five —
-Mark Constantine Kingsley

Our Youngest Son's Interview on Travel

I INTERVIEWED MY youngest son about his traveling experiences. He was fourteen years old at the time of this interview.

"My favorite thing about our trips is experiencing things you can't find in your hometown. The best parts are the beaches, new environments and seeing how different things can be.....like the bazaars we've been to. The worst part about traveling is going through the airports and not being able to get to what you want to do when you want to.

My favorite trip of all time was Switzerland because it started with Switzerland and it ended with Greece. The tiny little city of Churwalden up in the Alps was my favorite place. The weather was cool and the air was fresh. We didn't have to go into a city to sightsee....it was just calm. I also loved Hawaii because of the nice beaches and the natural wonders that are unique. We had fruit at breakfast that we've never even heard of before.

My advice is to always be ready to be going somewhere and be sure to have the energy to do it. Getting enough sleep and eating the right foods help you have the energy. The craziest thing I saw was a naked man walking down a major street in Spain. The best artifact I've seen was the thorn from Jesus's "crown of thorns" in the Seville Cathedral. The most fun thing I did was ride the waves in Hawaii and Mexico. My favorite transportation was ferries. I liked the short distance of going between countries. On the plane, it's good to always have music and earphones. Appreciate your time while you are there and keep a journal. I'm glad that my mom made me keep a journal because I enjoy reading it now!"

These interviews with my sons were simple and heartfelt summaries of such complex and intricate trip destinations and lessons. Remembering my oldest son's docent moments of Ireland, leading us to the Cliffs of Moher to St. Patrick's Cathedral and our middle son's docent tour of Spain from sights in Seville to facts of the Alhambra and our youngest son's docent moments of Scottish castles to the St. Andrew's birthplace of golf are all strong historic features among their simple pleasures of just appreciating the bonds of humanity and the diversity of global awareness and respect.

The DNA of Wanderlust

"You can't know where you're going unless you know where you've been." The latter quote always appealed to me because I grew up with a strong sense of roots. Reflecting on this quote, I think it's important to interject some my wanderlust "DNA" in analyzing how my family travels developed. I came from two parents who experienced exotic world traveling in their youth and it's appropriately romantic that they ended up together. My father traveled to fifty five countries between his time in the Merchant Marines and later because of his American Airlines employee benefits. My mother took six months off of high school to travel with relatives to Greece, France, Turkey and Egypt in the most original and authentic "travel abroad program" designed for her by my grandmother and great-aunt. What alchemy transpired when my parents ended up being able to combine their well rounded global awareness with airlines privileges later on in their marriage and family life! I conducted several interviews with my parents and relatives on my travel blog and I am including them here in their interview format for a conversational feel between the two of us.

Recently, I recorded a list of the countries my father has been to but I never knew specific details about his job duties until I interviewed him. Wisdom and resilience are two nouns that come to mind when people think of him. He has zillions of proverbs and inspirational quotes. He defines *swagger* and his story is as humorous as he is. I interviewed my father about his experience in the Merchant Marines and the conversation that evolved revealed more insight about him.

Why did you join the Merchant Marines?

I was nineteen years old and it was a good opportunity. I had to help support my family back home in Greece because my father died at fifty seven years old.

Did you have to take a test? Were there any requirements?

I needed a Seaman's Passport or Seaman's papers. I saw a job in the newspaper in the village square....an ad asking for people to work on ships. I worked in the Navy as an employee on the *Hephaestus* ship. That ship had 200-300 employees and we serviced other ships; their motors, pumps, pipes,....I spent three years like that. We picked up old WWII airplanes that had sunk in the ocean. I departed from Piraeus to go to Alexandria, Egypt then onto France because we were on a French ship. My duties were as an assistant electrician on the ship *Mediterranea* where I learned the skills on the job. On one ship we went to Istanbul, Israel, Lebanon, Turkey and Tunisia which is next to Libya. We took an airplane from Athens to Cairo and Suez, Egypt and from there took a ship to England transporting the oil. Then onto Venezuela and Argentina and back and forth to Venezuela before going onto San Francisco.

I was on the *Meditteranae* for 6 months, then went to Egypt by airplane. I worked for three years for the Royal Navy before this. After San Francisco, Curacao, New York and back and forth there, I went to Aruba, Cartagena, Columbia and loaded up to go to England. Back and forth. Then, onto Morocco. We spent a few days there and went onto Jamaica and Baton Rouge. Back and forth.

There was something that happened that was very significant. On a ship going to Jamaica, there was seaweed that made a big clump that floated close to the ship. If the ship got too close, the pump sucked it in and stopped up the pipes. Then we'd have no electricity and we'd be in emergency mode. We couldn't start the engines with no electricity. Everyone was desperate and confused. I had a thought that if I unplugged the weeds from one pipe, then, the water would go the other direction where the pipe was clean. It could've flooded the ship. When I cleaned that area, it was 140 degrees in the engine room and I was down there by myself. I started that generator back up and it fired the boilers and started the pump from the bottom of the ship and pushed the water out. The lights and fan came on, the ship cooled down and started running again. When I looked up, everyone came down to the boiler room cheering for me! The cook, the captain, the whole crew was surprised to find me there. They thanked me and the cook brought me a case of sodas as a gift. We started the engines and went to Jamaica. It was a controversial situation. If I failed, I might have flooded the ship. I was 23 years old at the time. They were supposed to give me a medal by the company who owned the ship….a badge of honor because we almost lost the ship. The whole crew was responsible. I never received the medal because I didn't stay on. I jumped ship in Baton Rouge and took a Greyhound Bus to Tulsa. I went there to visit relatives, met your mother and the rest was history. It was like I woke up and found myself with a baby and then two babies. (Another guy also jumped the ship and went to New York and found a job there.)

What happened leading up to this was that your mother's cousin- in- law came to Tulsa (from Greece). He was engaged to your mother's cousin. Your mom introduced him to me. He brought a bottle of wine for your mom from the doctor suitor who was intending to marry your mom. The doctor suitor was still back in Greece. I drank his wine with your mom's cousin in law. (He said this chuckling). So, he was never able to give her the bottle of wine from her suitor.

You drank his wine and you took his girl?!
Yes. And your mom's cousin in law told her that I was the better deal and that she'd be better off with me. The doctor suitor back in Greece wanted a dowry anyway. Your grandpa was confused about all this. He wanted the other man to marry your mother.

Writer's side note: (my dad and mom's cousin in law became dear friends and relatives. Their fathers-in-law were business partners and brothers-in-law. Their children were not just cousins but

best buddies and now their grandchildren are cousins and best buddies.

After a short courtship, we married. She arranged for me to get a lawyer so that we could handle the situation of me jumping ship. We went to the police station and the lawyer told them that I was confused and was supposed to go to New York but ended up in Tulsa. They fingerprinted me and told me I had 20 days to leave the U.S. My father in law was exhausted from worry about all this. (I stayed in the U.S.) We considered going to Mexico if we needed to but a few months after all this, I went to Canada on a Greyhound Bus alone and entered the states legally in order to stay married.

Back to the Merchant Marines job, did you encounter any other danger on your voyages ?

Yes, hurricanes! And icebergs. We never knew they were coming because there was no communication. ...only the wind. There were icebergs in the North Atlantic but we never saw them in the nighttime. We just watched the temperature of the water and if it dropped fast, we stopped because it meant the iceberg was coming. We'd turn and go the other way. I was caught in many hurricanes. We went against the waves of the ship, otherwise the ship would tilt. *"If you manage to face the waves, you have a good chance to survive."*

My father's experience in the Merchant Marines embodies everything about travel and adventure so I delved into another chapter in that story. This is what my father told me...

"In 1957 in New Orleans, two ships collided at midnight. I was on duty. Everyone was alert. I remember many bats gathering all over the ship. We stayed two days until better weather came. This collision was covered in the newspaper.

"November 30, 1957, the SS Ellin and SS Claiborne collided....The Coast Guard said Friday it will investigate a ship collision on the Mississippi River and dense fog about 11:55 PM Thursday 13 miles downstream from New Orleans...No injuries were reported but both cargo vessels had deep gashes in their bows...Neither ship took on water as the damage was above the waterline....Involved were the one-year-old SS Ellin 16,000 ton freighter of Liberian registry and the Waterman 15 ship corporation SS Laybourne AC 2cargo ship…The Ellin, according to Captain Michael Worden present at the Texas Marine transport company Inc. agents Alan was anchored in the thick fog…The Claiborne ran into Ellin's bow…."

(He explained the mechanics of what happens when they hit rough seas or hurricanes, too.) When a propeller comes up, we had to slow down the engine. When the ship goes down, we closed the steam…… when it goes up, we opened the steam. This went on for four hours. If you miscalculate, the engine goes too fast.

Did you ever regret being in the Merchant Marines?
No. I was lucky I never got seasick. Lots of guys vomited. A couple of times, we had the icon of Agios Nikolaos (St. Nicholas) for hope to save us.

Tell me about some of the dangers and disasters.
There was a time when the captain had his family posing for a picture and a wave came up and picked up the three year old boy. He fell in the ocean. We stopped the ship, turned around in big panic and confusion. We found him but he was dead. This was on a trip from Iran to London.

Another time, the assistant cook went to dump trash and he fell in, too. We never stopped that time…nothing…just "goodbye." The waves are so bad and you have to hit the waves a certain way. You can't always turn back.

On another ship, (going from San Francisco to Curacao) our propeller hit a whale and damaged the propeller. It took two months to sail because the propeller was going so slow. You can't change ships in the middle of the ocean. From San Francisco to Curacao, in the Los Angeles area, we had to go to Norfolk for repairs. We saw the whale with blood all over it.

What are the ports like? Which were the most exciting?
We found places to eat good food or buy things. The islands and the ports in the Caribbean were the best---Curacao, Colombia, Venezuela… The worst port was England I guess because there was no sunshine or good food.

Which country had the best looking women?
When you're on a boat for a month and come out, every woman looks good. (chuckling). Brazil, I guess.

When you left the Merchant Marines and moved to Tulsa- what was your first job there?
Shortly after the ships collided in New Orleans, I left the ship and went to Tulsa to visit relatives, get married and started a new life there. I worked at the Tulsa Hotel overseeing the boilers. They had two boilers and had to run both to keep up. There was steam for laundry and the air conditioning. An engineer at Wonder Bread (where your mom was working) told me about that job at Tulsa Hotel.

Around that time, immigration officers came to our house to deport me. Your mom told them I was working at the Tulsa Hotel. She called our priest (who was my uncle) and said, "Kosta's in trouble."

The priest came to my work to intervene. The immigration officers told me to go to the immigration office in Dallas. I did and then went on to Toronto to fix my papers and entered the states legally through the Detroit office.

What would you have done if they deported you?
I would've gone back to Greece. But by leaving Greece in the first place to join the Merchant Marines to help support my mother, sisters and younger brother back home, I wasn't drafted. In Greece, everyone has to go to the army at twenty years old.

Why is it called "Merchant Marines" ?
We transported merchandise. (the merchant part). A "marina" is another word for a "port" (the marines part). A better term for it is "merchant mariners." The Merchant Marines was very educational. On some legs of the voyages, we traveled to seven countries or so. In later years, fewer people signed up for it because they didn't want to do that type of work. But, it was a good opportunity and a very good financial opportunity for helping support my family back in Greece.

My Mother's Fabulous First Journey

MY MOTHER AND her two first cousins traveled with their mothers to Greece, Turkey, France and Egypt in 1950. It was the first time they were going to meet their grandmother. Mom was approximately fifteen years old at the time and she and her cousins took six months off of school to take this journey. They had to go to summer school to make up for the absence. They sailed on the ship Neptune (how appropriate for Greeks!) to Greece and they returned on the Queen Mary ship. Because my mother is deceased, I interviewed my two aunts about their journey. My aunt explained that they sailed on the lowest level of the ship to save money and this caused them much seasickness.

When they arrived in Greece after the long sailing trip, they changed their American money into Greek money. My grandmother and great aunt suspected that the cashier was trying to trick them into exchanging too much money in the plan that they'd have to leave the extra money with him. My spirited and strong great aunt raised her voice to the cashier proclaiming, "I'd rather throw the leftover money into the ocean than give it to you!"

They stayed three months in their grandmother's home in their ancestral village on the island of Imvros and were immersed into authentic and antiquated village life. They went from mid-century modern American living to outhouses, wood burning fireplaces and donkey rides. The outhouses were made out of bricks built up around a hole. Fortunately, they were provided with some type of toilet paper.

The home in the village has an interesting history of hardship. Decades before this time, my great-grandfather came to America briefly to earn money and return to his village in Asia Minor to build a home with the money he saved working on the American railroad for two years. Tragically, some time later, an earthquake destroyed their new home.

My aunt recalled that they thought of this stay in the village as being in the colonial times---no running water, no electricity and no toilets. Their grandmother had a fireplace with a stool to sit on to start the fire. A funny memory my aunts have from this time is when my great-aunt (their mother) was determined to start the fire herself. As she huffed and puffed to stoke the fire, she blew so hard that she fell backwards off the stool! Her mother, exasperated by this, told her to move over and let her handle it.

They remembered their walks through the village, noticing that the figs and grapes were very big and the only meat they ate was from hunted birds or chickens that were raised on their land. They even made their own bread dough and took it to the bakery across the street to bake in the ovens there. They attended festivals held on religious feast days, recalling donkey rides and bouzouki music though the village and the occasional sighting of a handsome boy.

They went to France together for awhile before splitting up into two directions. My aunts and great-aunt went to a wedding in another town in France while my mother and grandmother went to Cairo, Egypt to see relatives. While in Paris together, they stayed in an uncle's tiny apartment with a "2 x 2" foot kitchen that was so small, you had to shop daily for food because the refrigerators were the size of college dorm refrigerators. Their uncles in Paris worked as shoemakers so my mother and her relatives had special Parisian shoes made for them. When the relatives left their Turkish-occupied village decades before, two of the brothers became shoemakers but my grandfather and his brother in law did not want to be shoemakers so they went on to America to be restauranteurs.

My aunt recalled sightseeing with my mother in Paris, going to the Eiffel Tower and Versailles, specifically. When they walked on marble steps at a particular monument, my educated and intellectual mother wistfully remarked to her cousins, *"We are walking where kings and queens have walked!"*

In remembering this comment, my aunt explained that my mom paid more attention to history than she did and most other teenagers, probably. My mom thought about Napoleon, Marie Antoinette and other historic French figures while they explored the sights.

My mother's time in Cairo, Egypt is a mystery to me because there is no one alive who can tell me details about it. All I know from my aunts is that my mother's favorite uncle bought her a special Egyptian dress. We have a picture of her posing in a robe and veil and we think it is from this time in Egypt. The enthusiasm on her face shows me her youthful spirit and reminds me that my mother was not always sick with cancer –she was once a young, vibrant, intelligent woman on a trip of a lifetime in the most exotic places of Greece, Turkey, France and Egypt—walking among the ruins where royalty have walked. I keep this framed photo in my writing study to inspire me to carry on her legacy of adventure and learnedness.

I love this memory about my enigmatic mother. It's bittersweet that I have to excavate knowledge about her from her cousins. I know there is so much more information that is missing as my relatives are elderly now and have fading memories. Since I was only sixteen when my mother died, she is largely a mystery to me. This little snippet into her "wanderlust DNA" is meaningful and powerful to me and I'm grateful for it now as I piece together our rich travel history. It bonds me to her thirty years after her death as I hope my future generations will feel bonded to me.

A Magic Carpet Ride

My Step-mother's Story: Surviving the Armenian Genocide

MY PARENTS HAVE rich histories of travel and adventure but so does my stepmother. Although she may not be a part of my formative childhood history, she has been an influential part of my adulthood so I am including her history, too. Her multicultural, international identity contributes to my daily life and my family life.

My second mother is half-Armenian, half-Greek and was born in Istanbul, Turkey. She became my stepmother when I was eighteen years old. It wasn't until I was twenty seven years old, almost ten years later, that I asked her about her genealogical history. At the time, I was pregnant with my first child and I think I was subconsciously needing a maternal figure in my life in order to feel a sense of bonding in preparation for my own child. I began to appreciate my stepmother's affectionate nature as she nurtured me. I realized that since she had no biological children and us stepchildren were her kids, it might be nice to know her history so I could share it with this new baby I was bringing into the world. It was important to know where his grandmother came from and since she was such a caregiver in his life and his brothers later on, we eventually understood where her customs and mannerisms originated from and how they influenced her behavior.

She shared her knowledge with me about being a descendant of a survivor of the Armenian genocide. I am always fascinated to ask her about her upbringing in Istanbul from parents of mixed heritages. Exotic cuisine, homeopathic practices, religious customs and superstitions are all part of her background. I interviewed her about her Armenian background as well as her Greek lifestyle, growing up in Istanbul. I translated this somewhat as she is multilingual.

Where were you born?
I was born in Istanbul. My father was Armenian and my mother was Greek. My mother was born in Istanbul. People told my grandfather to take his family from Armenia and go to Istanbul in 1915 because of the genocides. There were many Armenians in Istanbul.

What can you tell me about the Armenian genocides?
My grandfather and his family were on a train when they witnessed people sabotaging the train and lighting it on fire. Many people got off the train but many people died. My grandfather's family got off the train. He lost his fortune and had to support his family by selling containers of water on the street. He also sold Turkish carpets and worked in the auctions, pricing carpets.
   (writer's side note: She also describe other violent acts to me that occurred during the genocide.)

How many years did you live in Istanbul? What heritage did you identify with?
I lived there thirty-one years before I moved to Greece. My father's last name was Armenian but the people changed it completely to sound more Turkish. My surnames were Armenian and then Turkish but I was raised more Greek.

What customs did you practice growing up? Did you have any Armenian customs?
Just receiving Armenian Orthodox communion. After fifteen years of age, you wear a headscarf to take communion. Armenian women cannot baptize others or be a koumbara (sponsor role) in a wedding. My mother told me once I married, I'd take on my husband's Orthodoxy. I

never found an Armenian Orthodox church in Greece so I found a Greek Orthodox church.

Tell me about the cuisine you grew up with?
My mother and grandmother cooked Greek foods and Turkish foods. For example, Imam bayildi, Youverlakia, Moussaka, Baklava and Kadaifi are Turkish in origin. My mother cooked dolmathakia and keftethes. Antranik was an Armenian restaurant in Bosphurus and the chef made Topik which is a garbanzo dish. (a vegetarian meatball with a chickpea-paste.)

Tell me about Istanbul. Describe it.
There are four islands near Istanbul, across from Bosphorus: Proti, Antigone, Halki and Pringipo. Halki had a seminary and a Turkish navy. Pringipo had beautiful houses! Every Sunday, after we went to a Greek Orthodox church in Istanbul, we'd have lunch in Bosphurus. It was beautiful in Istanbul, but in 1954 there was vandalism. Churches were burned and stores were looted. Cyprus was separated in 1974 in a Greek-Turkish conflict.

Describe the homeopathic practices that you've told me about before.
My dad took me to a hodja (a Muslim priest) who cut my skin between my eyebrows to help me heal from jaundice. Another jaundice treatment the hodjas recommended to people involved drinking urine. My mom gave us a daily, morning drink of mournolatho which is an oil. It smelled so bad, I closed my nose. (pinched her nostrils together). Then we ate an orange after it.

Tell me about the superstitions that were part of your background. I remember you telling me about them when I had my first son.
A superstition for mothers and newborns was for new mothers to put a dirty diaper under their doormat for forty days. When visitors came over and stepped on a doormat, they didn't know that they were stepping on top of a diaper. It was supposed to ward off the exposure of germs.

Another superstition I practiced was to never take a knife or scissors from a person's hand. They had to put it down first and then I'd take it. It was believed that you'd avoid a fight or conflict this way. Also, if someone gave you soap, you were supposed to give them back a coin.

(Writer's side note: my sons have noticed that she handles scissors and knives this way.)

What is your favorite thing about moving to America when you got married ?
Everything! It was so different.... the lifestyle. Having a house and car was new to me. I lived in a house in Istanbul but in Greece, I lived in an apartment and took public transportation. *I liked everything about moving to America.*

Now that my parents' stories have been shared, it embodies the quote *"if you know where you come from, you'll know where you're going."* Since I wasn't able to record my mother's chronicles from her directly, it has been a bittersweet and enigmatic process of searching for facts about her history but I feel fortunate that I could delve into my father and step-mother's pasts while they are alive.

A Peruvian Quinceanera in Tulsa

———— ⁂ ————

You don't have to travel far sometimes to learn about different cultures. In between trips, I was fortunate enough to be involved in the Latin celebration of the quinceanera here in my own hometown. I have always been curious about quincenaras and not only was I a guest but I was able to watch my son become part of the celebration by being one of the dancers for the guest of honor. I learned so much from this experience.

A Quinceanera is a celebration of a milestone. When a young lady becomes fifteen years of age (quince) in many Latin communities, she is celebrated with this coming of age party. The event has religious undertones and can include a mass service or a blessing. Reportedly, this tradition dates back more than six hundred years to when Aztec and Mayan cultures celebrated the marriage and family eligibility of a young girl. The tradition was eventually influenced by Spaniards and developed a Catholic relationship.

The priest or minister guides the girl about her responsibilities as a woman of faith and how she can grow from that. There is symbolism in every item used: the bible, rosary, ring, last doll, earrings, shoes, etc. The tiara that is worn by the guest of honor symbolizes that the daughter is still a princess in her parents' eyes. With her mom's permission, I am sharing this celebration for educational purposes and to celebrate the diversity that is alive in Tulsa and at my sons' private school. I compared it to Southern cotillions, debutantes, the American Sweet Sixteen party and other cultures celebrating the age they consider the child reaching "maturity" or presenting the young person to society. In the Jewish culture, the Bar or Bat Mitzvah is celebrated for thirteen year olds. I jokingly told my friends at the event that the Greeks don't have such an event because they never want to let their children grow up. But of course, I was being facetious. Kind of.

Being friends with the guest of honor and her parents was the icing on the Quinceanera cake for us! Not only were we lucky enough to be invited–but our son was asked to be a participant in the event! He was one of the salsa and waltz dancers for the honoree's special event. After several Saturday morning rehearsals in a row, the friends ordered costumes, took professional photos together and practiced other important details to prepare for the big day. My son was honored to be asked to do a bible reading, too. The Quinceanera was held at a venue in our downtown and was beautifully decorated. It was heartwarming to watch the guests and friends of the family arrive to celebrate the honoree's big day.

After the blessing, speeches and dinner, the dancers presented us with the meaningful waltz in which the couples alternated and rotated so that each young man could dance with the honoree. He held her, twirled her and with no words–only emotions and gazes– each boy got his turn to celebrate her through dance.

Next was the salsa dance! The girls sat down in chairs while the boys lined up opposite them. The music started and the boys humorously and in their suave way, approached the girls. As they danced their way to the girls, the boys teasingly backed off and danced back to their side of the dance floor.

Eventually, they met in the middle and started their couples dance of salsa. The honoree and her partner had color coordinated outfits that stood apart from the other dance couples who were in gray and silver. Everyone looked glamorous!

All of us parents were proud to watch our children's skills at these intricate dances. They seemed so grown up, and yet, we could remember when some of them were in Preschool, Kindergarten or Elementary school together. My son and his best friend have been friends from the womb since my friend and I went through pregnancy together.

My husband found it bittersweet that our youngest son is already old enough to do these grown up dances. It was like a glimpse into future wedding celebrations. It definitely made me feel emotional thinking that time is slipping away from us. I can't imagine how the guest of honor's parents must have felt that night to watch their beautiful daughter reach this age of maturity.

The friends' excitement for her was so touching. The appreciation in the room was so evident and the diversity was impressive. I was excited to realize how these children found such kindred spirits in each other and from such diverse backgrounds. In this dance group alone there were children from the following backgrounds: Swedish/Finnish, Cypriot, Greek, Peruvian, and Mexican. The friends that attended were from the following backgrounds: New Zealand, (Eastern) Indian, American, etc.

The kids weren't the only ones dancing the night away. The adults danced, too! My husband and I enjoyed watching the Latin people dance. They have a swagger that is so innate and joyful. The youngsters lit up when their modern tunes came on–the deejay knew all the right hits.

As grown up as they might be becoming, I noticed my son lingering by the candy table and sneaking some candy before going on the dance floor for his big moves. Priorities. Boys will be boys. Never too old for candy!

The parents' speeches to their daughter, as well as the priest's blessing, were absolutely heartfelt and life affirming. The carefully chosen words of love, guidance and resilience imparted to this child of God were sincerely crafted from unconditional love. The honoree was graceful, poised and reverent on her special day. She seemed groomed for this event. I have known her since she was a little girl– beautiful and elegant with bright eyes and a genuine love of friendship. She is a good reflection of her Peruvian and American heritage. I feel so fortunate to be included in this milestone and to be part of the Latin culture at this event.

"What's Down in the Basement?"

My Gypsy Family Travel blog led to magazine travel writing opportunities which coincided with epiphanic moments that lent themselves to more creativity. Objects I had around the house seemed to "make themselves known to me" or reappear from garage storage or even attic storage as I kept up with seasonal purging and editing. Was it a sign that as I prepare for the empty nest, I was finding items that contributed to the creativity that was helping my writing?

> "Imagination is more important than knowledge. For knowledge is limited to all we now know and understand, while imagination embraces the entire world, and all there ever will be to know and understand."
>
> -- Albert Einstein

This quote applies to everyone no matter what your vocation. I *imagine* (pun intended) we all relate to this quote. When I took the time to digest its words, it made me remember which childhood imagination events influenced me. Certain childhood imagination tools I had in my basement playroom influenced my future vocations and interests. The wonderful thing about the pre-electronic games era is that our playtime was perhaps more inventive, creative and definitely, more imaginative.

Now, in my season of travel writing, I've come across some items from my childhood had some epiphanies about the conception and origins of my desire for tourism and travel agencies.

Recently, I literally unearthed an item from my childhood home's attic-- an old Remington typewriter! It was covered with dust, soot and hopefully, not asbestos from our 1920's attic. It was a heavy antique but so pristine, dramatic and proud! I was immediately flooded with memories of a similar typewriter we had from Goodwill and how I used it in my childhood basement playroom. My older sister was always bringing home unique things from estate sales or Goodwill. I used to use a vintage typewriter as a pretend cash register with my best friends. I had a pretend grocery store in my basement because my parents stored overflow groceries down there as a pantry. One of the friends would go "shopping" and put the canned goods and boxed goods in her "shopping basket" and one of us would ring up the items on the antique typewriter which was posing as a cash register. Since the return bar had a wonderful "DING", it seemed like a cash register.

On the nearby table which we unknowingly fashioned as a partner desk, I had another business going on...a travel agency. My sister brought home some tourism department books she found at a school library that was closing. They were about all of the provinces of Canada. They were old and outdated but I thought they were fabulous and resourceful! I can still envision the photos of lush green forests in those old books. On a vintage rotary dial (again heavy) black phone, (which really worked) I chatted away with pretend customers, setting up wonderful trips to anywhere in Canada....and only Canada...because those were the only tourism books I had at my fingertips. At nine or ten years old, I could design you a trip to Nova Scotia. Later, I discovered this delicate Paris travel brochure that made it in my move to the new house. If I had it in my pretend travel agency, I could've designed you a trip to any province in Canada---and Paris.

It reminded me about a conversation I had at seven years old. I told my mom and brother that I wanted to be a tourist when I grew up...as my job. My mom skeptically asked me in her practical minded Greek mom way, "How are you going to make money doing that?!" My 16 year old brother waited for the reply to see if my critical thinking skills would apply here. I was kind of baffled and deflated and asked her, "what do you mean??". She replied, "That's a hobby but how is that a *job*?" I stated, "I don't know!" My brother chuckled but didn't want to discourage me.

My mom technically didn't discourage me either but she showed me there was a realistic side to consider when you're imagining and making plans. I wasn't ready to give up on this tourist job idea. Ironically, my grandmother's old passport was discovered years later when I moved to my new home. It was intact, glamorous, full of historic travels and a most important pilgrimage of taking her daughter, (my mother) back to Greece, Turkey, France and Egypt to meet relatives for the first time. My maternal grandparents were political refugees in the 1920's leaving their Turkish-occupied Greek island to come to America.

I worked well alone on this pretend travel agency and it became kind of hectic one day in the travel agency/grocery story basement when two playmates came over. Innovation turned to mischief and someone got the bright idea to change my serious travel agency ambience into a phone call pranking headquarters and we started calling random numbers and doing the usual 1970's pranking scripts, ("Did you order a pizza? etc,) "One of the playmates got nervous when someone answered and in handing the heavy vintage phone over to the other friend, it got too close to her face and she chipped our friend's tooth! That's how heavy the phone was. We panicked. The friend caught the piece of her tooth in her hands and went to find her parents. The playdate was OVER. And my travel agency was tainted, in my opinion. We had our first casualty! Our friend went to the dentist over this mishap. The phone sits innocently in a nook at my sister's home. Whenever I see it, I consider it a culprit to a prank....and a chipped tooth!

A calling to become an educator took center stage in my life when my baby cousins were born. They became my little students and there was no pretending about it! We had a true neighborhood style "homeschool" going on for a few years and a full curriculum designed by me, a seven to eleven year old and my little cousins were the experimental students.

The tourist job fantasy didn't exactly take a backseat though. I was able to travel extensively as a child of an American Airlines employee because of the flight privileges and hotel discounts. My mom was talented at making all of the complicated connections possible and I listened intently as she made our "non-rev" flights and details. This was the heyday of travel, in my opinion. When the flight attendants looked like Miss America contestants and people dressed up to fly! First class seats were so available to us "non-rev" (non-revenue) passengers and I even got to be a flight attendant on one flight.

I passed out peanuts, spoke on the intercom, saw the cockpit and sat with those stunning "glamazon" flight attendants in their special section when we were landing.

Years later, I helped friends with their trip itineraries and made recommendations to them on which stops and excursions to take off of cruise ships in Greece, etc. This was all for fun and I loved it when the recommendations were appreciated. But what a full circle moment from that pretend travel agency in my basement with all of my vintage and antique props!

On these wonderful family trips, I remember my dad's new camera--a Minolta Super 3 Circuit. That was a big deal. It even had a leather strap and case. I was able to use it later for a photography course at my high school. I remember my grandpa's old accordion style camera, too and I found a similar style camera and display it as a reminder of all of the meaningful vintage items that I was surrounded by in my childhood. It created an appreciation for historic items….things made with artistry and value. Those items represented challenges, adventures, voyages, journeys and risk taking for my immigrant ancestors entering into the New World for a New Life.

In this same childhood basement where imagination and discovery collaborated, there was one other item displayed which was a part of my daily images whenever I passed by the living room mantel….the GEISHA GIRL. That's what we called her. Geisha had a marvelous glass case box that in which she was displayed. It was as if she was stored away and protected from the elements. She could look out but she was untouchable. I was bewitched by the geisha girl. She had a Mona Lisa smile and a gaze that was averted. She was an enigma to me. I loved that my Greek mom and Greek household had this "oriental" (as we called it in the 70's) item prominently displayed over our fireplace! It was not a house only full of Greek columns, Greek keys and busts of Apollo or Aphrodite. We had those things, too- of course. But Geisha Girl had a presence in our home and conveyed that we appreciated international souvenirs of all kinds.

My best friend was always intrigued with the glass case that surrounded the geisha and strangely, years later, somehow the case broke. Geisha Girl was freed! I liked her even better that way. I felt like, finally, geisha was out of the case and not untouchable. We could enjoy her delicate details up close. She moved with us to our new house but she was not up high anymore on a mantel. She became the centerpiece of our dining room table or buffet. And in some ways, she represents to me that I, too, have passed down an appreciation for international culture for my sons. I appreciate that my family did not toss out those old items. We incorporated them into our childhood imagination play. As adults, we later displayed them in our homes. Currently, they are inspirational "props" for me in my writing study. They connect me to my roots. In creative writing, it is nostalgic to think of those childhood influences. Life was black and white but evolved towards gray. In those shades of gray, I delve into interviewing others about their travels, inspirations and passions. That has been good for the soul!

"When you're talking, you are only repeating what you already know. But when your'e listening; you're learning." In travel writing and interviewing people about their travels and stories, I am listening....and learning. As a travel writer, I am surrounded by my inspiration props-- an antique typewriter, antique cameras, and an antique phone while I use my modern day laptop, my modern camera and my handy cell phone as my tools. It's funny to think one day these modern day gadgets will be antiques to the next generations.

I love being surrounded by these childhood imagination props. They are from a pre-electronic game time; pre-social media, pre-computers, pre-cell phones. A time when we had imaginary play in droves in the backyard, neighborhood alleys or down in the basement. I am not quite fifty years old but I'm almost there. The props were there in the first half-century of my life and now they are being useful again in the next half-century. *And where knowledge is limited, imagination is limitless.*

Be Happy for This Moment

My favorite trip memories aren't necessarily the monumental moments like the Taj Mahal and elephant rides. Rather, they are the unexpected surprises of discovering yourself in a moment so foreign or exotic or so simple and esoteric. My favorite trip memories have ranged from tasting cardamom in my Arabic coffee for the first time in the Emirates Lounge to enjoying a surprise birthday cake served to me in the Emirates Business Class bar lounge and drinking champagne with the glamorous flight attendants, my sister-in-law and a mother with a baby. My favorite trip moments have included drinking wine, exhausted at night, on the hotel balcony overlooking the Taj Mahal and being delirious with excitement for the next morning's tour of the massive monument. Other favorite moments have included realizing a monkey ate our orange from the fruit basket of our hotel room balcony in India or our van breaking down in the middle of nowhere between Agra and Jaipur and having to find a restaurant with air conditioning. We ended up having a cold beer with the wait staff on their break and bonding instead of panicking.

Other spontaneous discoveries included being driven around in Manzanillo, Mexico by our villa's van driver and seeing a man sell Richard Pryor wigs on the street. One of us yelled out in disbelief, "Who would buy a Richard Pryor wig?!" And I think I was the one who replied, "**We** should!" **We** should buy a Richard Pryor wig!!" While most of our van seemed game for it, my thirty year old niece leaned her forehead against the back of the van seat in front of her and whispered, "No, no....no!" in embarrassment. As chic as our villa experience was in Manzanillo, it was this hilarious moment driving in downtown Manzanillo that exposed us to these wigs that define our trip memories. Our daily drive into downtown Manzanillo for an iced coffee at Starbucks was a little treat in the middle of the day.

Our talent show, poetry nights and margarita-assisted card games around the large patio table were favorite memories that probably ranked higher than deep sea fishing and all terrain vehicle rides. Again, it was that realization that "this moment is your life." Our lives are made of moments.

The Greek Muses

IT'S SERENDIPITOUS HOW things evolve and how vivid memories or concepts influence one's writing. When I was a girl, I was fascinated with the Greek muses. In mythology, it wasn't the goddesses and demi-gods that interested me—it was the nine muses: Calliope, Clio, Euterpe, Thalia, Melpomene, Terpsichore, Erato, Polyhmnia, and Urania. These creatures represented skills in the arts and sciences. They represented inspiration, not power like the gods. Rather than magic, power, rage and lust in the stories of the gods and goddesses, I was intrigued by the educational forces of the muses. Their power was their knowledge. They inspired the arts and sciences in the mythological realm.

As a young student, I learned more about the muses because of the movie Xanadu in which Olivia Newton-John played one of the muses. She recited part of the poem *Kubla Khan* by Samuel Taylor Coleridge. With the help of my twenty-one year old brother, I located the poem at the library and memorized it. My brother filled me in on Kubla Khan's place in history and I learned that Samuel Taylor Coleridge reportedly took opium when he wrote that poem. Concepts such as these were pretty advanced for a twelve year old but that's what I loved about my big brother---he was a Pandora's Box of information for me; you never knew what was going to come out of him.

Our middle school had a speech festival and in the category of poetry, I signed up to recite *Kubla Khan*. I felt such a connection to the poem because of my fascination with the muses and my love for the quirky, whimsical movie, Xanadu. Images like "an incense-bearing tree", "dulcimer, and "lyre" gave me such rich visuals for how I conceptualized art to look. A love of words was formed then. Years later, I subconsciously integrated the muses' influence again when I realized I had pursued degrees in both arts and sciences. They both held vocations for me and I couldn't and wouldn't "choose between them." "Greekmuse" became my email address name and my personalized license plate decades after my initial interest in the muses. It was all tongue in cheek, of course. My father and I had long conversations on car rides naming all nine Greek muses and their crafts and disciplines.

I was not referring to myself as a muse but rather, I was expressing that I hold the muses near to my heart and psyche. They inspire me.

When I began to work in more than one field area at a time, another subconscious thing happened. My home office was in my kitchen—a clinical and sterile environment with sunny windows and a big island to spread out my work. However, when I started travel writing, I found myself drawn to my dining room. This ambience was different from the kitchen—an inner sanctum. Rather than the sterile, bright, clinical kitchen which was fine for statistical writing with background noise going on and the view of my dog, cat and hens coming to the French doors to distract me, I was in a warm, eclectic and exotic "womb" of a room with no access from the pets to distract me. No background noise and no bright sun in the room ---just surrounded by travel souvenirs to inspire me and vintage items from my family. It lent itself to the creative mood I needed to be in to draw out the thoughts that were emotional and visceral---not statistical and editorial. It was like "wearing two hats"; I worked in two rooms.

When I wanted to put on my educational consultant hat, I worked in the kitchen. When I wanted to write creatively, I went into the new writing study which was my dining room. This was appropriate considering it was the dining room table where my sons and I created trip itineraries together, researched countries and played international board games. This purpose breathed new life into the dining room. A bookshelf went up and my wonderful vintage items which seemed to reappear in my life mysteriously, were displayed on the bookshelf.

A Magic Carpet Ride

Editing the garage and basement in an effort to purge and prepare for the empty nest was why I found many of these items. They found a proper place in the home again. My father and grandfather's old cameras were symbolic since I was experimenting more with photography and received my first photo credit in a magazine. The vintage typewriter that was discovered in my childhood home was symbolic of all the writing I was doing on my laptop computer. The antique phone in my sister's house and the vintage stores I covered on my blog were symbolic of my pretend travel agency I had as a kid. My writing study's bookshelf now had travel guides, books and magazines I referenced to create real travel guide stories---not pretend. My grandmother's passport and Paris travel brochure which has been displayed on a shelf, seemed to also reveal a new purpose to me—as they joined the items on my bookshelf.

Old black and white photos were given to me by a special aunt when I started interviewing my mother's relatives about her youth. My aunt had also been purging her items when she became a widow and had to make changes in her residence. She wanted my sister and I to have some of these treasured photos of our mother. A small globe joined the collection. My porcupine quills from Africa given to me by a dear friend went into a vase from India given to me by a former student. A wooden camel to remind me of our trip to Morocco, Africa stood next to a glass container of vintage postcards. My sister gave me a jewelry box of my mother's pins, brooches, earrings, and jewelry. Inside the jewelry box, a little mosaic guitar pin reminded me of my musical sons so I pinned it to the leash of the wooden camel. Typewriters of all sizes became my new collectible as well as vintage cameras in their original stately leather cases—a bit tattered and weathered but just how I liked them—showing their wear, tear and history. These cameras had *been* places and to me, they represented what I was trying to capture in travel writing---covering places where people have been. The manual leaflets in the camera cases were special to find because I was currently perusing camera manuals in the hopes to learn more photography skills and features. I related to the stranger who owned this manual at one time---knowing what it's like to be excited to be on a quest to figure out new equipment that will capture and record your photojournalism archives of adventures.

A basket to hold my numerous travel journals was also in my writing study for easy reference. Along with facts and itinerary resources, I found humorous anecdotal memories of things the boys said and did on these trips. Writing those travel journals for all these decades was something I felt compelled to do, not even realizing that they'd ever be used in publications someday.

Passing down this habit to my sons was so worthwhile because the boys have their journals as keepsakes, now, too. The mosaic bull from Spain to remind me of eating Rabo de Toro in Gibraltar was displayed on a table next to other souvenirs. The Moroccan pottery we bought, next to a small silver Mexican sombrero of my mother's, combined more global imagery. A photo of my mother dressed in Egyptian clothes next to a photo of her ancestors on camels in front of the Sphinx and Great Pyramids was displayed together on the bookshelf, too. In the writing process, I realized that while traveling with my husband and children to countries on "Mother Earth", I had rediscovered my *own* mother—her memory, influences and spirit. I found her spirit again by trying to emulate her in some ways. I reflect back on some of these chapters and realize how many healthy and creative mother figures I actively connected to through the years to gain inspiration and to fill that void.

Also on the bookshelf, is a picture of Patrick and me in our twenties. We were dressed in costumes at Shakespeare's Theatre in England and the photograph reminds me of our trip to London the year we decided to start having children. It was the end of a chapter to our life together as a "couple only" but on the brink of having babies. We stood atop the edge of Warwick Castle with our arms around each other and the heavy winds blowing my new London cashmere cape around. It was the most intensely romantic memory of our pre-kids relationship. We embraced each other talking about how we knew this trip was one last adventure and splurge before bringing children into the world together. We were fine with it, too. We had been to Greece for our honeymoon, Mexico, Bahamas and

England together in those four short years. Now, looking back, I think the force of the wind, as we teetered on the ledge, was almost symbolic of the whirlwind that was awaiting us. Holding on tightly was just a foreshadowing of bracing ourselves through the future journey of having three sons in five and a half years! We were ready for a new frontier---our kids! On top of this pinnacle, we looked out onto the English countryside in front of this foreboding castle, feeling like royalty ourselves. We felt like our life together was its own fairy tale---and now, we were ready to bring in some court jesters and little princes to the mix.

The muses had done their job and several years after this, it would be the gypsy spirit that would take over.

Philanthropic Connections and Opportunities

When Gypsy Family Travel was being created, I found myself drawn to philanthropic connections. As I set out to interview people about their travels and stories, I became very interested in stories of people's passions and hobbies; some of which turned professional (like it did for me). Before I knew it, there were enough interviews that I made a menu tab on the blog called "Philanthropy." Under that section, there were interviews which included the following philanthropies or passions: soap making, candy making family tradition, jewelry designer, camp counselor for terminally ill cancer patients and their families, an orphanage missions trip, a locks for love type program, equestrian and equine photography and much, much more. I enjoyed promoting my interviewee's passions, hobbies and philanthropies and I included information on the article directing people to donate to these charities.

When I was fortunate enough to earn the magazine writing free lance job, I decided that I should donate the paychecks from those articles to charity. Each month, I chose a different charity to donate to which would also raise my awareness and the awareness of others to that charity. I announced this plan to my husband who instantly liked it, as well. I felt like it was good karma for me to do this because the blog was created to put an intention out into the world---about positive stories about world travel. When good things came back to me because of this positive energy, I thought it was even more appropriate to put any income back out into the world from the success of the creative spirit which kept generating positive energy for me.

Connecting to people's stories brought so much new information into my life. I ordered gifts from the artisans that I promoted on my blog. I wrote a piece about a relative of mine who volunteered at an orphanage. Writing that piece with her felt very inspiring for me to see her in this light and spirit of "voluntourism". I reached out to her to write about her unique travel experience to Romania for an orphanage mission trip. Writing it was meant to inspire others to consider doing such a trip but it also inspired me to remember what I loved about her genuine love for children. My effort to spread positivity was working---on me! My first writing paycheck was joyfully donated to Camp Agape; the camp for terminally ill cancer patients and their families. I began to create a list in my head of all the worthy philanthropies I was excited to donate to and promote.

When it was time to design my logo for the blog, I instantly thought of my artist friend. She had recently experienced a family tragedy and I saw on social media that she was delving into art again.

She expressed that she was using art as her therapy for healing from her loss. I was drawn to her art and I wanted to collaborate with her and participate in the positive energy of her healing. I admired her talent and her journey in the healing process. More philanthropic undertones seemed to come to the forefront of my writing experience. My artist friend designed a whimsical logo for me with my ideas and synergistic spirit and we bonded in our creativity.

I discovered a mission church in a city in Missouri when I was invited to serve meals to the homeless with a church's ladies auxiliary group. When I asked for a tour of the mission church, the priest took me and a friend through the humble and quaint Orthodox mission church. I was mesmerized by the iconography in the church and the way they acquired their items. They ran a rehabilitative program through this church and many of their staff and clergy had experienced challenges in their lives that led them to their own conversions to Orthodoxy. I instantly thought of donating my next paycheck to this program. I remembered another charity that I learned about called Reading Partners which provides tutoring and resources for local school students. I learned about the program from the friends who I happened to sit on the beach with in Dominican Republic, in fact! The ladies who sat with me under a beach umbrella, enjoying the sunset and bonding had invited me months later to a charity event that taught us about the Reading Partners program. I had never been so excited before in my life to give money to others. Altruism has such healing effects and I was ready to accept this healing into my heart.

Expanding my Gypsy Family

"....WHEN YOU'RE LISTENING, *you're learning.*" I included this phrase in my last chapter and I began to internalize it when I started to expand my gypsy family by interviewing others about their travels. This was a transformative process for me. I was taking the emphasis off of me and my blogs and writing about my own travels to include others' wisdom from their transformative experiences. By doing so, I was inviting them to become part of my gypsy family. We are all one family in this world, from a humanist standpoint. When I took a class in college called Feminist Theology (which seemed very "out there"), I discovered about myself that I prefer to think of myself as a humanist and an activist.

The blog began as an educationally-based forum that students could read also, in addition to their parents. I "put it out into the universe" for parents and children to possibly gain inspiration to create trip itineraries like we did. The yoga videos and classes always seemed to end with "put your intention out into the universe" and I was taking that to heart. In a time of such negative world news in the media and such emotionally exhaustive narratives in the newspaper, I wanted to turn away from that negativity (not blindly) and create something positive. I wanted to "cover the globe" on my travel blog with beauty and wisdom about each place on God's earth. I had traveled to many countries, several which are not even covered in this book but I had not been to ALL of them, obviously. The best way I could do that was to interview others about places unknown to me. I wanted to educate local readers on travel trend buzzwords: agriturismo, glamping, voluntourism and worldschooling.

I contacted friends and acquaintances and made appointments to meet at coffee shops. The interviewees were happy to oblige and share their own wanderlust. Off I went with my notebook, audio recording application on my Iphone and my curiosity, open heart and mind to hear what they had to share. This was a huge step for me. I was used to being the one who tells, teaches, instructs, bosses, directs, etc.... in all of the vocations I had in life. First, as a young tutor to my cousins, mentoring them. Then, as a teacher, instructing my students and implementing my lesson plans. Later, as a psychometrist, telling parents what their children's strengths and weaknesses are and telling them how to "fix the problem." Also, as a youth director, guiding and instructing kids where to go, how to greet, how to present a speech, how to address and greet a hierarch clergy, etc. As a volunteer and committee chairperson, I was needed to tell the public in media interviews, how to attend our community events and what they were for, etc. My role in life seemed to be to *talk*, to direct.

But now, my soul was telling me it was time to *listen*. There had been a change lately in one of my volunteer positions and I had to somewhat adjust one of my directorial roles which was hard to do. This void left me less busy with directing my energy to something I loved; mentoring youth. The creative juices were there but didn't seem to have an outlet. God was leading me to something in the aftermath of trying to tolerate this change in my path and to understand its purpose. For various reasons, many positive steps were made that drove me to my next creative path. So here I was, in the aural mode for a change. The interlacing of my strengths and these new auditory skills were forming an alchemy to merge with other people in the driver's seat and me as the vessel to bring forth their stories.

An educational paradigm I learned in my degree was the model of the Empty Vessel vs. the Jigsaw Puzzle approach. Teachers and professors might look at students as "empty vessels" that you fill up with crystallized knowledge and information. Or, you can look at teaching as the "jigsaw puzzle" approach, where you put the pieces out there and let the student assemble fluid reasoning into meaning. Ideally, we were told that educators should combine both methods for successful teaching. The latter made a huge impact on me as a young teacher and I shared this paradigm on Back to School night presentations with my students' parents. Now, I was incorporating it in my Gypsy Family Travel blog design. The magic carpet became part of the logo to illustrate the spirit of adventure.

In every interview I conducted, I excavated the artifacts out of my friends' hearts. I felt the wistful love of Peruvian families when my friend taught me about Peru. I felt the post-divorce strength from my friend who climbed base camp at Everest and all of the "14'ers" she ascended and overcame. I felt the impassioned and epiphanic discovery of the photographer/artist grandmother who achieved her childhood dream to see Africa. I felt the quest of the single woman who attended dance seminars in Icaria, (one of the blue zone countries) as well as her author friend who attended an immersion course there. She immersed herself in village life for several weeks, learning Greek language and so many rituals.

Some of these travelers were healing their souls and moving forward in their lives. Some travelers I interviewed were merely augmenting their knowledge and filling up their passports. One had attended a Metropolitan's enthronement in Argentina. Another had gone on a science research expedition trip to Antarctica for his job and experienced a glacier calving. I felt the ecstasy of the young traveler who achieved her dream of seeing Egypt and the equestrian mother and daughter duo who race their horses at top speed through the Colorado meadows. I learned how a newlywed couple (on a budget) designed a trip to watch the Tour de France from tiny French villages.

I learned about so many different world travel nuances in this interview process, from the dances of the Maori tribe in New Zealand to dove hunting in Argentina, to the campesinas in Peru to the Romanian orphanage mission trip (and on and on and on.....) My brain was swimming with new knowledge and I was excited to record it all. (for a future book!)

The thread throughout the interviews seemed to include the following epiphanies: many travelers embraced the road less traveled, followed their passions and learned to give up control. People who make their dreams happen on complicated journeys at great expense are typically people who are "in control" and driven. In their world travel transformations, they were led to experiences which taught them to embrace "giving up control" and discovering that they'd be alright in doing so. I know what they mean about this relinquishing of control while in a foreign place. They are talking about trusting. They are talking about the trust you learn among situations where you feel your safety might be compromised. They are talking about being in the moment and people-watching. They are talking about "far niente" and "dolce vita" versus the American work ethic. Dolce far niente means the sweetness of doing nothing as Elizabeth Gilbert so eloquently illustrated in her incredible book <u>Eat, Pray, Love.</u> They are talking about adapting to a new environment, whether it's changing your routine and circadian rhythms, participating in different social mores or trusting the unknown of flying over the Sahara desert or driving into the dunes. It is the trust required to depend on your foreign tour guide who has your safety in his hands in a private tour van in a country that proclaims to hate Americans. It is the trust of the ferry boat captain unloading us into the hot sulphuric springs of Santorini and telling us to swim back to the boat-without life preservers. (We were not Olympic swimmers and neither were the elderly people swimming with us. I floated on my back to catch my breath in spurts and somehow made it back.) It was the trust on another Santorini trip to take my sons into the hot springs with only life preserver rings from another ferry boat captain. It is the trust you give the tour guide who asks you to trust him with your passports (rule #1: don't be without your passports) so he can get you to the front of the immigration line onto the ferry boat after a day of bonding and understanding the person from another faith and political viewpoint. It is the trust of the private school mom who sleeps in sub zero degree weather on Everest Base Camp, urinating in a bottle at night and getting there by landing at the world's highest airport. It is the trust of the preppy, professional middle aged man who drank goat blood in an African tribal ritual. It is the trust of an extended family taking a sunset cruise that turns into a storm tossing your boat around which is being driven by a maniacal pirate-looking captain.

Perhaps it is a subconscious magnet that pulls us to seek enlightenment through journeys. We must know on some level that our soul needs complex layering and substance. On the surface, we think we are planning a trip for relaxation, adventure or culture but we inevitably gain much more than the original goal. We change and grow a little bit more with each journey. Even if there is the rare chance that a trip is not a positive experience, at the very least, it might make us appreciate the comforts of home more.

The thread I was hearing in these interviews was about giving up control and giving into it. It was a cosmic lesson being sent to me that I can give up some control and I'll be alright. While my sons were young, I was grateful for the control within us that is needed in parenting. I think it has its time and place. Discipline is liberating.

As the nest empties, I am likewise grateful that I am giving up some control to embrace balance and flexibility. I want to continue my interviews and magazine articles in my quest to share my spirit and the spirit of others and spread a positive message. Whether I take more trips or just continue to interview others about their trips, I look forward to spending my time in the empty nest penetrating this subject matter. Like Virginia Woolf, who wrote *A Room of One's Own*, celebrating the freedom and privacy to write, I curl up in my writing study or vacation condo to savor my thoughts and share my words.

Having the luxury of personal time now to sleep in and curl up in bed with books or notes almost seems like the last time I was in this position. Twenty years ago when I gave birth to my first son, I stayed in the hospital one day only with nurses attending to me and my newborn son being brought to me. It was the last time I probably really cocooned like that in bed for one day before embarking on the journey of motherhood which makes you think of someone else first for the first time in your life and for the rest of your life. Here I am, curled up in a bed in my condo, (my "room" of one's own) and while I'm not delivering a baby now, at age forty eight, I am "delivering" a book. My new baby is my travel writing and the newness of it.

I "put something out in the universe" and did not expect anything in return. The creativity brought balance to my scientific vocation and allowed me to connect with people in new ways. It brought me a wonderful distraction from the deafening silence that will happen when each of my sons leaves the nest, one by one. I now know that I can turn my focus to something creative and productive as I, ironically, become less productive physically as a mammal. The eggs inside me will decrease as I mature and the baby chicks will be hatching out in the real world instead of my nest and that's fine because that is what's needed in order for them to fly. Just like the airplanes we took together to see the world on our magic carpet ride, I know they will fly and I pray they will soar. The rest is still unwritten.

A Magic Carpet Ride

absorb this....

Gina Michalopulos Kingsley

A Magic Carpet Ride

The End

The following recipes have been included to relate to some of the trips that have been described in various chapters of A Magic Carpet Ride. While they are not all of the recipes and meals that we sampled on our trips, they are examples of some of the ones we prepared at home while entertaining friends. Bon appetit, Kali Orexi and Salud!

Chicken Cacciatore ala Orvieto

THIS RECIPE IS a combination of what I learned in a cooking class and how I added my own items.

Ingredients:
whole chicken in cut up pieces
drain water from chicken
add ½ bottle of white wine, simmer again
add bay leaf and peppers
reduce chicken down, drain wine off chicken. Let it stand for 5 minutes.
Collect herbs.
Add 1 cup of olive oil to chicken and garlic.
Strain pureed or stewed tomatoes and add to garlic olive oil.
Add parsley to the tomato sauce, add salt and sugar.
Cover sauce, reduce heat to slow cooking.
Add in fresh and dried mushrooms.
Serve with pasta.

Greek Lamb Chops

VACATIONING IN GREECE always offers a treasure chest full of comforts and culinary delights. of A day of Greek cuisine on the island of Crete consisted of a variety of mouth watering dishes. An excerpt from my travel journal of Crete in 2009 revealed the following delicious day of delicacies!

In Chania, Crete we ate at Taman Taverna after seeing the outdoor Maritime Museum and going out on the lookout tower.

One of our sons ordered rabbit in Mavrodaphne (wine) and it tasted like nutmeg. Another son ordered Giartoula--baby lamb in yogurt sauce, feta and tomato sauce. Our youngest son ordered french fries in Cretan goat cheese. My husband and I split "Taman salad"--slaw, tomatoes, shredded carrots, shredded relish, dill, avocado sauce and walnuts.

Lamb chops seem to be our favorite Greek meat to serve friends and family and we enjoyed many a moonlit night in Greece, savoring these delicious chops.

Greek Lamb chops:
1 tablespoon dried oregano
2 tablespoons lemon juice
1/2 teaspoon salt
1/4 teaspoon black pepper
8 (4-ounce) lamb loin chops, trimmed

Dakos Salad in Crete

CRETE WAS AN earthy, raw, agricultural and authentic island experience. Its flavor was unique because of its geology, customs and cuisine. One of the highlights of Crete was definitely the cuisine! The food is marvelous, the ambience of every restaurant is quaint and the presentation and hospitality is authentic. Depending on which islands and regions you visit, the delicacies and local flavor can vary.

For example, on the island of Crete, we discovered a *different kind of Greek salad*. The usual Greek salads are called horiatiki salata: country (style) salad. But in Crete, they feature the Dakos salad. This was incredible!! The main difference was the crouton-bread on top! This salad was so filling and satisfying, that many times we filled up just on this delicious salad for a "light" lunch and feasted more at night on a bigger dinner. When we came back to America, after the trip, we tried to copy the Dakos salad by finding the big crouton style bread or drying out bread ourselves to add to the salad. It was close---but the major ingredient lacking was the Cretan vibe, the ocean breeze and the vacation feeling of being in Greece!

A Dakos Salad recipe I use combined from various recipes:

1 loaf rustic bread, cut into chunks
1 cup Greek olive oil, Salt and freshly ground pepper capers (optional) dill, oregano
1/4 cup fresh lemon juice

1 red onion thinly sliced

1-2 English cucumbers diced 2 tomatoes, diced 12 ounces creamy (or French style) feta cheese, crumbled

Parsnip Soup of Ireland

WE HAD NEVER had a parsnip or a turnip until we went to Ireland and Scotland in 2010. In my opinion, these are a much more delicious version of potatoes! (sorry, potato)

Parsnip Soup Recipe:
1/2 cup finely chopped onion
1 garlic clove, minced
1 teaspoon ginger
1/2 cup sliced carrot
1/2 cup sliced celery
2 tablespoons unsalted butter
3 parsnips peeled and cut into slices
2 cups chicken broth
nutmeg to taste cook the onion, garlic, ginger, carrot, celery, and the thyme in the butter in a saucepan over low heat Add the parsnips and broth and boil. simmer, covered, for 15 minutes until the vegetables are very tender.
Purée the soup in a blender and return to the pan. Stir in the nutmeg add dash of salt and pepper

Tagines of Morocco

Our meal in Morocco was such a highlight for our family, I immediately tried to duplicate the dishes back home. I bought and borrowed cookbooks and best of all, I bought a tagine! A tagine is a North African casserole dish that has two pieces - a bottom "bowl" and a conical shaped lid. Historically, the bottom also had the purpose of a serving dish, which came in handy for nomads. These can be found at popular kitchen stores. The food cooks quickly and everything is tender, juicy, flavorful, and healthy! The meat falls off the bone. It seems like a combination of the effects of a pressure cooker and a crock pot. You can use it stove-top or in the oven. They can crack because they are made of clay or ceramic so you have to watch out for this. Ras-al-hanout is a mixture of spices that I mix up on my own and bottle in a cute spice jar to keep handy.

Ras-al-hanout recipe
cardamom,
cumin,
clove,
cinnamon,
nutmeg,
mace,
allspice,
dry ginger,
chili peppers,
coriander seed,

peppercorn,
sweet and hot paprika,
fenugreek, dry turmeric.
(there are various combinations of the ingredients above)

Rabo de Toro recipe ingredients (Gibraltar)

The ingredients that might be included for this Spanish stew are:

bull's tail or oxtails olive oil
saffron threads
prosciutto
onions,
carrots,
tomato paste
leeks,
red bell pepper,
cloves of garlic
In a pan, heat the olive oil and brown the oxtails.
Saute onion and garlic
Add the leeks, peppers, onions and carrots
Add herbs or spices
Boil it and simmer for 4 hours.
or.....grill it!
We grilled our oxtails and basted them with olive oil and garlic.

Neeps and Tatties in Scotland

"NEEPS AND TATTIES" are the terms for Turnips and Potatoes which is a famous Scottish mashed potatoes dish. In America, we have "tater tots" (potato-er) and in Scotland, they have tatties! We loved neeps and tatties and haggis!

Recipe:
1 lb potatoes (tatties)
1 tablespoon chopped chives a little garlic
1 lb. turnips (neeps)
1 tablespoon of butter dash of salt and pepper
Peel the potatoes and cut into chunks or cubes. Boil in lightly salted water. Cook for 20 minutes and drain well.
Peel the turnips and cut into small chunks. Boil and cook for 20 minutes until tender, then drain. mash the cooked neeps and tatties together in the same bowl.
Add salt, pepper, butter. (Or white pepper)
Garnish with chopped chives.

When we returned from the trip that included Scotland, we hosted a "Scottish Night" dinner party and invited our friends in Tulsa who were from Scotland or had been to Scotland. I served neeps and tatties and some kinds of meat that was similar to haggis. We had whiskey for our beverage and a dessert similar to benofee (banana toffee pie). The centerpiece of the table was a Scottish tea towel I bought at Stirling Castle which illustrated historic moments. Scottish bagpipe music played in the background and we all shared memories of our Scottish trips.

Similar dinner parties were held like this throughout the year celebrating other countries. I had a Moroccan night that evolved spontaneously one night while showing my Morocco slideshow to my inlaws. Moroccan music played in the background while I whipped up a copy of the multi course meal we had in Tangier at Popeye's Mediteraneo Ristorante Popular. All of this transpired on my intricate Moroccan tablecloth I bought at the rug factory. Moroccan pottery adorned the table and I distributed Moroccan pottery souvenirs to my inlaws.

Years later, we grilled oxtail for our friends, inspired by our Rabo de Toro meal in Gibraltar.

Many a night, we served chicken cacciatore which we learned to make at the cooking class in Orvieto, Italy. The most frequent meals I served though were the Moroccan tagines. Our dinner guests looked forward to Greek food the most but it was fun to also expose them to other international cuisine. Cooking regional foods and listening to foreign music is definitely one way to reminisce about the memorable and magical trips. Why not extend the magic carpet ride into our daily lives!?

Paella in Marbella....Sangria and Tapas

IN SOUTHERN SPAIN, we had a scrumptious meal of paella and sangria. Nothing said "welcome to Espana!" quite like the pairing of paella and wine. The presentation of it was perfect. Fresh from the sea and perfectly symmetrical in its design. We were beachfront in Marbella (Mar-bae-ya) with sea breezes and sweet sangria. I have made paella before but I must admit, it's much better when it's served to you with a Spanish band strolling nearby!

Paella isn't impossible to make; it's just time consuming. When I've just experimented on the spot with sangria ingredients, it ironically turns out to be the one my guests will enjoy the most! A pitcher of sangria looks festive on a buffet table or dinner table and Occasionally, I'll whip up a pitcher of sangria for parties back home that remind me of our Spanish feasts seaside in Southern Spain.

While paella was among the grand entrees in Spanish cuisine, the show stopper in Spain is the custom of tapas. Tapas are a recent treat in the United States restaurants, but they've been around for a long time in Spain! Tapas are appetizers or small plates. There are many versions of how tapas originated. My favorite reason of the origin of tapas is that the Spaniards covered their wine glasses with small plates of appetizers to *keep the flies out of their wine!* In Spain, we tried the tapas method by strolling from one beautiful restaurant or tavern to the next, ordering a few small plates of tapas. We absorbed the environment of the specific restaurant we were in and we moved on to the next one and tried some more! We didn't do this every night because it could get expensive. But we tried it to get into the culture and cuisine of Spain. It is a popular belief, in the Mediterranean countries, that people should not drink alcohol on an empty stomach so tapas are a perfect way to mix a little food with a little drink!

Some of our favorite tapas were: chorizo sausage, olives, calamari, croquettes and manchego. What a fantastic custom of Spain! Tapas provide variety while strolling and extending the night!

Since paella, tapas and sangria recipes vary, I'll just include my favorite sangria recipe here:

Simple Sangria
orange slices
apple slices
blackberries
red wine, possibly Spanish wine
ice
1/3 cup brandy
chill in refrigerator

Made in the USA
Charleston, SC
15 August 2016